39.95

Professional Sports and Antitrust

Recent Titles from Quorum Books

Arts Administration and Management: A Guide for Arts Administrators and their Staffs
Harvey Shore

Hazardous Waste: Confronting the Challenge
Christopher Harris, William L. Want, and Morris A. Ward, with the Environmental Law Institute

Choosing Effective Development Programs: An Appraisal Guide for Human Resources and Training Managers
James Gardner

Investing in Japanese Real Estate
M. A. Hines

Planning, Implementing, and Evaluating Targeted Communication Programs: A Manual for Business Communicators
Gary W. Selnow and William D. Crano

The United States Trade Deficit of the 1980s: Origins, Meanings, and Policy Responses
Chris C. Carvounis

The Legal Handbook of Business Transactions: A Guide for Managers and Entrepreneurs
E. C. Lashbrooke, Jr., and Michael I. Swygert

Federal Statutes on Environmental Protection: Regulation in the Public Interest
Warren Freedman

The Marketer's Guide to Media Vehicles, Methods, and Options: A Sourcebook in Advertising and Promotion
Ann Grossman

Corporate Asset Management: A Guide for Financial and Accounting Professionals
Clark E. Chastain

The Control of Municipal Budgets: Toward the Effective Design of Tax and Expenditure Limitations
David Merriman

Business Strategy and Public Policy: Perspectives from Industry and Academia
Alfred A. Marcus, Allen M. Kaufman, and David R. Beam, editors

Professional Sports and Antitrust

Warren Freedman

Quorum Books
NEW YORK · WESTPORT, CONNECTICUT · LONDON

Library of Congress Cataloging-in-Publication Data

Freedman, Warren.
   Professional sports and antitrust.

   Includes index.
   1. Sports franchises—Law and legislation—
United States. 2. Professional sports—Law and
legislation—United States. 3. Antitrust law—
United States. I. Title.
KF3989.F74   1987   343.73′072   87-2499
                           347.30372
   ISBN 0–89930–191–6 (lib. bdg. : alk. paper)

British Library Cataloguing in Publication Data is available.

Copyright © 1987 by Warren Freedman

All rights reserved. No portion of this book may be
reproduced, by any process or technique, without the
express written consent of the publisher.

Library of Congress Catalog Card Number: 87-2499
ISBN: 0-89930-191-6

First published in 1987 by Quorum Books

Greenwood Press, Inc.
88 Post Road West, Westport, Connecticut 06881

Printed in the United States of America

The paper used in this book complies with the
Permanent Paper Standard issued by the National
Information Standards Organization (Z39.48-1984).

10 9 8 7 6 5 4 3 2 1

Contents

1. Definitions and Terminology   **1**

1.1 "Sports Law" and "Sports Business": A Brief History   1
1.2 The Goal of Serving the Public Interest   3
1.3 Antitrust Perspectives   4

2. Legal Relationships in Professional Sports   **17**

2.1 Sports Agents and Athletes   17
2.2 Leagues, Parent Teams, and Subsidiaries   22

3. Exemption and Non-exemption of Professional Sports from the Antitrust Laws   **31**

3.1 Baseball   31
3.2 Football   35
3.3 Basketball   40
3.4 Hockey   42
3.5 Boxing   44
3.6 Tennis and Golf   46
3.7 Soccer, Bowling, Automobile Racing, and Harness Racing   47
3.8 The Labor Exemption   49

4. Aspects of Monopolies and Restraints of Trade in Professional Sports   **71**

4.1 Introduction   71
4.2 Control of Playing Facilities   75

4.3 The Franchise Market	76
4.4 Control of Professional Athletes	80
4.5 Control of Media Coverages	82
4.6 Cross-Ownership	83

5. Other Anti-Competitive Practices Against the Professional Athlete — 91

5.1 Eligibility Rules	91
5.2 Disciplinary Rules	94
5.3 Discrimination Based on Sex, Color, or National Origin	95

6. State Regulation of Professional Sports — 99

6.1 State Antitrust Statutes	99
6.2 Rights of Athletes and the State	102
6.3 Anti-Competitive Restraints	104

7. Aspects of Tort and Contract Liability in Professional Sports — 109

7.1 Injuries to Players, Spectators, or Officials	109
7.2 Municipal Liability	112
7.3 Other Business Practices	114

8. Professional Sports As First Amendment Expression — 117

8.1 Commercial Speech	117
8.2 Performative and Symbolic Speech	118
8.3 Professional Sports As Speech	121

Appendix: NBA Uniform Player Contract — 129
 NFL Player Contract

Index to Cases — 139

Subject Index — 143

Professional Sports and Antitrust

1

Definitions and Terminology

1.1 "SPORTS LAW" AND "SPORTS BUSINESS": A BRIEF HISTORY

It has been said that sports is a mirror of society in that as the world has expanded sports too has expanded into national and even international business. Today professional sports is linked solidly with business, and the business of professional sports may be defined as the range of business activities which are necessary to, or an integral part of, the purchase or sale of rights to, or the promotion or conduct of, a professional sporting event which is presented for profit, as well as those multifaceted activities by which a professional athlete obtains money in return for applying his or her skills in a sporting competition or display.[1] "Sports business," while encompassing these many business activities, also refers to business activities which are incidental to the presentation of a professional sporting event, such as the operation of the sports facility, the manufacture and distribution of sports equipment, and the business of endorsement of products and services for advertising purposes by professional athletes.[2] "Sports law" indeed embraces more than playing contracts, commercial endorsements, and personal injuries; today labor law and antitrust law in the sports context are included along with municipal law involving cities that have gained or lost a valuable franchise for professional sports teams or sports events.

Beginning with the Olympic Games in 776 B.C.E., which developed out of an earlier Greek tradition of localized sports festivals, sports has been linked with business.[3] A class of professional sportsmen known as *athletai*, well-paid, recruited from the mercenary armies, and trained exclusively for their brutal and fierce competition, participated in the early Olympic Games, along with legitimate Greek competitors, i.e., participants who were the legitimate sons of free Greek parents, without a criminal record and officially registered as Greek citizens of a native city, and registered for training one month prior to the commencement of the Olympic Games.[4] Bribery and corruption were rare, for the athlete "felt that any violation of the rules . . . especially any unfairness or corruption, was an act of sacrilege and displeasing to the gods . . . a feeling which undoubtedly tended to preserve the purity of sport at Olympia.[5] The first recorded instance of "game-fixing" occurred at the 98th Olympiad in 388 B.C.E. when the boxer Eupolis of Thessaly bribed his opponents to throw the competition.[6] In addition to boxing and wrestling,[7] the Olympic Games included footraces, chariot races, horse races, the pentathlon, and other contests of skill and endurance.[8] Interestingly, an official corps of "whip-bearers" had the task of watching the innumerable peddlers who surfaced at this quadrennial sports event.[9] Women in Greece were barred from attending the Games, although late in the pre-Christian era women were allowed to compete in sporting events of other festivals.[10] And "death was one of the recognized risks in sporting competitions; hence, the law exempted fatal accidents from a charge of homicide."[11] While the only prizes one could win at the Olympic Games was a crown of ivy (cut with a golden sickle by a boy, both of whose parents were living, from the sacred olive tree that grew at the west end of the Temple of Zeus)[12] and perhaps an animal to sacrifice to the gods, the winning athlete could look forward to many years of royal treatment in his native city-state: "He was granted a seat of honor . . . and provided with board at the public table for the rest of his life."[13]

The Roman emperors in the first and second centuries considered the public sporting events to be "entertainment," a major element of imperial Roman policy.[14] In addition to the popular barbaric gladiator and wild animal fights there were other competitive sporting events, although in nearly every instance the main attraction was the lottery tickets strewn among the crowd and entitling the recipient to prizes from gold to fine clothing to land. By the second century associations of gladiators (axwielders or swordsmen) sprang up to commercialize further the sporting events.

In the early fourteenth century in England the favorite sports were archery for the common folk and jousts and tournaments for nobility.[15] The English played the game of bowls during the thirteenth century, and cricket about the year 1600, although rugby has been played for well over six centuries.[16]

In the United States sports were frowned upon during colonial days as a waste of precious time.[17] But even a succession of anti-sport laws did not stop the development of sports, and team sports grew alongside individual sports competition. It was not until recently that the magical quality of sports was soiled by the hurly-burly of American business. Judge Irving Ben Cooper in the 1970 case of Flood v. Kuhn[18] remarked: "Baseball's status in the life of the nation is so pervasive that it would not strain credulity to say that the Court can take judicial notice that baseball is everybody's business." The businessmen who ran the early sports leagues of professional athletes argued convincingly that baseball was not subject to the same laws and regulations affecting other businesses.[19] Admittedly, professional sports leagues, associations, and organizations have endeavored to engage in self-regulation to offset the impact of antitrust laws as well as to insure that players of professional caliber (the product) are developed and distributed in such a way as to make the quality of competition and the resultant financial rewards as high as possible.[20] How well these sports entrepreneurs succeeded is the reason behind this volume on professional sports and antitrust.

1.2 THE GOAL OF SERVING THE PUBLIC INTEREST

At the outset it is well to distinguish between the "amateur athlete" and the "professional athlete," although the distinction is somewhat blurred today, for even amateurs like the U.S. gold medalists in the 1984 Olympics have set up trust funds through which to channel their winnings.[21] For a discussion of amateur sports in relation to the federal antitrust laws, see Amateur Softball Association v. U.S.[22]

The professional athlete is more than an individual entrepreneur or a unionized employee of a sports enterprise because, it is submitted, he or she also has a responsibility for serving the public interest. Indeed, "professional sports are set up for the enjoyment of paying customers and not solely for the benefit of the owners or the benefit of the players."[23] The destiny of sports is ultimately controlled by the "fans," not only those actually attending the games but perhaps more significantly by those listening on radio or watching on television.[24] Another interested party is the municipality or state whose name is identified with the professional franchise or team. To be certain that the public's interest is protected beyond the ambit of the federal antitrust laws, two suggestions have been made, to wit: (1) federal regulation of the business of sports, but such a national agency might be insensitive to local needs and would undoubtedly degenerate into an inefficient and expensive bureaucracy; or (2) local legislation that would establish local priorities, especially since public monies have given professional sports huge tax subsidies in the form of stadiums and tax abatement; legislation requiring reduced ticket prices for the communities' elderly, poor, or handicapped might be a logical step.[25] Self-regulation of professional sports has also been a vehicle for serving the public interest, but self-regulation has hardly succeeded, as the professional athlete seeks to feather his nest monetarily at the expense of fans loyal to a particular team or sport; indeed, the public's tolerance for highly paid, free-living, and arrogant professional athletes seems to be at an end, and a less businesslike attitude is inevitable. Self-regulation has not solved the problems of the team owners, who must come up with winning teams to merit the support of fans or there can be no marketable competition.[26] There must be a balance between short-term and long-term award for both the professional athlete and the organization which he or she serves.

In 1946 the collectivization of professional sports players commenced as professional baseball players sought to equate their powers with the powers of the club owners. In 1952 the National Basketball Association Players' Association was created; it became a viable power in 1963, three years before the professional baseball players' association emerged with real powers. In 1967 the players in the National Hockey League obtained formal recognition from the team owners, and in 1956 the National Football League Players' Association was born, only to wait 12 more years for full recognition.[27]

1.3 ANTITRUST PERSPECTIVES

The federal antitrust laws embodied in the Sherman Act,[28] for example, express the national belief that "preserving free and unfettered competition" was the summum bonum and the most effective and productive method of regulating economic activity.[29] It was not the intent of the Sherman Act to outlaw every type of agreement or restraint upon competition, but to declare illegal those which unreasonably restrained trade and competition. This "Rule of Reason" meant that an unreasonable restraint which suppressed or destroyed competition rather than promote competition was in violation of the Sherman Act.[30] In Molinas v. National Basketball Assn.[31] the restraint in the form of "blacklisting" a professional basketball player who had engaged in certain corrupt practices was upheld as reasonable since the restraint was designed to protect the integrity of the National Basketball Association. But courts have ruled as illegal per se such restraints on competition as division of markets,[32] concerted refusals to deal,[33] group boycotts,[34] price-fixing,[35] and contracts not to compete,[36] inter alia. However, the courts have treated the professional athlete and the professional sports entrepreneur differently than other business people. Due to the unique nature of professional sports operations, such as the necessity of members of a league agreeing to abide by predetermined rules and regulations, the courts have found justification for violations of antitrust laws.[37] The 1972 case of Flood v. Kuhn[38] preserved professional baseball's continued and curious immunity from the antitrust laws; but at the same time the court gave the professional athlete an enormous amount of freedom to offer his services freely in the marketplace. The dilemmas here are abundant: (a) if the antitrust laws are administered to afford protection to the professional athlete, then competition among the teams might lessen; (b) if the antitrust laws are administered to protect the teams and the leagues, players will necessarily be less free to compete with each other for positions on teams paying the highest salaries; (c) if the antitrust laws are administered so as to promote free competition for player resources among the leagues, then the quality of competition within the leagues may drop; but (d) if the antitrust laws are administered so as to protect the interests of a particular team or particular league as against newcomers, the protected team or league would enjoy a monopoly of that sport.[39] It should be noted that the Sherman Act has three prerequisites: (1) the activity alleged to have a restraining effect on interstate trade or commerce does in fact have that effect; (2) the activity in fact must be an unreasonable restraint; and (3) the activity is not exempt from the antitrust laws. These attributes, however, change with the times, for in 1922 professional baseball was declared exempt from the antitrust laws because then baseball was "local" in nature and the teams' travel did not necessarily involve them in interstate travel.[40] The reluctance of the judiciary to remove baseball's immunity today constitutes an anomaly, since the business of baseball has grown to the extent that vast expenditures of money directly affect millions of people as professional baseball engages in interstate commerce, interstate travel, and worldwide distribution of the "product" via radio and television.

Professional sports leagues, whether characterized as a market of competing entities, a joint venture, a partnership, or a single entity,[41] have been deemed to be lawful joint enterprises by many courts. Mr. Justice William Rehnquist in his dissent from the denial of certiorari in National Football League v. North American Soccer League[42] stated that "NFL owners are joint venturers who produce a product . . . which competes with other sports and other forms of entertainment in the entertainment marketplace." And in Arizona v. Maricopa County Medical Society[43] the U.S. Supreme Court opined: "In such joint ventures (in which persons who otherwise would be competitors pool their capital and share the risks of loss as well as the opportunities for profit) the partnership is regarded as a single firm competing with other sellers in the market."[44] Thus, it would appear logically that the professional sports league is immune from liability under Section 1 of the Sherman Act, in that the league is not a "contract, combination . . . or conspiracy in restraint of trade or commerce." However, Section 2 of the Sherman Act, which declares that "every person who shall monopolize, or attempt to monopolize, or combine or conspire . . . to monopolize" is subject to liability, may mean that a professional sports league may be exercising monopoly power and therefore be guilty of monopolization. To resolve the inquiry, reference must be made to the relevant product market, the relevant geographic area, the degree of market power required, and the appropriate measure of market power. Once that inquiry is answered the plaintiff must establish that the defendant league misused that monopoly power or undertook actions to secure harmful monopoly power.[45] But certain business practices which adversely affect competitors of the league may be little more than legitimate business practices dictated by sound judgment. What is required is a specific intent on the part of the league to discourage or to destroy any semblance of competition.[46]

A professional sports league requires a certain amount of cooperation among competitor-members for the league to survive, and it is this fact that troubles the antitrust plaintiff. Self-regulation is but an aspect of this "cooperation" among competitors that have formed and operate the professional sports league. For example, there are restraints on owners of teams seeking to move their franchises; Section 4.3 of the National Football League Constitution and By-

Laws requires prior approval of not less than three-quarters, or 20 of the 28, club owners before a team can be moved to a different geographical location. There are restraints upon potential owners attempting to acquire franchises within the league,[47] and even restraints upon amateur athletes entering league play.[48] The leagues have in the past imposed upon the players or professional athletes the greatest burdens and the greatest restraints. It was in the late 1960s that professional athletes themselves began the assault on player restraints through the formation of players' associations which pooled the strength of the athletes so as to gain leverage at the bargaining table with the management.[49] Antitrust actions by the professional athletes also contributed to a lessening of the monopoly power being exercised by the leagues.[50] But leagues still exercise monopoly power, for example, when they invoke deliberate acquisition of exclusive rights to a significant portion of the athletes, or where they restrict use of arenas or stadiums, or even control media coverage of the professional sporting event.[51]

The antitrust perspective on professional sports, it is submitted, should be concerned with the needs of the consumer. While professional sports is a business pure and simple, it is also an emotional involvement of people with a professional team or a professional athlete.[52] Therefore, it is understandable why the consumer favors unlimited and unrestricted competition with a maximum number of professional teams and professional athletes, while the owners of those professional teams and the professional athlete believe that competition is harmful in the sense that an increasing number of teams and athletes would erode the quality of play and diminish fan interest. Indeed, the key to management of professional sports in recent years has been a realization that professional sports is a long-term business investment that must grow and prosper as part of a community of people.[53] The National Football League (NFL) is an excellent example of the business of professional sports: founded in 1920 in a Hupmobile showroom in Canton, Ohio, it is still described by its constitution as an "unincorporated association."[54] Each of the 28 franchised-team owners has one vote, and all decisions require at least three-quarters agreement; the NFL Commissioner is hired by the team owners and charged with "full, complete and final jurisdiction and authority to resolve disputes between league members." Today the NFL sells its collective television rights as a single package and shares the broadcast revenues equally among all franchise owners. Prior to 1975 the NFL Commissioner under the so-called Rozelle Rule had complete authority over player grievances; when a player reached the end of his contract and signed with another NFL team, the NFL Commissioner could unilaterally award "equal compensation" to the team suffering the loss of the player. In Mackey v. NFL[55] the Rozelle Rule was deemed to violate the Sherman Act, and as a result "free agency" for players came into being. The NFL granted the union an agency shop, put an end to the Commissioner's authority over player grievances, and paid the players' association $13.6 million in damage settlements. Cross-ownership (whereby an NFL team owner might have an investment or ownership in another professional team in another professional sport) was sanctioned in North American Soccer League v. NFL,[56] which held that the NFL's proposed ban on cross-ownership was in restraint of trade; the plaintiff soccer league won the battle but lost the war, as it went out of business in 1985. The NFL is today a strikingly successful business monopoly in professional sports which becomes vulnerable only when it restricts competition for reasons that have nothing to do with the need to cooperate to produce professional football games.[57] The National Basketball Association's "salary cap" on professional basketball players, it has been argued, constitutes a "monopsony," or a one-buyer market, that is violative of the Sherman Act in that the salary cap adversely affects a player's mobility and thereby restrains competition among professional basketball teams as well as among professional basketball players.[58] The offense of monopolization was defined by the U.S. Supreme Court in its 1966 case of United States v. Grinnell Corp.[59] as containing two elements: (1) "the possession of monopoly power in the relevant market, and (2) the willful acquisition or maintenance of that power as distinguished from growth or development as a consequence of a superior product, business acumen, or historic accident." Almost 20 years later in 1985 in Aspen Skiing Co. v. Aspen Highlands Skiing Corp.[60] the highest court restated this legal test of monopolization, holding here that a monopolist's refusal to participate in a joint ticket-selling venture with a competitor could be considered by the jury as evidence of the monopolist's intent to exclude competition by improper means. Here the monopolist's refusal to participate in the sale of joint ski slope lift tickets with a competitor changed an existing ticket distribution pattern to the detriment of the competitor. The court observed that participation in the sale of joint ski slope lift tickets would have been profitable, in terms of increased consumer demand, to both the monopolist and the competitor. But refusal to participate was more profitable to the monopolist in the long run, for the refusal to participate would cause the competitor to lose a substantial market share to the monopolist, who was simply unable "to offer any efficient justification whatever for its pattern of conduct" other than retrenchment of its monopoly position. In the business of professional skiing the defendant had made a "kill," as would any monopolist in a similar position. Such monopolization is condemned under Section 2 of the Sherman Act, but there is no objection to "no fault" monopolization, for being a monopolist is legal as long as the monopolist does not engage in impermissible exclusionary practices such as the defendant hereinabove. Other "impermissible exclusionary practices" might include refusal to deal, and tying arrangements, inter alia, as delineated hereinafter.

In addition to monopolization there is the offense of attempt to monopolize, also under Section 2 of the Sherman Act. Mr. Justice Oliver Wendell Holmes is said to have delineated the offense of attempt to monopolize in Swift & Co. v. United States[61] as encompassing three elements: (1) specific intent to control prices or eliminate competition in some market; (2) predatory or anti-competitive conduct directed at accomplishing this unlawful purpose; and (3) a dangerous probability that the conduct, if permitted to run its course, would have created a monopoly. The "specific intent" element in the offense of attempt to monopolize is complex, for there are legitimate and illegitimate ways of intending to injure one's competitors. Lowering prices unnecessarily or failing to disclose a technical innovation can be construed either way; in United States v. Empire Gas Corp.[62] the Eighth U.S. Court of Appeals concluded that the "mere intention . . . to exclude competition . . . is insufficient to establish specific intent to monopolize by some illegal means. . . . To conclude otherwise would contravene the very essence of a competitive marketplace, which is to prevail against all competitors." The second element of "anti-competitive conduct" undoubtedly involves conduct that is capable of giving the defendant monopoly power and yet that "anti-competitive conduct" may be socially beneficial conduct creating substantial market power. And the third element of a "dangerous probability of success" is perhaps repetitious of the second element, but most courts do not evaluate the probability carefully, as illustrated in Blanton v. Mobile Oil Corp.,[63] where the Ninth U.S. Court of Appeals found a per se violation of Section 1 of the Sherman Act without a showing of the dangerous probability of success.

In addition to monopolization and attempt to monopolize, Section 2 of the Sherman Act condemns every "person who shall . . . combine or conspire with any other person or persons, to monopolize." This conspiracy to monopolize, however, can be more easily condemned under Section 1 of the Sherman Act as a conspiracy in restraint of trade or commerce. The U.S. Supreme Court in the 1947 case of United States v. Yellow Cab Co.[64] set forth the necessary elements of the conspiracy offense: (a) the existence of a combination or conspiracy among two or more participants; (b) specific intent to monopolize some part of "trade or commerce"; (c) some overt act carried out in furtherance of the conspiracy; and (d) an adverse effect upon interstate commerce. A conspiracy to monopolize does not require a showing of a "dangerous probability of success," only proof of the existence of the agreement plus the overt act carried out in furtherance of the conspiracy.[65]

The "impermissible exclusionary practice" of refusal to deal takes on significance only when the refusal to deal is (1) "concerted," as when two or more competitors agree not to deal with a third competitor or competitors, and (2) an attempt to create or maintain a monopoly. In 1919 the U.S. Supreme Court in United States v. Colgate Co.[66] observed that, in the absence of the above two factors, a private company or person may freely "exercise his own independent discretion as to parties with whom he will deal." Fourteen years later in Appalachian Coals, Inc. v. United States[67] the highest court examined an exclusive joint selling agency created by several competing producers of coal. The selling agency was instructed to sell all of its members' coal at the highest prices it was able to obtain, and the agency priced all of its coal at the identical price. But the court viewed this "price-fixing" and refusal to deal at lower prices as justifiable under the depressed market conditions of 1933. Forty-six years later in 1979 the highest court sanctioned the activities of a nonexclusive joint sales agency engaged in blanket licensing of the right to perform musical works in Broadcast Music, Inc. v. Columbia Broadcasting System.[68] The court found an absence of any requirement that the members must refuse to deal except through the blanket licensing arrangement, and therefore the arrangement was not a coverup for price-fixing or for refusal to deal. However, where there is "concerted" activity, the refusal to deal is condemned as shown in Eastern States Retail Lumber Dealers' Assn. v. United States,[69] where the U.S. Supreme Court condemned the agreement among lumber retailers to identify and refuse to deal with lumber wholesalers who dealt directly with customers as well as retailers. Where the offending defendant or defendants do not have market power, the Rule of Reason must be applied to find a refusal to deal, as exemplified in 1985 in Northwest Wholesale Stationers, Inc. v. Pacific Stationery & Printing Co.,[70] which case delineated a concerted refusal to deal involving expulsion of a member of a buying cooperative. Where the offending defendant has the market power, as in Klor's Inc. v. Broadway-Hale Stores, Inc.,[71] the highest court held that, since the defendant used its "monopolistic buying power" to force major appliance manufacturers to refuse to deal with the plaintiff, the offense constituted a cause of action under the per se rule. Similarly, in United States v. General Motors Corp.[72] there was a per se violation for refusal to sell "discounters"; and in Fashion Originators' Guild of America v. FTC[73] the refusal to deal with or sell to stores which purchased clothing from design "pirates" was condemned as a per se violation of the Sherman Act. In 1979 the Rule of Reason was, however, applied to a refusal to deal situation in Berkey Photo, Inc. v. Eastman Kodak Co.;[74] here noncompetitors Kodak and General Electric agreed to develop a camera and flash attachment and not to predisclose their research to any company; as a result of this concerted refusal to deal or predisclose technical data, the plaintiff was not able to enter the market for either the camera or the flash attachment. The U.S. Supreme Court in condemning this concerted refusal to deal observed that Kodak was a monopolist in the market for cameras, and therefore the scheme was part of the monopolist's conduct to maintain its monopoly. Thus, the concerted refusal to deal was in essence an illegal monopolization or an attempt to monopolize or a conspiracy to monopolize under Section 2 of the Sherman Act.

Admittedly, the exclusionary practices of a professional sports enterprise do not necessarily fit the patterns of business activity seen in the above refusal to deal cases. But there are practices that can be described as concerted refusals to deal, as shown in United States Trotting Assn. v. Chicago Down Assn.[75] and in Gunter Harz Sports, Inc. v. United States Tennis Association.[76] In the former case the Illinois legislature had required all horses entering harness races to be registered by the United States Trotting Association (USTA) and have current USTA eligibility certificates; only USTA members could have their horses registered. The Chicago Down, a racetrack with no USTA affiliation, challenged the refusal to deal, but the Seventh U.S. Court of Appeals in 1981 applied the Rule of Reason and saw no antitrust violation. In the latter case the tennis association imposed a temporary ban on the use of "double-strung" tennis rackets and then excluded all double-strung rackets from use in competition; and the rule was challenged by a tennis racket manufacturer on the grounds of a concerted refusal to deal with dire anti-competitive effect upon his business. But the court held that the restriction was properly evaluated under the Rule of Reason. Such restraints as in the case of harness racing are for the promotion of the professional sport, to ensure the integrity of the events, and to guarantee the highest level of on-the-field competition. The tennis racket rule was enacted, according to the court, to preserve the essential character of the game of professional tennis as it had always been played; apparently double-strung rackets impart significantly more spin on the ball than other tennis rackets. Above all, neither of the sponsoring associations had a competitive interest in the restraint adopted. In the Chicago Down case[77] the court found no indication that groups of drivers or owners were using the association as a means of eliminating other participants or that certain tracks were conspiring or combining behind the facade of the association to eliminate competing tracks. Similarly, the court in Gunter Harz Sports[78] found no restraining agreement between the association and producers of tennis equipment to prevent manufacturers of double-strung rackets from competing.

Another "impermissible exclusionary practice" is the tying arrangement, which is cited in Siegel v. Chicken Delight Inc.[79] as involving the following elements: "The scheme in question involves two distinct items and provides that one (the tying product) may not be obtained unless the other (the tied product) is also purchased. . . . The tying product possesses sufficient economic power appreciably to restrain competition in the tied product market . . . [and] a 'not insubstantial' amount of commerce is affected by the arrangement." In essence, the illegal tying arrangement is a forced "package" sale such as limiting tickets to World Series baseball games to those persons who purchased entire season tickets, for example. Tying arrangements are condemned under the per se rule of Section 1 of the Sherman Act if the plaintiff can show both market power in the tying product and a "not insubstantial" amount of interstate commerce adversely affected in the tied product market. Tying arrangements are also condemned under a Rule of Reason test in Section 3 of the Sherman Act if the scheme involved the forced, combined sale of separate products and the seller had either substantial market power in the tying product market or the tying arrangement affected a "not insubstantial" amount of interstate commerce.[80] The Section 1 illegal per se characteristic of tying arrangements is described by the U.S. Supreme Court in Northern Pacific Railway Co. v. United States[81]:

"Tying agreements serve hardly any purpose beyond the suppression of competition. . . . " They deny competitors free access to the market for the tied product, not because the party imposing the tying arrangements has a better product or a lower price

Definitions and Terminology 11

but because of his power or leverage in another market. At the same time buyers are forced to forego their free choice between competing products. For these reasons . . . they are unreasonable *in and of themselves* whenever a party has sufficient economic power with respect to the tying product to appreciably restrain free competition in the market for the tied product and a "not insubstantial" amount of interstate commerce is affected.

As recently as 1984 the highest court approved the per se violation under Section 1 of the Sherman Act for tying arrangements.[82]

The Rule of Reason as applicable to tying arrangements under Section 3 of the Sherman Act is seen in action in Times-Picayune Publishing Co. v. United States.[83] Here the defendant newspaper publisher was charged with forcing buyers who wanted to advertise in one of its newspapers to advertise in the other newspaper also. (One paper was a morning paper and the other was an evening paper.) Justice Tom Clark of the U.S. Supreme Court in 1953 was impressed by the fact that, when the sale of the morning and evening advertising was combined into a single transaction, many of the costs of advertising were reduced, including the costs of soliciting and billing as well as the costs of setting type. No violation of Section 3 was found.

Virtually all tying arrangement litigation is initiated by private plaintiffs seeking damages which are trebled like any antitrust violation. However, in recent years, victories for damaged plaintiffs have been few and far between, as illustrated by Principe v. McDonald's Corp.,[84] where the Fourth U.S. Court of Appeals held that it was not illegal for McDonald's Corporation to require all its franchises to rent their McDonald's restaurant locations from the defendant at a rental rate based on gross sales volume.

There can be no doubt that the Sherman Act and other antitrust legislation has been influential in forcing a fundamental restructuring of the basic relationships in all professional sports. And yet the impotence of the U.S. Supreme Court in 1922 in declaring professional baseball exempt from the antitrust laws even prompted professional baseball to develop institutional mechanisms which closely followed the nonrestrictive practices of other professional sports not the beneficiaries of exemptions from the antitrust laws.[85] The intervention of the antitrust courts in professional sports has prompted leagues, professional teams, and professional players to reformulate on more competitive lines, although the "labor exemption"[86] is undoubtedly the most important vehicle rendering professional sports more competitive. The labor exemption, afforded to employment-related agreements arrived at through collective bargaining, is a selective form of immunity from the antitrust laws in that there are always numerous issues which come within its coverage. Since there is no assurance that the present patterns of collective bargaining will endure in all professional leagues, it would appear that substantive antitrust review remains as a potent control device in the business of professional sports.

A word about amateur sports and the antitrust laws can be understood by noting National Collegiate Athletic Association (NCAA) v. Board of Regents,[87] a 1984 decision of the U.S. Supreme Court. The focus of attention was the college association's television plan, which limited the number of college football games that appeared on television and limited the number of television appearances of any one college team. The highest court ruled that the plan violated the antitrust laws; and, for the first time, applied the antitrust laws to an internal amateur athletic association in the area of college sports.[88] Amateur sports, like professional sports, must be tested against the goal of enhancing consumer preferences. Here the litigation arose when the University of Oklahoma and the University of Georgia complained about the NCAA limitations that were imposed on their abilities to sell broadcast rights apart from opportunities under the NCAA television plan. Both the federal district court in Oklahoma[89] and the Tenth U.S. Court of Appeals[90] had agreed that the NCAA television plan was impermissible under the Sherman Act; the federal appellate court found the plan to be both a per se violation as well as an unreasonable restraint upon interstate commerce. The U.S. Supreme Court, however, found the per se standard to be inappropriate; the plan was an unreasonable restraint, for it constituted an agreement among potential competitors to limit output in the form of telecasts of college football games as well as an agreement to price-fix. The highest court rejected three NCAA arguments, to wit: (1) the NCAA television plan protected live attendance at games not being televised; (2) television controls are necessary to maintain competitive balance; and (3) television controls were a cooperative marketing effort that increased the desirability of the product being sold and enabled that product to compete effectively against other forms of entertainment. (The dissents of Justice Byron White and William Rehnquist rested upon the argument that college sports were not "purely commercial ventures.")

The court in effect identified the activities of the NCAA as similar to those of professional sports leagues: the essential activity of NCAA is directed toward the marketing and selling of a product, i.e., amateur football. Educational rules for college players were delineated as "product-defining." The court observed that the absence of the NCAA television plan would mean that "the television exposure of all schools would increase. . . . smaller institutions appealing to essentially local or regional markets would get more exposure if the plan is enjoined, enhancing their ability to compete for student athletes."[91]

NOTES

1. See generally 18 ALR Fed 489.
2. See 62 Yale L J 576 (1952), 81 Harv L Rev 418 (1967), and 57 Cornell L Rev 297 (1971).
3. See Insight Magazine (Aug. 25, 1986) at p. 9.
4. See generally 8 Ohio Northern L Rev 433 (1981). Also E. N. Gardner, Greek Athletic Sports and Festivals (1910), and J. B. Bury, A History of Greece to the Death of Alexander the Great, 3rd ed. (1910).

Definitions and Terminology

5. Supra note 4 [Gardner at p. 33].
6. Supra note 3.
7. See Chapter 3 herein.
8. See Finley and Pleket, The Olympic Games: The First Thousand Years (1976), at p. 54.
9. Id.
10. Id. at p. 45.
11. Id. at p. 40.
12. Supra note 4 (Gardner at pp. 35–36).
13. See Leonard, A Guide to the History of Physical Education, 2nd ed. (1927), at p. 26.
14. Supra note 3.
15. See Guttman, From Ritual to Record (1973), at pp. 30–31.
16. Supra note 13 at p. 200, and supra note 15 at pp. 37–38.
17. See Twombly, Two Hundred Years of Sport in America (1976), at p. 18.
18. 309 F Supp 793 (SDNY, 1970).
19. See Section 3.1 of Chapter 3 herein, and note the U.S. Supreme Court's decision in Flood v. Kuhn, 407 US 278 (1972), discussed hereinafter in Section 3.1 of Chapter 3.
20. Supra note 1 at p. 493.
21. Supra note 3 at p. 9. The Amateur Sports Act of 1978 (Pub L No. 95-606,92 Stat 3049) was designed "to promote and coordinate amateur athletic activity in the United States, to recognize certain rights for United States amateur athletes, to provide for the resolution of disputes involving national governing bodies, and for other purposes." Each sport is to have a National Governing Body (NGB), and any amateur sports organization will be eligible to be recognized as an NGB only if it

> (1) is incorporated domestically as a not-for-profit corporation having as its purpose the advancement of amateur athletic competition, and has the managerial and financial capability to plan and execute its obligations;
> (2) submits an application for recognition . . . ;
> (3) agrees to submit, upon demand of the USOC, to binding arbitration conducted in accordance with the commercial rules of the American Arbitration Association in any controversy involving its recognition as an NGB . . . or involving the opportunity of any amateur athlete, coach, trainer, manager, administrator or official to participate in amateur athletic competition, as provided for in the USOC's constitution and bylaws;
> (4) demonstrates that it is autonomous in the governance of its sport, in that it independently determines and controls all matters central to such governance, does not delegate such determination and control, and is free from outside restraint, and demonstrates that it is member of no more than one international sports federation which governs a sport included on the program of the Olympic Games or the Pan-American Games;
> (5) demonstrates that its membership is open . . . ;
> (6) provides an equal opportunity to amateur athletes, coaches, trainers, managers, administrators, and officials to participate in amateur athletic competition, without discrimination on the basis of race, color, religion, age, sex, or national origin, and with fair notice and opportunity for a hearing to any amateur athlete,

coach, trainer, manager, administrator, or official before declaring such individual ineligible to participate;

(7) is governed by a board of direction or other such governing board whose members are selected without regard to race, color, religion, national origin or sex, except that, in sports where there are separate male and female programs, it provides for reasonable representation of both males and females on such board of directors or other such governing board;

(8) demonstrates that its board of directors or other such governing board includes among its voting members individuals who are actively engaged in amateur athletic competition in the sport for which recognition is sought . . . ;

(9) provides for reasonable direct representation on its board of directors or other such governing board for any amateur sports organization which, in the sport for which recognition is sought, conducts . . . a national program . . . ;

(10) demonstrates that none of its officers are also officers of any other amateur organization which is recognized as a national governing body;

(11) provides procedures for the prompt and equitable resolution of grievances of its members;

(12) does not have eligibility criteria relating to amateur status which are more restrictive than those of the appropriate international sports federation; and

(13) demonstrates, if it is an amateur sports organization seeking recognition as a national governing body, that it is prepared to meet the obligations imposed on an NGB.

22. 467 F2d 312 (10th Cir., 1972). The relationship between athletes and academics was addressed in Hall v. University of Minnesota, 530 F Supp 104 (Minn., 1982):

This Court is not saying that athletes are incapable of scholarship; however they are given little opportunity to be scholars and few persons care how the student athlete performs academically, including many of the athletes themselves. The exceptionally talented student athletes are led to perceive basketball, football, and other athletic programs as farm teams and proving grounds for *professional sports leagues*. It may well be true that a good academic program for the athlete is made virtually impossible by the demands of their sport at the college level. If this situation causes harm to the University, it is because they have fostered it and the institution rather than the individual should suffer the consequence." (p. 109)

23. See Reynolds v. National Football League, 584 F2d 280 (Minn, 1978) at P. 287.
24. 2 Comm/Ent (1979) at p. 440.
25. See "Protecting Cities and Fans" (editorial), Sporting News (June 25, 1984) at p. 6.
26. Supra note 1 at p. 494.
27. See generally 38 Law & Contem Prob 3 (1974).
28. 15 USC 1 to 7 (1976).
29. Note the landmark case of Northern Pacific Railway Co. v. United States, 356 US 1 (1958).
30. See Paramount Famous Lasky Corp. v. U.S., 282 US 30 (1930).
31. 190 F Supp 241 (SDNY, 1961).
32. See Timken Roller Bearing Co. v. U.S., 341 US 593 (1951).
33. See generally 71 Harv L Rev 1531 (1958).

34. See Klor's Inc. v. Broadway-Hale Stores, Inc., 359 US 207 (1959); but courts have found excuses for the professional sports participants and justified their conduct, as illustrated by Denver Rockets v. All-Pro Management, Inc., 325 F Supp 1049 (CD Cal., 1971).
35. See United States v. Socony-Vacuum Oil Co., 310 US 150 (1940).
36. See Lektro-Vend Corp. v. Vendo Co., 660 F2d 225 (7th Cir., 1981), cert den 102 S Ct 1277 (1982).
37. For example, see Mackey v. National Football League, 543 F2d 606 (8th Cir., 1973).
38. Id.
39. Supra note 26.
40. See Section 3.1 of Chapter 3 herein, and Federal Baseball Club of Baltimore Inc. v. National League of Professional Baseball Clubs, 259 US 200 (1922).
41. See 25 Ariz L Rev (1983) at pp. 998–999.
42. 103 S Ct 499 (1982).
43. 457 US 332 (1982).
44. Id. at p. 336.
45. Supra note 41 at p. 1000.
46. See, for example, United States v. Crescent Amusement Co., 323 US 173 (1944).
47. See Washington Professional Basketball Corp. v. National Basketball Assn., 147 F Supp 154 (SDNY, 1956).
48. See Tondas v. Amateur Hockey Association of United States, 438 F Supp 310 (WDNY, 1977).
49. See generally 81 Yale L J 1 (1971).
50. Note 15 USC 15, which provides that "any person who shall be injured in his business or property by reason of anything forbidden in the antitrust laws may sue therefore. . . ."
51. See 18 ALR Fed 489.
52. See New York Times (Aug. 3, 1986) at p. S2: "The principal concern of antitrust law is not whether a particular competitor wins in court, but whether the market is catering to the needs of the consumers."
53. See Insight Magazine (Aug. 25, 1986) at pp. 8 et seq.
54. See New York Times Magazine (Sept. 7, 1986) at pp. 31 et seq.
55. 407 F Supp 1000 (Minn., 1975), modif 593 F2d 606 (8th Cir., 1976).
56. 465 F Supp 665 (SDNY, 1979).
57. See generally 59 So Cal L Rev 157 (1985), and also 4 Whittier L Rev 217 (1982) at p. 238.
58. Note the implications for professional sports from Cascade Cabinet Co. v. Western Cabinet & Millwork, Inc., 710 F2d 1366 (9th Cir., 1983) at p. 1373.
59. 384 US 563 (1966).
60. 105 S Ct 2847 (1985).
61. 196 US 375 (1905).
62. See Lessig v. Tidewater Oil Co., 327 F2d 459 (8th Cir., 1964), cert den 377 US 993 (1964).
63. 721 F2d 1207 (9th Cir., 1983), cert den 105 S Ct 1874 (1985).
64. 332 US 218 (1947).
65. See American Tobacco Co. v. United States, 328 US 781 (1946).
66. 250 US 300 (1919).

67. 288 US 344 (1933).
68. 441 US 1 (1979).
69. 234 US 600 (1914).
70. 105 S Ct 2613 (1985).
71. 359 US 207 (1959).
72. 384 US 127 (1966).
73. 312 US 457 (1941).
74. 603 F2d 263 (2nd Cir., 1979), cert den 444 US 1093 (1980).
75. 665 F2d 781 (7th Cir., 1981).
76. 511 F Supp 1103 (Neb., 1981), aff 665 F2d 222 (8th Cir., 1981).
77. Supra note 6.
78. Supra note 7.
79. 448 F2d 43 (9th Cir., 1971), cert den 405 US 955 (1972).
80. See United States v. Loew's Inc., 371 US 38 (1962).
81. 356 US 1 (1958).
82. See Jefferson Parish Hospital District No. 2 v. Hyde, 466 US 2 (1984).
83. 345 US 594 (1953).
84. 631 F2d 303 (4th Cir., 1980), cert den 451 US 970 (1981).
85. Note comments of the U.S. Supreme Court in International Boxing Club v. United States, 358 US 242 (1959), and Section 3.1 of Chapter 3 herein.
86. See Section 3.8 of Chapter 3 herein.
87. 104 S Ct 2948 (1984).
88. See, for example, Justice v. NCAA, 577 F Supp 356 (Ariz., 1983).
89. 546 F Supp 1276 (WD Okla., 1982).
90. 707 F2d 1147 (10th Cir., 1982).
91. Supra note 88 at p. 2971.

2

Legal Relationships in Professional Sports

2.1 SPORTS AGENTS AND ATHLETES

The unprecedented growth of the business of professional sports in recent years, coupled with million-dollar player contracts and their widespread publicity, has attracted a flock of agents and managers (lawyers and non-lawyers) into the legal relationship. The influx of these persons, in particular, has spawned new and unique problems bordering upon the antitrust laws. It is primarily the "sports agent" whose legal relationship has important implications for the professional sports industry.

The professional athlete as a member of a professional sports team has traditionally been a victim of restraints upon his or her services, which restraints have been imposed by team owners and by the leagues of team owners.[1] But the professional athlete and player associations have been successful in asserting that such restrictions or restraints violated federal and state antitrust laws.[2] The result has been an influx of player's agents or managers who represent the professional athlete in good faith, arm's-length negotiation about million dollar salaries. Efforts have been made to license or regulate the agent or manager, such as the certification requirements of the NFL Players' Association and Section 1500 et seq. of the California Labor Code; but to date these and other efforts have been unsuccessful.

To understand the role of the agent or manager of the professional athlete a review of some of the restraints on players must first be made. Briefly, there are and have been the following restraints (a) an option clause, which provides the professional team with the right to renew the player's contract for an additional year, often at a stated lower percentage of the salary;[3] (b) the compensation rule, which provides that after an athlete plays out his or her option, any team or club that then signs him or her must compensate the original employer in the form of cash, player contracts, or player draft choices;[4] (c) the player draft system, which allows the team to select, in reverse order of the league standings for the previous season, an equal number of graduating high school or college players;[5] (d) the eligibility rule, which authorizes an athlete to enter the league and negotiate a contract;[6] and (e) the reserve system, which delineates the very restraints in the Standard Player's Contract.[7] It was in 1975 that "free agency" came into its own as professional baseball's impartial arbitrator Peter Seitz ruled on December 23, 1975:

The grievances of Messersmith and McNally are sustained. There is no contractual bond between these players and the Los Angeles and the Montreal clubs, respectively. Absent such a contract, their clubs had no right or power, under the Basic Agreement, the uniform player contract or the Major League Rules, to reserve their services for their exclusive use for any period beyond the "renewal year" in the contracts which these players had heretofore signed with their clubs."[8]

Obviously, the Seitz decision in creating free agency dramatically and irrevocably changed professional sports. But the impetus of free agency truly came from the 1970 court decision in a case brought by Curt Flood, a talented and proud outfielder for the St. Louis Cardinals who in 1970 was traded to the Philadelphia Phillies. Flood challenged the teams' right to barter players like chattel, a form of "indentured servitude." Flood lost his suit and finished his career as a forgotten man, but the case signaled the end of the reserve system, thereby allowing major league baseball players to play an option year without a signed contract, if necessary.[9]

The free agency system which gave rise to the influx of agents or managers of professional athletes may be illustrated by reference to the National Hockey League (NHL). Its By-Law Section 9A, adopted November 27, 1973, states that "a player who becomes a 'free agent' pursuant to subsections 2 or 3 of this By-Law shall have the right to negotiate and contract with any Member Club or with any club in any other league."[10] There is a free agent list[11] and an obligation to make "equalization payment" by the acquiring club to the former club.[12] It should be noted that the 1972 National Hockey League contract terms concerning matters other than salary and length of service were fixed through the use of the Standard Player's Contract, and among its restrictive conditions was the Option Clause. But in the Philadelphia World Hockey Club case[13] the federal district court for the Eastern District of Pennsylvania found that the reserve system was in violation of the Sherman Antitrust Act and entered a preliminary order preventing NHL teams from seeking injunctions against former players who had "jumped" to the World Hockey Association (WHA). In February 1974 the parties reached a settlement, and a consent decree was filed; more than two years later, in May 1976, the NHL and its players' association reached agreement on a collective bargaining arrangement that incorporated By–Law 9A.[14] In McCourt v. California Sports, Inc.[15] in 1979 the Sixth U.S. Court of Appeals upheld NHL By-Law 9A on the grounds that federal labor policy deserves preeminence over antitrust policy and that the non-statutory labor exemption (a judicial tool created to effectuate federal labor policy)[16] insulates reserve systems from antitrust attack. On the other hand, in the case of basketball, the federal district court for the Southern District of New York in Robertson v. National Basketball Assn.[17] in 1975 upset the existing reserve system; the court held that the two control mechanisms of player draft and the perpetual reserve system were analogous to price-fixing devices condemned by the antitrust laws. These mechanisms allowed competing teams to eliminate competition in hiring of players and to lower invariably the cost of "doing business" for the team owners. But the next year the same Robertson case[18] approved until 1987 a right of first refusal system, i.e., a free agent's former team has a right of first refusal which allows it to match an offer made by another team and thereby possibly retain the free agent.[19] Professional baseball has a free agent system without equalization provisions.[20] A notewriter in 81 Harvard Law Review summed it up best:

Recognition that player restraints of some sort are necessary and justified does not mean that all features of the present system should be held immune from antitrust attack. Indeed, where defenses are allowed for restraints which would otherwise be summarily condemned, it is appropriate for courts to require not only convincing evidence that the restraint genuinely promotes the ends asserted to justify it but also that these benefits could not be obtained by devices with less anticompetitive potential.[21]

The option system, which is part and parcel of the overall reserve system, is a restrictive device precluding a drafted player from negotiating or signing with any other team.[22] He is bound to his team for the term of the contract plus one option period; if the professional athlete and his team do not come up with a new contract he may "play out his option" and then negotiate and sign with another team at the end of the option period.[23] But in the NFL, for example, if the player signs with another team, "equalization payment" to the former team is still required. Professional baseball has a similar restrictive system but does not provide for "equalization payment."[24] Professional hockey has similar restrictions, as evidenced in the NHL Standard Player's Contract.[25]

Another restrictive device or mechanism is the player draft, whereby the professional teams acquire virtually all their players. In the NFL, for example, each team is allowed to select a player and acquire exclusive rights to his services; the drafted player must sign with the team that drafted him or not play in the NFL that year. But in Kapp v. National Football League[26] the Ninth U.S. Court of Appeals held the player draft to be patently unreasonable insofar as it permitted a virtually perpetual boycott of the draft prospect even when the drafting club refuses or fails within a reasonable time to reach a contract with the player. Similarly, in Smith v. Pro-Football, Inc.[27] the court found the "group boycott'' to be violative of the Sherman Act and the Clayton Act, i.e., the rule that no team is permitted to negotiate prior to the draft with any player eligible to be drafted and that no team may negotiate with or sign any player selected by another team in the draft. However, in Saunders v. National Basketball Assn.[28] the federal district court in Illinois refused to recognize the claim of a professional basketball player that the National Basketball Association (NBA) league had refused him the opportunity to play basketball in the NBA league by not "drafting" him. The court pointed out that plaintiff had never made a demand or request on the NBA league to deal with him prior to the instant lawsuit.

The "eligibility rule" delineates the restriction upon professional athletes' ability or nonability to enter the leagues of professional sports. This rule bars certain athletes and at the same time requires those athletes that do enter the league to participate in the draft. Professional baseball makes a high school athlete eligible for the baseball draft if he drops out of school and remains out of school for one year after graduation; he is also eligible for the draft at any time after losing eligibility to participate in high school athletics due to age, completion of the maximum number of semesters of attendance set by the high school, or completion of the maximum number of seasons in which he was eligible to participate in any major high school sport.[29] Rule 3(k) of Professional Baseball Rules set forth the college requisites for the professional baseball player.[30] The NBA eligibility rules are somewhat more liberal, for any athlete may become eligible for the draft if his high school class has graduated and he renounces his intercollegiate basketball eligibility by written notice to the NBA at least 45 days before the draft.[31] The NFL eligibility rules are perhaps the most restrictive because they generally assume that an athlete has attended college, to wit: the athlete must have exhausted his college football eligibility and five years must have elapsed since he first attended college, or he must have graduated from a college before September 1 of the next NFL season.[32] Generally the professional athlete seeking employment in the NFL must therefore be over 22 years of age. A notewriter in 47 Nebraska Law Review contends that eligibility rules are secondary boycotts illegal per se under the Sherman Act and that such rules perpetuate economic injury through the use of economic or coercive pressure on a third party who has or is attempting to do business with the competing parties.[33]

The role of the sports agent can be vividly seen in Zinn v. Parrish,[34] where the courts considered the sports agent's duty to register under an Illinois employment agency law, the applicability of the federal Investment Advisory Act, and the general question of the legal standard against which the sports agent's performance must be measured. In April 1971 the agent Zinn entered into a professional management contract with Parrish, who was then under contract to the Cincinnati Bengals professional football team. The professional management contract contained provisions for the agent to furnish Parrish with advice on business investments, assistance with tax matters, endorsements of products, and efforts to find off-season employment for Parrish. In 1974 Parrish signed a four-year agreement at a substantial salary with the Cincinnati Bengals, and in 1975 he dismissed agent Zinn for unsatisfactory performance. When Zinn sued him for his agent's commission, Parrish defended on the ground that Zinn had not been licensed as a private employment agency under Illinois law.[35] The federal district court for the Northern District of Illinois, upon remand, rejected this argument, pointing out that the professional career services management offered by Zinn did not come within the scope of the Illinois law because the statute related only to undertaking a general public job placement for the client, which Zinn did not do. Parrish's second argument that Zinn functioned as an investment advisor under the federal Investment Advisory Act[36] and had failed to register, rendering the professional management contract void, was accepted by the federal district court; but the Seventh U.S. Court of Appeals reversed, concluding that any investment advice given pursuant to the contract was merely incidental to the main purpose of the management contract.[37] Furthermore, the federal statute in question was limited to situations involving advice about securities and not general business advice.[38] (Subsequently, the federal Investment Advisory Act of 1940 was amended to cover those who possess general management authority with respect to the money of their clients.)[39] The Seventh U.S. Court of Appeals deemed the services of the sports agent Zinn to be similar to the professional services rendered by lawyers,[40] brokers,[41] and trustees.[42] If Zinn had received specific compensation for investment advice (which was apparently not the case), he would have been required to register.[43] On the issue of the competence of the sports agent the federal appellate court found that Zinn had satisfied his legal obligation by his good faith efforts to fulfill the tasks he had assumed. "Each of these obligations was subject to an implied promise to make 'good faith' efforts to obtain what he sought. . . . The district court confused success with good faith efforts in concluding that Zinn's failure to obtain in many cases jobs or contracts for Parrish was a failure to perform."[44] But unfortunately this decision does not set forth any definition of the sports agent's legal duty with some sensitivity to the needs of the professional athlete whose relative youth and lack of business experience make him particularly vulnerable to malperformance or misperformance on the part of the sports agent.

The legal implications of conflicts of interest of the sports agent are seen in Detroit Lions, Inc. v. Argovitz.[45] Here the defendant sports agent had negotiated a contract on behalf of his client Billy Sims, a professional football player, with a professional football club in which the agent held a substantial ownership interest, to wit, the Houston Gamblers of the U.S. Football League (USFL). Subsequently Sims signed a contract to play for the Detroit Lions of the NFL. The federal district court in Michigan found that the sports agent had acted improperly in breach of his fiduciary duty to Sims, and the court entered an order rescinding Sims' contract with the Houston Gamblers. The fact that Sims knew of his agent's financial interest in the Houston Gamblers did not change the ruling: "It is not sufficient for the agent merely to inform the principal that he has an interest that conflicts with the principal's interest. Rather, he must inform the principal of all facts that come to his knowledge that are or may be material or which might affect his principal's rights or interests or influence the action he takes."[46]

In 1981 the state of California passed the first state legislation on sports agents in the form of the California Athletic Agencies Act.[47] Any agent who represents an athlete for the purpose of negotiating employment with a professional sports team must register with the California Labor Commissioner.[48] Employees of the teams are exempt, as are business advisors, tax consultants, and even personal managers.[49] Attorneys who are members of the State Bar of California "when acting as legal counsel for any person" are exempt,[50] but presumably out-of-state attorneys are not exempt and must register. The scope of the California statute is to require registration by any agent who solicits or contracts with athletes within the state of California;[51] failure to register means that the agency contract is unenforceable in California.[52] The fees charged by the sports agent as well as records of the clients are apparently subject to review by the California Labor Commissioner,[53] who also had authority to make initial findings in some controversies between agents and clients.[54] An adversely affected party is afforded the opportunity to seek de novo review in the California Superior Court.[55]

In 1983 the NFL Players' Association (NFLPA) adopted a regulatory scheme governing the conduct of sports agents[56] so as to improve the quality of representation and to preserve the integrity of the union-negotiated collective bargaining agreement. The union certifies agents as authorized contract advisors, and the agents agree to abide by a series of regulations including a limitation on fees and a prohibition on agent ownership of an interest in an NFL team.[57] The legitimate theatre industry in H. A. Artists & Associates v. Actors Equity Assn.[58] set a pattern for NFLPA regulations which are exempt from the Sherman Act under the labor exemption.[59]

2.2 LEAGUES, PARENT TEAMS, AND SUBSIDIARIES

Legal relationships in professional sports also include the professional sports team and its farm clubs or teams, which may engage in conduct that is violative of the antitrust laws. The 1984 decision of the U.S. Supreme Court in Copperweld Corp. v. Independence Tube Corp.[60] is illustrative of a complacency on the part of the judiciary to find agreements between a corporation and its wholly owned subisidiary to exclude one of the subsidiary's competitors from the market as in violation of the antitrust laws. The court flatly rejected the intra-enterprise conspiracy, holding that a parent corporation and its subsidiary are a single enterprise with a "complete unity of interest," and therefore Section 1 of the Sherman Act does not extend thereto.[61] This important decision naturally raises the question whether the professional sports league and its member teams,

Legal Relationships

which have a common interest in collective decisions, constitute a single enterprise or a "joint venture," the former being free of antitrust attack and the latter perhaps being in violation of Section 1 of the Sherman Act.[62] Undoubtedly, some forms of coordinated conduct among the member teams of the professional league are "unilateral" and therefore outside Section 1 of the Sherman Act, while other forms of conduct are "concerted" and therefore subject to Section 1 of the Sherman Act.[63] The Copperweld case[64] considered the restrictive practices of the parent and its subsidiary corporation to be "unilateral" and therefore immune from antitrust attack. The highest court compared that form of conduct to a multiple team of horses drawing a vehicle under the control of a single driver![65]

Of course, "unilateral" conduct, it must be pointed out, can be violative of Section 2 of the Sherman Act if the court deems the conduct to be a monopoly or an attempt to monopolize; Section 2 also reaches "conspiracies to monopolize."[66] But plural conduct, as opposed to singular conduct, is reached by Section 1 of the Sherman Act, and is illegal if its anti-competitive effects outweigh its pro-competitive benefits, even if the conduct poses no danger of monopolization.[67] Indeed, the Copperweld Corp. case[68] follows the Congressional belief that "concerted" or plural conduct should be treated more sternly than "unilateral" conduct because "concerted" conduct is especially "fraught with anti-competitive risks."[69] And yet the professional sports league presents a complicated mixture of "unilateral" and "concerted" conduct; consumer demand, it is explained, requires some aspects of league production to be undertaken collectively and other aspects to be taken independently. To coordinate a league championship, for example, collective conduct as well as unilateral conduct is mandatory. Unity and autonomy are vital to protect competition and to enhance revenues for all teams. A professional sports league is not an independent legal entity but an entity owing its very existence to the contractual relationships with the teams or clubs comprising the league. The clubs or teams themselves are organized as solely held private corporations, public corporations, Subchapter S corporations, ordinary partnerships, limited partnerships, and even sole proprietorships.[70] League constitutions and by-laws generally divide league operations into three categories, to wit: (1) activities controlled primarily by the individual teams or clubs; (2) activities controlled by the collective decisions of the league; and (3) activities governed by both the league and the individual teams or clubs. The day-to-day operations of the professional sports team are generally within the prerogative of the individual club or team; for example, in major league baseball, clubs control all rights to regular season games that are not sold by the league as part of the league network television or radio agreements; the league controls the rights to national broadcasts and telecasts of the regular season, playoffs, and World Series games.[71] The individual club or team determines ticket prices for its games and controls the sale of concessions at the sports facility.[72] Revenues from professional sporting events are generally shared by the member teams or clubs, although the sources and proportion of shared revenue vary from league to league; generally shared are revenues from the sale of broadcasting and televising rights, fees paid by new members of the league, actual gate receipts, and league merchandising proceeds. The importance of broadcasting and television rights is seen by the fact that in 1980 the average NFL team received 40 percent of its gross revenue from that source.[73] Indeed, approximately 97 percent of all NFL revenues are pooled for sharing by member teams or clubs.[74]

In practice, the judiciary has rejected the "single-entity" defense of the action by a league and its member teams, as illustrated by Los Angeles Memorial Coliseum Commission v. NFL[75] wherein the Ninth U.S. Court of Appeals was concerned with an NFL rule that barred the Oakland Raiders from moving to Los Angeles without the approval of other teams or clubs of the NFL. The court concluded that the collective decisions of a professional sports league are always "concerted" activity subject to Section 1 of the Sherman Act.[76] Clearly this ruling appears to be in conflict with the U.S. Supreme Court determination in the Copperweld Corp. case,[77] which rejected the legal entities approach to plurality in finding a single entity of parent and subsidiary corporation. But there is a world of factual difference between a league existing by virtue of contractual commitments of its member teams, and two corporations which legal entities happen to have a financial kinship. Many legal commentators find professional sports leagues to be single entities for all purposes relating to the production of professional sports events.[78] As the federal district court in North American Soccer League (NASL) v. NFL[79] expressed it:

The single economic entity concept finds some support in the [idea] that joint activity, inherently necessary to produce a marketable . . . product, creates a single, "separate seller" of that product. . . . A professional sports team cannot play or market itself. The sport's league product can exist only as the result of joint effort. In that context, I conclude there is no combination in restraint of trade.[80]

In summary, it is readily discernible that the legal relationships in professional sports are complex and competitively harsh in the sense that legal status may change from day to day depending upon the popular view of the particular professional sport.

NOTES

1. See generally 32 Univ of Fla L Rev at pp. 670 et seq. (1980).
2. See Robertson v. National Basketball Assn., 389 F Supp 867 (SDNY, 1975), aff. 556 F2d 682 (2nd Cir., 1977); Kapp v. National Football League, 586 F2d 644 (9th Cir., 1978), cert den 441 US 907 (1979); and Philadelphia World Hockey Club, Inc. v. Philadelphia Hockey Club Inc., 351 F Supp 462 (ED Pa., 1972).
3. See 6 Cal West L Rev 133 (1969).
4. See 4 Pepperdine L Rev 285 (1977).
5. See 43 Cornell L Rev 566 (1958).

Legal Relationships 25

6. See 46 Missouri L Rev 798 et seq. (1981).
7. See 15 New England L Rev 3 (1980).
8. See New York Times (Dec. 22, 1985) at p. S3.
9. See Insight Magazine (Aug. 25, 1986) at pp. 8 et seq.
10.

9A.2. A player who enters into a 1974 Form Standard Player's contract shall have the right to become a free agent in accordance with the terms of Section 17 of said contract and in accordance with the Player's Option contract to which said Section 17 refers.

9A.3. Any other player under contract to any Member Club on the date this By-Law is adopted, the final year of whose contract ends on or after September 30, 1974, shall become a free agent on June 1 of the final year of that contract, except that any such player whose contract is a 1972 Form Standard Player's contract whose final year ends on September 30, 1974, shall become a free agent on June 1, 1975. For purposes of this subsection 3, the "final year" of a contract shall be the last year of its fixed term specified in Section 1 of said contract, including, however, any period added to that term by any addendum or exercised special option contracted for by the Member Club and player.

9A.4. The foregoing subsection 3 shall not be construed to derogate in any way from the rights of any player under any contract but constitutes instead a waiver of any and all rights by each Member Club under the contracts to which said subsection is applicable to require the services of players for periods beyond those set out in said subsection.

11.

Free Agent List
9A.5. On or before May 15 in each year each Member Club shall deliver to the President a report in writing, by TWX, telegram or by mail, (which report shall remain confidential until the issuance of the Free Agent List described below), setting forth the name of each player under contract to it who, unless signed to a new contract with said Club prior to June 1 of that year, will become a free agent as of that date. Each Member Club shall also furnish to the President after May 15 of such year, by immediate TWX or telegram, information as to any change of status of any such player. The President shall, on June 1 of such year, issue to all Member Clubs a Free Agent List setting forth the names of all players together with the name of the Member Club with which each such player was last under contract, and shall thereafter promptly issue such bulletins correcting, amending, or updating such list as may be necessary to ensure its accuracy and currency. Except during a period that a player's name remains on the Free Agent List, no Member Club other than the Club with which he was last under contract may sign a contract or negotiate with such player, directly or indirectly, without the prior written consent of the Member Club with which he was last under contract, or otherwise take any action which would violate Section 15 of these By-Laws.

12.

Obligation to make equalization payment
9A.6. Each time that a player becomes a free agent and the right to his services

is subsequently acquired by any Member Club other than the club with which he was last under contract or by any club owned or controlled by any such Member Club, the Member Club first acquiring the right to his services, or owning or controlling the club first acquiring that right, shall make an equalization payment to the Member Club with which such player was previously under contract, as prescribed by subsection 8 of this By-Law. Each Member Club may acquire the right to the services of as many free agents as it wishes, subject to the provisions of subsection 9 of this By-Law. Determination of Equalization Payment.

Purpose

9A.7. The purpose of the equalization payment shall be to compensate a player's previous Member Club fairly for loss of the right to his services when that player becomes a free agent and the right to his services is acquired by another Member Club or a club owned or controlled by another Member club.

Procedure

9A.8.(a) The Member Club acquiring the services of a free agent, or owning or controlling the club acquiring such services, shall immediately notify the player's previous Member Club and the President of that fact by TWX or telegram. The equalization payment shall be determined, if possible, by mutual agreement of the two Member Clubs involved. If no such agreement is reached within three business days after the date on which the player's services are acquired, each of the Member Clubs involved shall within two additional business days submit by TWX or telegram its proposal for an equalization payment to a neutral arbitrator selected from time to time by majority vote of the Board of Governors of the League.

9A.8.(b) Within two business days after the deadline for receipt of the Clubs' proposals, the arbitrator shall, unless notified by both Clubs in writing, by TWX or by telegram that they have reached agreement on the equalization payment, select without change one of the proposals submitted to him, and his determination shall be final and not subject to review.

9A.8.(c) The Clubs' proposals and the arbitrator's determination of equalization must be limited to:-

(i) the assignment of a contract or contracts for the services of a player or players binding upon such player or players for at least the next season; and/or

(ii) choices in any intra-league, inter-league and/or amateur drafts to be held at any time subsequent to such a proposal and/or unsigned draft choices or negotiation nominees; and/or

(iii) cash.

In making his selection the arbitrator shall be governed by the policy that cash shall be used for equalization purpose only as a last resort.

9A.8.(d) The contracts of all players under contract to the acquiring Club at the time a free agent is acquired shall be available for equalization purposes.

9A.8.(e) The cost of the arbitrator shall be borne by the League.

9A.8.(f) To facilitate a good faith effort to reach agreement on the equalization payment, the acquiring Club shall furnish to the Club entitled to that payment such information as may reasonably be required with respect to any player the assignment of whose contract is proposed by either party as an equalization payment, in whole or in part, including, but not limited to, the salary, bonus, and other compensation of such player, a copy of the player's contract, and any adverse information with respect to the physical, mental, or emotional condition of such player.

9A.8.(g) The details of the procedure to be followed in the event arbitration is required shall be set forth in the agreement entered into by the League and the arbitrator.

Satisfaction of Equalization Obligation

9A.9. No Member Club, or any club owned or controlled by such Member Club, shall be entitled to sign or acquire the right to the services of any free agent until it has satisfied in full its equalization obligation under these By-Laws as to each other free agent, the right to whose services it has acquired, by assigning the player contracts and/or draft rights and otherwise consummating the equalization payment required by mutual agreement or by arbitration. It shall be the responsibility of the acquiring Club to notify the President that it has satisfied its equalization obligation.

9A.10. The President shall disallow the right of any acquiring Member Club to use the services of any signed free agent if he has not received the notice specified in subsection 9 or otherwise finds that the equalization payment for that player or for any other free agent previously signed has not been fully satisfied by said Member Club in accordance with this By-Law.

13. Supra note 2.
14. Supra notes 10, 11, and 12.
15. 600 F2d 1193 (6th Cir., 1979), reversing 460 F Supp 904 (ED Mich., 1978).
16. See Sections 6 and 20 of the Clayton Act (15 USC 17 and 29 USC 52) as well as Sections 4, 5, 6, and 13 of the Norris-LaGuardia Act (29 USC 104, 105, 106, 113).
17. 389 F Supp 867 (SDNY, 1975).
18. 72 FRD 64 (SDNY, 1976).
19. See 45 Antitrust L J 290 (1976).
20. Supra note 1 at p. 573.
21. (1967) at pp. 418 et seq.
22. See 25 Baylor L Rev 20 (1973).
23. The Standard Player's Contract of the NFL, for example, provides in part:

> 5. The Player promises and agrees that during the term of this contract he will not play football or engage in activities related to football for any other person, firm, corporation, or institution, or on his own behalf, except with the prior written consent of the Club and the Commissioner. . . .
>
> 8. . . . [T]he Club shall have the right, in addition to any other rights which the Club may possess, to enjoin him by appropriate injunction proceedings against playing football or any other professional sport, without the consent of the Club, or engaging in activities related to football for any person, firm, corporation, institution, or on his own behalf. . . .
>
> 9. It is mutually agreed that the Club shall have the right to sell, exchange, assign or transfer this contract and the Player's services hereunder to any other Club in the League. Player agrees to accept such assignment and to report promptly to the assignee Club and faithfully to perform and carry out this contract with the assignee Club as if it had been entered into by the Player with the assignee Club instead of with this Club.

10. The Club may, by sending notice in writing to the Player, on or before the first day of May following the football season . . . renew this contract for a further term of one (1) year on the same terms as are provided by this contract, except that (1) the Club may fix the rate of compensation to be paid by the Club to the Player during said further term, which rate of compensation shall not be less than ninety percent (90%) of the sum set in #3 hereof . . . and (2) after such renewal this contract shall not include a further option to the Club to renew the contract.

24. The Uniform Player's Contract in baseball provides in part:

4.(a) . . . The Player agrees that, in addition to other remedies, the Club shall be entitled to injunctive and other equitable relief to prevent a breach of this contract by the Player, including, among others, the right to enjoin the Player from playing baseball for any other person or organization during the term of this contract.
5.(a) The player agrees that, while under contract, and prior to expiration of the Club's right to renew this contract, he will not play baseball otherwise than for the Club, except that the Player may participate in post-season games under the conditions prescribed in the Major League Rules. . . .
6.(a) The Player agrees that this contract may be assigned by the Club (and reassigned by any assignee Club) to any other Club in accordance with the Major League Rules and the Professional Baseball Rules. . . .
10.(a) On or before January 15 (or if a Sunday, then the next preceding business day) of the year next following the last playing season covered by this contract, the Club may tender to the Player a contract for the term of that year by mailing the same to the Player at his address following his signature hereto, or if none be given, then at his last address of record with the Club. If prior to the March 1 next succeeding said January 15, the Player and the Club have not agreed upon the terms of such contract, then on or before 10 days after March 1, the Club shall have the right by written notice to the Player at said address to renew this contract for the period of one year on the same terms, except that the amount payable to the Player shall be such as the club shall fix in said notice; provided, however, that said amount, if fixed by a Major League Club, shall be an amount payable at a rate not less than 80% of the rate stipulated for the preceding year.
  (b) The Club's right to renew this contract, as provided in subparagraph (a) of this paragraph 10, and the promise of the Player not to play otherwise than with the Club have been taken into consideration in determining the amount payable under paragraph 2 hereof.

25.

6. . . . The player therefore agrees that the Club shall have the right, in addition to any other rights which the Club may possess, to enjoin him by appropriate injunction proceedings from playing hockey for any other team. . . .
11. It is mutually agreed that the Club shall have the right to sell, assign, exchange and transfer this contract, and to loan the player's services to any other professional hockey club, and the Player agrees to accept and be bound by such sale, exchange, assignment, transfer or loan, and will faithfully perform and carry

> out this contract with the same purpose and effect as if it had been entered into by the Player and such other Club.

26. 390 F Supp 73 (ND Cal., 1976), aff 586 F2d 644 (9th Cir., 1976), cert den 441 US 907 (1977).
27. 420 F Supp 738 (DC, 1976), modif 593 F2d 1173 (DC Cir., 1976).
28. 348 F Supp 649 (Ill., 1972).
29. Rule 3 (h) of Professional Baseball Rules; see generally 46 Missouri L Rev (1981) at p. 799.
30.

> A college athlete is a member of his college baseball team in the following situations: (a) if he is a freshman in a college that does not have an intercollegiate freshman baseball program, or if his college does have such a program and he is a member or a prospective member of the freshman squad; (b) if he is a sophomore and is a member or a prospective member of the varsity baseball squad; (c) if he is a junior and is a member or a prospective member of the varsity baseball squad; or (d) if he is a senior and is a member or a prospective member of the varsity baseball squad.

College is defined as

> any university or other institution of higher education located in the continental United States, including but not limited to, all members of the National Collegiate Athletic Association, which confers degrees upon students following completion of sufficient credit hours to equal a four-year course, provided the college is represented by a baseball team which participates in intercollegiate competition.

31. See 46 Missouri L Rev (1981) at p. 799.
32. See Article XII, Section 12.1 (A) of NFL Constitution.
33. (1968) at pp. 82 et seq. However, the article cited Molinas v. National Basketball Assn., 190 F Supp 241 (SDNY, 1961) as a reasonable restraint case prohibiting an athlete convicted of the crime of betting.
34. 461 F Supp 11 (ND Ill., 1977), rev 582 F2d 1282 (7th Cir., 1978), and 644 F2d 360 (7th Cir., 1981).
35. See Ill Rev Stat, Ch 11, Sections 901–918 (1978).
36. See 15 USC 80 (b)-2(a)(11).
37. 644 F2d at p. 364.
38. See 15 USC 80(b)-2(a) (18).
39. See Abrahamson v. Fleschner, 568 F2d 862 (2nd Cir., 1977).
40. See Sullivan v. Chase Investment Services, 434 F Supp 171 (ND Cal., 1977).
41. See Securities and Exchange Commission v. National Executive Planners, Ltd., 503 F Supp 1066 (MDNC, 1980).
42. See In Re August P. Loring, Jr., 11 SEC 885 (1942).
43. Supra note 41.
44. 644 F2d at p. 366.
45. 580 F Supp 542 (ED Mich., 1984).
46. Id. at p. 548.
47. Sections 1500-1547 of California Labor Code.
48. Sections 1500 and 1510 of California Labor Code.

49. See Raden v. Laurie, 262 P2d 61 (Cal DCA, 1953).
50. Supra note 47 at Section 1500(b).
51. Section 12500(a) of California Administrative Code, Title 8 (1982).
52. Supra note 47 at Section 1546.
53. Supra note 47 at Sections 1531 and 1532.
54. Supra note 47 at Section 1543.
55. Id.
56. See NFLPA Regulations Governing Contract Advisors (1983).
57. Cf. Detroit Lions, Inc. v. Argovitz, supra note 45.
58. 451 US 704 (1981), aff'g 622 F2d 647 (2nd Cir., 1980), aff'g 478 F Supp 496 (SDNY, 1979).
59. See Section 3.8 of Chapter 3 herein.
60. 104 S Ct 2731 (1984).
61. See, for example, the holding in Perma Life Mufflers, Inc. v. International Parts Corp., 392 US 134 (1968).
62. See generally 52 U of Chi L Rev 999 (1985).
63. Id. at p. 999.
64. Supra note 60.
65. Supra note 60 at p. 2742.
66. 15 USC 2.
67. Note Northern Pacific Railway Co. v. United States, 356 US 1 (1956).
68. Supra note 60 at p. 2741.
69. Supra note 62 at p. 1005.
70. Supra note 62 at p. 1010.
71. See Select Committee on Professional Sports, Inquiry Into Professional Sports, H. R. Rep. No. 1786, 94th Cong., 2d Sess., 45–46 (1977).
72. See Los Angeles Memorial Coliseum Commission v. National Football League, 519 F Supp 581 (CD Cal., 1981), aff 726 F2d 1381 (9th Cir., 1984), cert den 105 S Ct 397 (1984).
73. See National Football League Economics: 1970–1980 (1982) at p. 9.
74. See Professional Sports Antitrust Immunity: Hearings Before the Senate Committee on the Judiciary on S. 2784 and S. 2821, 97th Cong., 2d Sess. (1982) at p. 34.
75. Supra note 72.
76. Id.
77. Supra note 60.
78. See 82 Mich L Rev 1 (1983), and 41 Antitrust L. J. 5 (1971); also 32 De Paul L Rev 625 (1983).
79. 670 F2d 1249 (2nd Cir., 1982), cert den 459 US 1074 (1982).
80. Id.; district court opinion in 505 F Supp 659 at p. 688 (SDNY, 1980).

3

Exemption and Non-exemption of Professional Sports from the Antitrust Laws

Of all the professional sports rampant on the American scene today only the professional sport of baseball is the proud owner of an exemption from the antitrust laws. Hereinafter under Section 3.1 baseball is examined for its purity; Section 3.2 deals with professional football, while Section 3.3 is concerned with professional basketball. Professional hockey is the subject of Section 3.4, and boxing occupies center stage in Section 3.5. Tennis and golf, as professional businesses, are found in Section 3.6, and Section 3.7 covers soccer and other professional sports. Section 3.8 delineates ''labor's exemption,'' perhaps an anomaly in the very nature of professional sport businesses.

Organized professional sports in the United States have in general operated apart from normal business considerations, and their rules of business conduct have not been subject to governmental scrutiny to the same extent as any ordinary business.[1] The history of antitrust application to the businesses of professional sports is an absorbing tale of sentimentality and of special interests.

3.1 BASEBALL

Professional baseball has been described as America's national pastime, part of American folklore, and as a loveable integration with the entertainment industry. Professional baseball possesses enormous economic power affecting millions of Americans in their daily lives. This monopolistic power stems in great measure from the 1922 decision of the U.S. Supreme Court in Federal Baseball Club of Baltimore Inc. v. National League of Professional Baseball Clubs.[2] The complaint recited the formation and attempted operation of the

Federal Baseball League, the combination and conspiracy of the National League and "organized baseball" to destroy such competition, and the ultimate elimination of the Federal Baseball League as a competitor of the National League. The trial court was impressed with the mounting evidence that the National League had violated the antitrust laws, and held, as a matter of law, that the defendant had attempted to monopolize the business of professional baseball as part of interstate trade or commerce. On appeal the U.S. Court of Appeals for the District of Columbia reversed: "A game of baseball is not susceptible of being transferred. . . . Not until the players come into contact with their opponents on the baseball field and the contest opens, does the game come into existence. It is local in its beginning and in its end . . . a game effects no exchange of things according to the meaning of 'trade or commerce'." The appellate court dismissed the reserve clause, the publication of lists of ineligible players, and other restrictive provisions and practices as "relating directly to the conservation of the personnel of the clubs" which did not "directly affect the movement . . . in interstate commerce. Whatever effect, if any, they had was incidental, and therefore did not offend against the statute."[3] Upon writ of error the case came before the U.S. Supreme Court, and the illustrious scholar Mr. Justice Oliver Wendell Holmes wrote the opinion of the court affirming the appellate court's holding that professional baseball clubs were not subject to the antitrust laws:

The business is giving exhibitions of baseball which are purely state affairs. It is true that in order to attain for these exhibitions the great popularity that they have achieved, competitions must be arranged between clubs from different cities and States. But the fact that in order to give the exhibitions the Leagues must induce free persons to cross state lines and must arrange and pay for their doing so is not enough to change the character of the business . . . the transport is a mere incident, not the essential thing. That to which it is incident, the exhibition, although made for money, would not be called trade or commerce in the commonly accepted use of those words. As it is put by the defendant, personal effort, not related to production, is not a subject of commerce. That which in its consummation is not commerce does not become commerce among the States because the transportation that we have mentioned takes place.[4]

Thus, professional baseball in 1922 was granted an exemption from the application of the federal antitrust laws upon the ground that this professional sport was not engaged in interstate commerce or trade, and furthermore baseball was in essence not a commercial activity. To appreciate the significance of Mr. Justice Holmes' decision (which the Second U.S. Court of Appeals 48 years later charitably described as "not one of Mr. Justice Holmes' happiest days"[5]) a bit of baseball history is in order. In 1879 the "reserve clause" system was created when seven surviving teams of the National League secretly agreed to reserve five players each for the next season.[6] Eight years later, in 1887, the National League of Baseball Clubs and the American Association of

Baseball Clubs agreed to a provision affording all teams the right to reserve a stated number of players so as to reduce a team's operating expenses by decreasing salaries of players and by restricting the influx of superior players at higher salaries.[7] This "reserve" system carried over to the player contracts under which players agreed to be bound in perpetuity to the same team. As the New York Supreme Court had expressed it in 1914, "If a baseball player . . . desires to be employed at work for which he is qualified . . . he must submit to dominion over his personal freedom and the control of his services for sale, transfer, or exchange, without his consent, or abandon his vocation and seek employment at some other kind of labor."[8] Sanctions imposed upon the recalcitrant player or the player breaching such a contract included injunctions to prevent contract "jumping" as well as "blacklisting" by all other baseball clubs in the professional leagues.[9]

This monopoly and these various restrictive practices by professional baseball were not challenged in the courts for the next 24 years until the 1946 Pasquel case.[10] Here the New York Yankees sought a temporary injunction to restrain officials of the Mexican League from inducing Yankee players to repudiate their contracts with the Yankees. Mr. Justice Miller of the New York Supreme Court, New York County, found ample evidence that the defendant Pasquel and the Mexican League had attempted and were continuing to "entice away plaintiff's players," which conduct the court deemed to be "wrongful and illegal under well-settled principles of law." The court dismissed defendants' argument that an injunction should not be granted, finding that professional baseball was a monopoly and was engaged in offensive restrictive practices.[11] Three years later in 1949 Danny Gardella, a former New York Giants baseball player, challenged the epochal decision of the Federal Baseball Club case.[12] Gardella had been placed on an ineligible list of players who were barred from employment in professional baseball because he had contracted with and played for a baseball team in the Mexican League. The federal district court in New York granted the motion of the Commissioner of Baseball to dismiss the case upon the authority of the 1922 Federal Baseball Club case that baseball in 1949 was not "trade or commerce." The Second U.S. Court of Appeals,[13] however, did not agree that professional baseball was not "trade or commerce" and remanded the case for trial. But before the U.S. Supreme Court could review the matter the Commissioner of Baseball reinstated the players who had "jumped" to the Mexican League and the action for damages was discontinued. In 1953 the highest court entertained Toolson v. New York Yankees[14] on the question of organized baseball's reserve clause as being violative of the Sherman Act; plaintiff, a minor leaguer in the New York Yankees organization, contended that the reserve clause precluded him from reaching the major leagues. In a 7-2 decision the court upheld the 31-year-old decision in the Federal Baseball Club case that professional baseball was not "trade or commerce": "If there are evils in this field which warrant application to it of the antitrust laws, it should be by legislation." The court opined further:

In Federal Baseball Club case . . . this Court held that the business of providing baseball games for profit between clubs of professional baseball players was not within the scope of the federal antitrust laws. Congress (as of 1953) has had the ruling under consideration, but has not seen fit to bring such business under these laws by legislation having prospective effect. . . . the judgments below are affirmed on the authority of Federal Baseball Club of Baltimore v. National League of Professional Baseball Clubs, supra, so far as that decision determines that Congress had no intention of including the business of baseball within the scope of the federal antitrust laws.[15]

In 1972 Curt Flood, an outfielder with the St. Louis Cardinals, sued organized baseball, contending that, due to baseball's reserve system he was given no opportunity to negotiate his involuntary trade to the Philadelphia Phillies. The federal district court for the Southern District of New York opined at the outset:

Baseball's status in the life of the nation is so pervasive that it would not strain credulity to say the Court can take judicial notice that baseball is everybody's business. To put it mildly and with restraint, it would be unfortunate indeed if a fine sport and profession, which brings surcease from daily travail and an escape from the ordinary to most inhabitants of this land, were to suffer in the least because of undue concentration by any one or any group on commercial and profit considerations. The game is on higher ground; it behooves everyone to keep it there.

The U.S. Supreme Court in Flood v. Kuhn[16] simply continued the exemption of professional baseball from the federal antitrust laws based upon its prior decisions in 1922 and 1953. Justice Harry Blackmun, writing for the majority of the court, held that professional baseball is a business and is engaged in interstate commerce; but

with its reserve system enjoying exemption from antitrust laws, baseball is, in a very distinct sense, an exception and an anomaly. . . . It is an aberration that has been with us now for half a century, one heretofore deemed fully entitled to the benefit of stare decisis, and one that has survived the Court's expanding concept of interstate commerce. . . . If there is any inconsistency or illogic in all this, it is an inconsistency and illogic of long standing that is to be remedied by Congress and not by this Court.[17]

The highest court also affirmed the position of the lower federal courts that, although baseball is exempt from the federal antitrust laws, the states are precluded from antitrust regulation of baseball because the nationwide character of organized baseball required uniform resolution and that uniformity would be lost if diverse state antitrust laws were applied.[18] The Court here refused to consider the argument of the major leagues that the non-statutory labor exemption[19] immunized the reserve system from the federal antitrust laws. The strong dissenting opinion of Justice William Douglas as referred to the 1922

Federal Baseball Club case as "a derelict in the stream of the law that we, its creator, should remove."[20]

The clear inability of the courts to overcome the 1922 precedent that professional baseball is exempt from the antitrust laws prompted two baseball players, Andy Messersmith and Dave McNally, to challenge the restraints upon baseball players by resorting to arbitration in 1981,[21] some eight years after the grievance procedure had been established by a collective bargaining agreement.[22] Both professional baseball players argued that they were free agents at the end of their option year, while the team owners contended that when the club renewed the contract it renewed all terms including the term giving the club the right to renew the option clause. But the arbitrators, headed by Peter Seitz, ruled that the players' contracts encompassed only a limited right of renewal due to the personal nature of the employment relationship, and therefore the two ball players were indeed free agents! The Eighth U.S. Court of Appeals in Kansas City Royals Baseball Corp. v. Major League Players' Assn.[23] affirmed the arbitrators' decision, and observed that, although professional baseball was exempt from the antitrust laws, the business of professional baseball affected interstate commerce and was therefore subject to other federal laws including national labor laws.[24] In 1978 the Seventh U.S. Court of Appeals in Charles O. Finley & Co. v. Kuhn[25] strengthened the hand of the Commissioner of Baseball as the sole and exclusive holder of the right to decide disputes, and the court continued baseball's exemption from the antitrust laws.[26]

3.2 FOOTBALL

Professional football is today a multimillion dollar business that stretches across the United States and involves thousands of professional athletes and team owners as well as countless satellite businesses. Professional football was organized in 1920 as the American Professional Football Association, truly a loose federation of teams.[27] Schedules were flexible, and teams were frequently sponsored by local businesses; top college players played for pay under assumed names. By the 1930s the popularity of professional football spread, but it was not until the 1950s that rules defining player relations were promulgated in the form of the college draft and the waiver system for release of veteran players. Other restrictions compelled a player who chose to play out the final year of a contract and switch teams to play at 90 percent of the previous year's salary. In 1953 in United States v. National Football League[28] professional football was found wanting in its restraints upon the sale of radio and television rights, and the federal district court in Pennsylvania subjected football to antitrust attack. The court reasoned that radio and television were clearly involved with interstate commerce, and therefore professional football was an interstate business subject to the antitrust laws. It was the case of Radovich v. National Football League[29] in 1957 that cemented the fact that professional football was subject to the antitrust laws.

It all began in 1946 when Bill Radovich, a professional football player for four years with the Detroit Lions of the National Football League, requested a transfer to an NFL team on the West Coast so as to be near his ill father. The Detroit Lions refused the transfer, and Radovich broke his player contract and signed with the Los Angeles Dons of the competing All-American Football Conference. In 1948 the San Francisco Clippers of the competing Pacific Coast Football League offered Radovich a job as player-coach, but withdrew the job offer when the NFL advised the San Francisco Clippers that Radovich had been "blacklisted" and could not be employed by any organized professional football team. Radovich thereupon sued the NFL for treble damages, alleging a conspiracy to monopolize interstate commerce in the business of professional football. The federal appellate court in California dismissed the complaint on authority of the Federal Baseball Club case,[30] and held that football, like baseball, was not "trade or commerce" within the meaning of the Sherman Act. But the U.S. Supreme Court reversed, and refused to extend the exemption for baseball to the professional sport of football because Congress had not done so and "the volume of interstate business involved in organized professional football places it within the provisions of the Sherman Act." The court observed that the NFL and its member teams scheduled football games in various metropolitan centers and contracted for the transmission of reports of the games over radio and television into several states by entering into contracts which produced a significant portion of the gross receipts of the clubs and the NFL, and without which the business of operating professional football teams would not be profitable.[31] In 1961 in United States v. National Football League[32] the federal district court invalidated a $9.3 million television contract between the NFL and the Columbia Broadcasting System as in violation of the antitrust laws: "By this agreement (an exclusive contract to televise regular season football games by the 14 professional football teams) the member clubs . . . have eliminated competition among themselves in the sale of television rights to their games. . . . Clearly this restricts individual clubs from determining from which areas the telecasts of their games may be made. . . . "[33] Just two months later, on September 30, 1961, the 87th Congress enacted Public Law 87-331 and obviated the decision by providing that the antitrust laws "shall not apply to any joint agreement . . . by which any league of clubs participating in professional football . . . sells or otherwise transfers all or any part of the rights of such league's member clubs in the sponsored telecasting of games . . . engaged in or conducted by such clubs." Nevertheless, courts have subjected other practices of professional football to the antitrust laws, as illustrated by Dallas Cowboys Football Club, Inc. v. Harris,[34] but have found justification for some player restrictions, to wit: the provision in the Standard Player Contract that allowed a club to extend unilaterally the contract for an additional year at a 10 percent reduction in salary, at the end of which year the player becomes a free agent and can negotiate with another club, was held to be not so unreasonable or harsh as to be unenforceable in equity.

Exemption and Non-exemption

In the 1960s a veritable myriad of cases about professional football was heard by the courts, beginning in 1962 with American Football League v. National Football League[35] when the Fourth U.S. Court of Appeals opined that "it is not disputed that (the plaintiff league and the defendant professional league and their member teams) are engaged in interstate commerce and subject to the provisions of the antitrust laws." Nine years later in 1971 in Hecht v. Pro-Football, Inc.[36] the federal district court in the District of Columbia referred to the "unusual applicability of the antitrust laws" to contracts by, between, or among those who engage in the business of professional football. It was at the January 1972 meeting of the National Football League Players' Association Board of Representatives that the "Rozelle Rule," one of the many devices of the NFL to control interteam player movement, was attacked, and Mackey v. National Football League[37] resulted in a federal district court finding that the Rozelle Rule was not the "product of bona fide arms-length bargaining" because the NFLPA was comparatively weak financially and the Rozelle Rule was unilaterally created. The Eighth U.S. Court of Appeals affirmed,[38] relying upon a 1965 decision of the U.S. Supreme Court in Meat Cutters v. Jewel Tea Co., Inc.,[39] which expounded the principle:

The issue in this case is whether the . . . restriction . . . is so intimately related to wages, hours and working conditions that the union's successful attempt to obtain that provision through "bona fide, arms-length bargaining" in pursuit of their own labor union policies, and not at the behest of or in combination with nonlabor groups, falls within the protection of the national labor policy and is therefore exempt from the Sherman Act.[40]

Clearly, the Rozelle Rule cannot be unilaterally imposed upon a union when it is not consonant with the self-interest of the NFLPA. But the court explicitly encouraged the parties nevertheless to "resolve this question through collective bargaining,"[41] and the court developed a three-pronged test to determine whether the non-statutory labor exemption[42] applied to the labor management agreement, to wit: the exemption applied if the restraint on trade affected only the parties to the collective bargaining relationship, if the restriction was classifiable as a mandatory subject of collective bargaining, and if the agreement was the product of bona fide, arm's-length negotiations.[43] In applying its own test the federal appellate court observed that the Rozelle Rule had no appreciable impact upon competing leagues or others outside the bargaining relationship and was a condition of employment; but there were no bona fide, arm's-length negotiations, and therefore the Rozelle Rule was a violation of the antitrust laws, and labor policies in favor of collective bargaining would not be furthered by a judicial grant of immunity to the NFL from antitrust attack. Furthermore, the Rozelle Rule was unreasonably broad in its application, lacked procedural safeguards, and unlimited duration, and substantially restricted the player's freedom of movement.[44] In 1974 the federal district court in California in Kapp

v. National Football League[45] had held that the Rozelle Rule, the player draft, and the prohibition on tampering with players, were unreasonable restraints of trade; the court recognized that, while the monopolistic combinations engaged in by the NFL would be per se antitrust violation in other businesses, the uniqueness of the professional sports business required the application of the "Rule of Reason" standard.[46] The court concluded that the contractual restrictions on the employee's right to pursue his profession with other employers were so patently unreasonable that it was unnecessary to determine whether the restrictions were mandatory subjects of collective bargaining or whether the agreement itself had been the subject of genuine negotiations.[47] Interestingly, the plaintiff Kapp, who alleged that he had been improperly boycotted by the NFL because he refused to sign a standard player contract, was awarded no damages by the jury; the jury apparently was of the mind that an unsigned contract did not give rise to damages.

The college draft system of the NFL was held to violate the Sherman Act in Smith v. Pro-Football, Inc.[48] The plaintiff was a first-round draft pick of the Washington Redskins whose career prematurely ended when he suffered a neck injury; he alleged that the college draft system prevented his negotiating a contract that would have contained adequate guarantees against loss of earnings due to injury. The court agreed that the college draft system was thrust upon a weak players' association by the team owners so that the labor exemption would not grant immunity from antitrust review; furthermore, the college draft system virtually eliminated economic competition among team owners for the services of the professional football player. Note that the federal district court here had labeled the 1968 college draft system a "group boycott," a per se violation of the Sherman Act. That same year in Reynolds v. National Football League[49] the Eighth U.S. Court of Appeals had held that the Rozelle Rule and other restrictions upon players were inconsistent with the competitive purpose of the federal antitrust laws as an unreasonable restraint on football players' marketing of their services. That case was indeed a class action and was based upon Section 4 of the Clayton Act:[50] "all professional football players who have been under contract to one or more of the defendants at any time since September 17, 1972."[51] Under the settlement of the case (the entire record of the trial transcript of Mackey v. NFL,[52] some 12,000 pages, was incorporated into the Reynolds record) the NFL agreed to pay the plaintiff class the sum of $13,675,000. That sum was divided among "all professional football players" according to a point system under which varying amounts of points were allotted for each year played in the NFL, whether the player had played out his option, and the relative strength of the rival World Football League in the year the option was played out. But 16 members of the plaintiff class were dissatisfied with the terms of the settlement and appealed under Rule 23(b)(3), which allows class members to "opt out"; but the Eighth U.S. Court of Appeals found no abuse of discretion and affirmed certification of the entire plaintiff class under Rule 23(b)(1) of the Federal Rules of Civil Procedure[53] because the settlement was fair, reasonable, and adequate. The new NFL first refusal principle, a part of the settlement package, was not more restrictive, although that principle was not directly before the federal appellate court.

In 1981 Leonard Tose, owner of the Philadelphia Eagles professional football team in the NFL, sued various banks and defendant team owners, alleging a conspiracy to force the distress sale of plaintiff's controlling interest in his football team.[54] The Third U.S. Court of Appeals affirmed the trial court's order directing summary judgment in favor of certain defendants because plaintiff did not prove any conspiracy to interfere with the credit market by tampering with the interest rates so as to deny plaintiff a loan. The decision of the NFL in another context to deny a qualified applicant a professional football franchise was held not to be a violation of the antitrust laws in Mid-South Grizzlies v. NFL[55] since the action had no anti-competitive effect as persons seeking franchises were not competitors of the NFL. But in Los Angeles Memorial Coliseum Commission v. National Football League[56] a $14.5 million treble damage award was upheld against the NFL for NFL restrictions upon the use of a stadium which occupies "an indispensable and intimate connection with professional football and football teams."

In July 1986 in the federal district court for the Southern District of New York the United States Football League (USFL) engaged the NFL in a battle for survival, seeking $1.69 billion in damages. But the jury, although holding that the NFL monopolized, awarded the USFL only $1 in damages. The four-year-old USFL promptly announced that it would not operate in 1986–1987.[57] Further, there are not plans for the USFL to ever operate again. The *New York Times* in May 1986 had announced that the USFL was "born to litigate" because the NFL "happens to have a relationship with all three major networks. The 1961 Sports Broadcasting Act gave the NFL an antitrust exemption in regard to a contract with 'any' television network."[58] Therefore, the issue, according to the *New York Times*, was "whether the USFL was harmed by conditions and attitudes it had to have known were in existence before it began. Like the salmon that knows to swim before it is hatched, like the thoroughbred that knows how to run before it is foaled, the USFL was preparing for this day from the day it was born."[59] A month before the trial in USFL v. NFL[60] the court had made several rulings on admission of evidence that frankly favored the defendant NFL; the court struck allegations that the NFL previously had caused the breakup of the defunct All-American Football Conference, that NFL conduct directed against the American Football League was predatory, that the NFL was politically favored by Congressional passage of special legislation in 1961 and 1966 giving partial exemption to the NFL from the antitrust laws, that the NFL had been sued 18 times for antitrust misconduct, that the NFL engaged in numerous acts to prevent existing and potential USFL clubs or teams from gaining access to suitable stadiums to play their games, that the NFL engaged in a deliberate and widespread campaign to disparage the USFL and its business prospects, and that the NFL held, as a matter of law, monopoly power in the market of persons qualified to officiate at professional football games. The court also preliminarily ruled that the fact of NFL contracts with the three major television networks "does not by itself" violate the antitrust laws: "Whether the intent or effect of such arrangements [is] to exclude a competing league . . . from selling any of its television rights presents material questions of fact that cannot be decided on a summary judgment motion."[61] The 159-page charge to the jury before the trial included the NFL defense that the estimated $200 million in losses the USFL claimed it sustained since it began playing a spring and early summer schedule in 1983 was the result of USFL mismanagement, poor business planning, and an attempt to bring about a merger with the NFL. Nevertheless, the jury found that the NFL willfully monopolized the major league professional football market in the United States under Section 2 of the Sherman Act, causing injury to the USFL. The jury also found a conspiracy to monopolize, but no overt action was taken to further that conspiracy; the jury did find a conspiracy in restraint of trade under Section 1 of the Sherman Act, but that conspiracy was not unreasonable, nor were the television contracts of the NFL, which the jury believed did not have the ability to deny actual or potential competitors access to national television broadcast contracts.

3.3 BASKETBALL

The business of professional basketball may have been the first professional sport to have its system of player restraints challenged under the antitrust laws. In 1956 in Washington Professional Basketball Corp. v. National Basketball Assn.[62] the court stated that "the business of professional basketball, as conducted by the National Basketball Association and its constituent teams on a multistate basis, coupled with the sale of rights to televise and broadcast the games for interstate transmission, is trade or commerce among the several States within the meaning of the Sherman Act." The court therefore denied a motion to dismiss the complaint in which it was alleged that the plaintiff, a prospective team owner who had acquired professional basketball players from a defunct team, had been prevented from entering the business of professional basketball by an illegal conspiracy entered into by the defendants.

Courts have from time to time declared player restrictions to be in violation of the antitrust laws, as illustrated by Central New York Basketball, Inc. v. Barnett;[63] here the restriction involved an interpretation of the uniform player contract, and the Ohio court enjoined players from "jumping" from the National Basketball Association (NBA) to the American Basketball Association (ABA). Another clause, the compensation or indemnity rule, provided that any team signing an athlete who played out his option must compensate the original team in accordance with its demands; failure to meet these demands resulted in the basketball commissioner determining the amount to be paid as compensation, and if the compensation was unpaid, all professional teams had to boycott the player. It was not until 1975 in Robertson v. National Basketball Assn.[64] that the compensation or indemnity clause was stricken due to its illegal restraint on a player's right to renew or not to renew a contract. The court also held that the plaintiffs had standing because the risks that the restraints posed to the ideals of free competition outweighed the maintenance of the labor-management relationship.[65] The court opined that it was difficult to conceive "of any theory or set of circumstances pursuant to which the college draft, blacklisting, boycotts and refusals to deal could be saved from Sherman Act condemnation, even if defendants were able to prove at trial their highly dubious contention that these restraints were adopted at the behest of the Players' Association."[66] The court specifically ruled that, although the basketball reserve system and player draft affected the employment relationship, these illegal practices did not constitute "terms and conditions of employment."[67]

As a result of the Robertson decision[68] the NBA management reached an out-of-court settlement with the players' association. Under the new agreement, at the end of the stated term of a contract that covers at least two basketball seasons, the club no longer has a unilateral right to renew a player's contract; the player becomes a free agent and may negotiate with any team, although the original contracting club or team retains a right of first refusal. The compensation or indemnity system, however, was allowed to continue until 1980; and a college draft player had one year in which the winning club must sign the player or the player returns to the college draft and is eligible to be drafted by another team.[69] However, the professional basketball is still subject to restrictive practices such as the no-tampering provision, the assignment provision, and the waiver of judicial recourse rule, as shown in Erving v. Virginia Squires Basketball Club,[70] which held that the arbitration clause in the player contract mandated that both parties resort to arbitration over any disputes, and that the arbitration award is final, binding, and conclusive.[71]

In 1971 in Haywood v. NBA[72] the U.S. Supreme Court was concerned about the status of Spencer Haywood, a brilliant basketball player who not only represented the United States in the 1968 Summer Olympics but also was chosen an All-American basketball player at the University of Detroit. With two years of college eligibility remaining he chose to turn "professional," although both the NBA and its rival league, the ABA, had rules which prohibited the signing of a player until four years after his graduation from high school; the ABA, however, had a hardship exemption which permitted the signing of the contract, and Haywood thereupon signed with the Denver Rockets. He played during the 1969–1970 season, but after a dispute arose with his team owner, Haywood signed a contract with the Seattle Supersonics of the NBA. But the NBA Commissioner disapproved the contract since Haywood was not yet eligible under the four-year high school rule. Haywood then sued the NBA, claiming a group boycott in violation of the Sherman Act, and the federal district court in California issued a preliminary injunction permitting Haywood to play with the Seattle team.[73] On appeal by the NBA, the Ninth U.S. Court of Appeals reversed and stayed the injunction; Mr. Justice Douglas of the U.S. Supreme Court decided to "allow the preliminary injunction of the District Court to be reinstated" because professional basketball "does not enjoy exemption from the antitrust laws." The highest court, sitting en banc, upheld Justice Douglas' order.[74] Thus, the restrictive four-year high school rule did constitute an illegal boycott under the Sherman Act. On the other hand, in Molinas v. National Basketball Assn.[75] the anti-betting rule of the NBA, which called for the suspension of any basketball player guilty of betting, was upheld, even though a restraint of trade was involved; the court found the NBA rule against gambling "about as reasonable a rule as can be imagined."[76]

One interesting restriction by the NBA involved team ownership, and relocation of franchises; guidelines were issued, presumably to aid and abet competition,[77] as more particularly delineated herein in Section 4.3 of Chapter 4.

3.4 HOCKEY

The professional sport of hockey came under judicial scrutiny in the 1958 case of Peto v. Madison Square Garden Corp.[78] when the federal district court impliedly recognized that the business of professional hockey is subject to the antitrust laws. Plaintiffs here claimed that the defendants, three of the member teams of the National Hockey League (NHL) had combined to restrain trade or commerce and establish a monopoly in the operation of major league professional hockey teams. The court refused to dismiss, but apparently nine years later in 1967 summary judgment was entered for the defendants on the ground that the action was barred by the statute of limitations.[79]

In 1972 in Philadelphia World Hockey Club v. Philadelphia Hockey Club[80] the reserve system of professional hockey was expressly found to violate Section 2 of the Sherman Act, as Judge Higginbotham made 212 specific findings of fact and 19 conclusions of law in enjoining enforcement of the NHL reserve clause, subject to the World Hockey Association posting a $2.5 million bond to protect the NHL against costs and damages resulting from a possible wrongful injunction.[81] The court cited the lack of any joint activity between the NHL and the players' association in creating and retaining the reserve system, which therefore was not the result of a bona fide, arm's-length negotiation; also the court pointed to attempts by the NHL to use the reserve system to exclude entry into the professional hockey business of a newcomer. The court enjoined the NHL from "further prosecuting, commencing, or threatening to commence, any legal proceeding pursuant to and/or enforce the so-called 'reserve clause' . . . against any player, coach or other person." Similarly, the Massachusetts federal district court in Boston Professional Hockey Assn. v. Cheevers[82] refused to enforce the reserve clause in two players' contracts; in Nassau Sports Inc. v. Hampton[83] the federal district court in Minnesota ruled that the reserve clause was "one aspect of a contractual scheme constituting a violation of Sections 1 and 2 of the Sherman Antitrust Act."[84]

Exemption and Non-exemption 43

In 1979 the leading case of McCourt v. California Sports, Inc.[85] was decided by the Sixth U.S. Court of Appeals, and resulted in a victory for professional hockey team owners. Here plaintiff, a 21-year-old Canadian, signed a contract in 1977 to play hockey with the Detroit Red Wings of the NHL. His stipulated compensation was $325,000, payable over three years. About the same time one Vachon, an outstanding goaltender with the Los Angeles Kings, declared himself a free agent and signed a contract with the same Detroit Red Wings for $1.9 million over a five-year period. Under the NHL By-law 9A[86] the Detroit club was obligated to compensate the Los Angeles club for the loss of Vachon, but the teams failed to agree on an "equalization payment." In arbitration Los Angeles demanded an assignment of the contract with the plaintiff, and the arbitrator agreed; thereupon plaintiff brought suit against Los Angeles team to enjoin the arbitrator's decision that plaintiff play for the Los Angeles team. The federal district court for the Eastern District of Michigan[87] entered a preliminary injunction restraining enforcement of the reserve system, thus keeping plaintiff in Detroit; but the federal appellate court later reversed, ruling that even if the reserve system incorporated in the NHL collective bargaining agreement was subject to the antitrust laws, the non-statutory labor exemption applied where the reserve system was incorporated in the collective bargaining agreement as the result of bona fide, arm's-length negotiation. A strong dissent by Judge Edwards stated that he knew of no instance "where profit making businesses have succeeded in justifying a cartel arrangement which suits their purposes by dint of securing that arrangement's introduction into a collective bargaining agreement and thus acquiring the right to the 'labor union exemption'. The majority's approval of this arrangement in this case stands the labor union exemption squarely on its head."[88] Judge Edwards pointed at the express language of the Free Agents and Equalization Rule of the NHL[89] and the labor exemption claim,[90] and found such measures to be "anticompetitive agreements banning or restricting competition between clubs for players. Such clauses adopted by an already dominating league will also have the effect of restricting competition from other leagues and thus promoting monopoly." In essence, the majority opinion simply took the position that where the agreement sought to be exempted was "the product of a bona fide arm's length bargaining," it will be exempted: "The evidence here, as credited by the trial court, compels the conclusion that the reserve system was incorporated into the agreement as a result of good faith, arm's length bargaining between the parties. As such it is entitled to the exemption, and the trial court's conclusion to the contrary must be deemed clearly erroneous."

The NHL has truly led a charmed life, as evidenced by the 1980 decision in Shayne v. NHL,[91] which found that the NHL did not monopolize or attempt to monopolize major league professional hockey or engage in any conspiracy to injure plaintiff or prevent plaintiff from forming his own professional hockey club under the aegis of a newly organized rival league. A discharged hockey referee lost his suit against the NHL and the World Hockey Association in

Dowling v. United States[92] because he failed to allege and prove a purported conspiracy to deprive him of the right to employment and because the purported conspiracy had no impact on interstate commerce.

3.5 BOXING

The multibillion dollar business of professional boxing has also drawn the attention of the federal government and the courts to the exhibition of professional championship boxing contests, the promotion and execution of which involve valuable rights to broadcast, televise, and film for sale in interstate commerce. The far-flung activities of the International Boxing Club were attacked by the United States Department of Justice in March 1952 as a conspiracy to monopolize and as a monopoly of the professional boxing business in the United States. Specifically, the government alleged that the promoters of professional championship boxing contests made a substantial utilization of the channels of interstate trade or commerce in such activities as (a) negotiating contracts with boxers, advertising agencies, seconds, referees, judges, announcers, and other persons living in states other than those in which the promoters resided; (b) arranging and maintaining training quarters in states other than those in which the promoters resided; (c) leasing arenas and arranging other details for boxing contests, particularly when the boxing contests were being held out of state; (d) selling tickets across state lines and negotiating for the sale of motion pictures of boxing contests; (e) negotiating for the sale of and selling rights to broadcast boxing contests throughout the United States; and (f) negotiating for the sale of and selling rights to closed-circuit telecast of boxing contests to some 200 motion picture theatres throughout the United States.[93] The conspiracy to exclude competition allegedly began in 1949 with an agreement among the defendants and Joe Louis, then heavyweight champion of the world, that Louis would resign his title and procure exclusive rights to the services of the four leading title contenders in a series of elimination bouts which would recognize a new heavyweight champion. Louis also agreed that he would obtain exclusive rights to broadcast, televise, and film those elimination bouts and then he would assign all such exclusive rights to the defendants. As the result of such restraints the defendants promoted or participated in promoting all but 2 of the 21 boxing championship matches held in the United States between June 1949 and March 1952.

The federal trial court dismissed the action on the authority of the baseball immunity doctrine[94] that professional boxing was not "trade or commerce." The federal government appealed directly to the U.S. Supreme Court, which on January 31, 1955, reversed the lower court, and held that the promotion of professional championship boxing on a multistate basis, coupled with the sale of rights to televise, broadcast, and film the contests for interstate transmission, constituted "trade or commerce" within the meaning of the Sherman Act.[95] Chief Justice Earl Warren declared that a boxing contest is not a local affair if the business itself is engaged in interstate commerce; he readily distinguished the baseball immunity anomaly as not holding that "all businesses based on professional sports were outside the scope of the antitrust laws. The issue confronting us is, therefore, not whether a previously granted exemption should be granted in the first instance. And that issue is for Congress to resolve, not this Court."[96] Mr. Justice Warren went on to find that defendants' business imposed illegal restraints upon interstate commerce and furthermore monopolized trade or commerce through a conspiracy to exclude competition.

On March 8, 1957, the International Boxing Club was found guilty after trial of violating Sections 1 and 2 of the Sherman Act.[97] Federal Judge Ryan held that defendants' monopoly of championship fights was the "relevant market," and that "the promotion of professional championship boxing contests is a pure and simple money-making, profit-seeking business." He found that defendants had accomplished their illegal business through (a) purchasing promotional control of championship contests; (b) acquiring the exclusive use of physical facilities like stadiums and arenas for the presentation of such contests; (c) acquiring the assets of competitors; and (d) contracting with boxers who won championship contests to engage in future title contests exclusively with defendants for periods of three to five years. In his June 24, 1957, opinion Judge Ryan ordered the "dissolution of the combination which will permit the re-establishment of the competitive positions of the defendants and the entry of others in the market."[98] Judge Ryan mandated "an immediate and complete severance of the interlocking ownership of Norris and Wirtz in Madison Square Garden," necessitating the resignation of both men as officers and directors within 30 days and divestiture of their stock within five years. The defendants were enjoined from promoting more than two championship contests in any one year, and were ordered to open competitive leasing of Chicago Stadium and Madison Square Garden on a reasonable rental basis. The court also placed certain restrictions upon defendants with respect to radio and television which would open up the boxing business to "legitimate and healthy competition." An appeal to the U.S. Supreme Court resulted in affirmance of Judge Ryan's orders on January 12, 1959, Mr. Justice Clark noting that without such stringent curbs "the government in its effort to free the professional boxing business of monopoly . . . would have won the battle, but lost the war. . . . "[99]

The business of wrestling, closely related to the business of boxing, was prohibited in 1956 by a federal district court in Iowa from conspiring under the auspices of the National Wrestling Alliance with the purpose or effect of recognizing a booker or promoter as the exclusive booker or promoter in a designated territory, preventing a booker or promoter from doing business in any other territory; restricting promotion and booking of wrestling matches to certain arenas and to promoters and bookers who are members of the National Wrestling Alliance; requiring a booker to book wrestling matches only through promoters who are members of the National Wrestling Alliance and to discriminate in favor of promoters who are members of the National Wrestling Alliance; requiring a promoter to promote wrestling matches only through the services of members of the National Wrestling Alliance, and to discriminate in favor of bookers who are members of the National Wrestling Alliance; and preventing any wrestler, booker, or promoter from participating in studio exhibitions.[100] Federal Judge Riley found these practices to be in violation of the antitrust laws and left no doubt that the federal district court had "jurisdiction of the subjectmatter of this action and of the parties thereto" as the consent decree cancelled all existing regulations and by-laws of the National Wrestling Alliance that were inconsistent with opening the business of professional wrestling to competition.[101]

3.6 TENNIS AND GOLF

The businesses of professional tennis and professional golf have received little, if any, attention by the courts with respect to their impact upon federal antitrust laws. In Drysdale v. Florida Team Tennis, Inc.[102] the federal district court in Pennsylvania examined the draft system utilized by the defendant tennis association that required that a chosen player could only negotiate with a certain franchisee, and ruled that the practice would stifle competition between franchisees for obtaining the services of tennis players. Plaintiff alleged that he had suffered injury because he was forced as a result of such draft system to sign with a team that was not financially stable. The court found violation of Section 1 of the Sherman Act.[103] However, in Gunter Harz Sports, Inc. v. United States Tennis Association[104] (USTA) the Eighth U.S. Court of Appeals found that the restrictive practice of USTA which banned the tennis racket manufactured by the plaintiff was reasonable because USTA rules included a provision whereby any interested party could obtain approval of its tennis racket upon showing that the use of its tennis racket would not significantly change the character of the game of tennis. Interestingly, the court also determined that the United States Tennis Association wielded enormous economic clout by virtue of its exclusive control over the conduct of the sport of professional tennis. But the court was of the opinion that this monopoly power was reasonably exercised to promote competition in that the USTA wielded its power to conduct the game of tennis in an orderly fashion without any intent to injure plaintiff or any other tennis racket manufacturer.

Golf is also a business, as exemplified in the 1966 case of Deesen v. Professional Golfers Assn. of America[105] and is therefore subject to the antitrust laws. Here plaintiff, who was a member of the Professional Golfers Association (PGA), was expelled because of his poor golf scores; when he was refused reinstatement, he sued the PGA, claiming that the PGA had combined and conspired to monopolize the business of professional golf. But the Eighth U.S. Court of Appeals disagreed and found that the restraint was reasonable and therefore there was no antitrust violation. The court reviewed the standards and procedures of the PGA in selecting and discharging members, which included test rounds and a review of record scores; it was found reasonable to limit the number of golfers on tour, for only a reasonable number of golfers may play an 18-hole golf course under tournament conditions during the daylight hours of a single day. The court also found that the combination and conspiracy alleged by the plaintiff were nonexistent.[106]

In Blalock v. Ladies' Professional Golf Assn.[107] the court specifically stated that professional golf was subject to the federal antitrust laws. Apparently the successful professional woman golfer Barbara Jane Blalock had illegally moved her ball during the course of tournament play and was disqualified on the spot and placed on probation for the rest of the golfing season.

3.7 SOCCER, BOWLING, AUTOMOBILE RACING, AND HARNESS RACING

Soccer did not emerge as a professional sport until 1960 in the United States, although soccer is and has undoubtedly been the world's most popular team sport.[108] It was in 1960 that several European and South American soccer teams participated in a summer tournament in New York City, and within five years interest in the sport of soccer prompted the formation of professional soccer leagues in the United States. The North American Soccer League did poorly, as did its rival National Professional Soccer League, even with television contracts. The 1978 soccer season, however, was the most successful for the North American Soccer League, and the prime time for its suit against the National Football League, which had sought to enforce a ban that would prevent all NFL franchise team owners from owning any other major league sports team such as a professional soccer team.[109] Plaintiffs sought and obtained a preliminary injunction against the NFL ban,[110] alleging serious competitive harms in that the market for soccer franchises was substantially diminished. The federal district court for the Southern District of New York weighed the competitive consequences of cross-ownership against the competitive consequences of the NFL ban, and concluded that plaintiffs met the burden of proof requisite for a preliminary injunction.[111] In effect, cross-ownership was considered to be a classic per se horizontal boycott in violation of Section 1 of the Sherman Act.[112]

Interestingly, the applicability of antitrust laws to the professional soccer industry has been tested in England in Eastern v. Newcastle United Football Club, Ltd.[113] An English court held that England's professional soccer's "retain system," in which a professional soccer player whose contract had expired was nonetheless "retained" by his original team, constituted an unreasonable restraint of trade. The English court observed that the restraint went further than was reasonably necessary to protect the owner's interest in his players. Indeed, the system was established for the employers' benefit, which caused the employers' negotiating strength to be disproportionate to the negotiating strength of the players.

The professional sport of bowling was found in violation of the antitrust laws in Washington State Bowling Proprietors' Assn. v. Pacific Lanes, Inc.[114] Here the Ninth U.S. Court of Appeals held that certain regulatory procedures of the defendant were violative of the Sherman Act. Defendant was found guilty of combining, conspiring, and acting in concert to organize and sponsor bowling tournaments only for those bowling proprietors who agreed to restrict their league and tournament bowling activities to those who were members of the defendant bowling association. Three years later in 1969 the federal district court for the Central District of Georgia in Manok v. Southeastern District Bowling Assn.[115] refused to consider a judicial review of plaintiff's suspension from membership in the voluntary bowling association without a clear showing of bad faith. Plaintiff, a professional bowler, was suspended by the American Bowling Congress and its local association for selling a bowling device called "Mono-Grip," which he had invented; he also was charged with knowingly bowling in tournaments with a partner who was using an assumed name and for collecting prize money from these tournaments. Plaintiff's complaint alleged that the bowling associations' officers treated him unfairly by making malicious statements about his associating with blackballed members and by curbing the use of his invention. The court held that plaintiff was not entitled to relief in the absence of any proof that the bowling associations had intentionally and purposefully restrained trade or commerce; the size and strength of the American Bowling Congress and its local association would be material if it was linked to some conspiracy by individuals to restrict competition and control prices, for example.

The professional sport of automobile racing was deemed subject to the antitrust laws in STP Corp. v. United States Auto Club, Inc.[116] On the other hand, the rules of the United States Trotting Association were deemed in May 1960 to be reasonable restraints in United States v. U.S. Trotting Assn.[117] because the restraints merely regulated and standardized the business of harness racing. The U.S. Trotting Association exercised control over horse owners, drivers, trainers, tracks, sponsors of stakes and futurity races, and officials. But there was no proof that the association "unreasonably, arbitrarily, or capriciously excluded any person or organization from membership, or prevented any interested party from obtaining the benfits or 'products' of the USTA."[118] On the other hand, the U.S. Supreme Court in Barry v. Barchi[119] ruled that the suspension of a horse trainer after tests showed the presence of drugs in a horse to be constitutionally defective, for there was no "prompt post-suspension hearing" by the state commission:

> As the District Court found, the consequences to a trainer of even a temporary suspension can be severe; and we have held that the opportunity to be heard must be "at a meaningful time and in a meaningful manner." . . . Here, the provision for an administrative hearing, neither on its face nor as applied in this case, assured a prompt proceeding and prompt disposition of the outstanding issues between Barchi and the State. Indeed, insofar as the statutory requirements are concerned, it is as likely as not that

Barchi and others subject to relatively brief suspensions would have no opportunity to put the State to its proof until they have suffered the full penalty imposed. Yet, it is possible that Barchi's horse may not have been drugged and Barchi may not have been at fault at all. Once suspension has been imposed, the trainer's interest in a speedy resolution of the controversy becomes paramount, it seems to us. We also discern little or no state interest, and the State has suggested none, in an appreciable delay in going forward with a full hearing. On the contrary, it would seem as much in the State's interest as Barchi's to have an early and reliable determination with respect to the integrity of those participating in state-supervised horse racing.

In these circumstances, *it was necessary that Barchi be assured a prompt postsuspension hearing, one that would proceed and be concluded without appreciable delay.* Because the statute as applied in this case was deficient in this respect, Barchi's suspension was constitutionally infirm under the Due Process Clause of the Fourteenth Amendment.[120]

Indeed, there are factual questions also with respect to whether the drug testing was performed by an appropriate party and whether the drug testing was scientifically reliable.[121] In Austin v. Garrett[122] the court found that the suspension of a trainer by the commission was manifestly erroneous, for the commission had failed to preserve properly the urine samples from the horse.

3.8 THE LABOR EXEMPTION

Section 1 of the Sherman Act states that "every contract, combination in the form of trust or otherwise, or conspiracy, in restraint of trade or commerce among the several States, or with foreign nations, is hereby declared to be illegal." As a result of controversies engendered by its application to labor union activities, the Clayton Act of 1914[123] was enacted "to equalize before the law the position of workingmen and employer as industrial combatants."[124] Section 20 of the Clayton Act withdrew from the general interdict of the Sherman Act specifically enumerated practices of labor unions by prohibiting injunctions against labor unions (since the use of the injunction had been a major source of dissatisfaction to labor unions). Section 20 also relieved such practices of all illegal taint by the catch-all provision "nor shall any of the acts specified in this paragraph be considered or held to be violative of any law of the United States." Courts generally restricted the scope of Section 20 of the Clayton Act to trade union activities directed against an employer by his own employees.[125] In 1932 Congress enacted the Norris-LaGuardia Act,[126] which removed the fetters upon trade union activities which might have been left untouched by the judicial construction of Section 20 of the Clayton Act. The 1932 act further narrowed the circumstances under which the federal courts could grant injunctions in labor disputes; the 1932 act promoted the principle that the allowable area of labor union activity was not to be restricted to an immediate employer-employee relationship.[127] In both Allen Bradley Co. v. Local 3, IBEW[128] and United Mine Workers of America v. Pennington[129] the

U.S. Supreme Court pointed out that the exemption from the antitrust laws made available to labor unions would be lost if the exemption was used in connection with corporations organized for profit to aid them in controlling prices of their products or creating a monopoly or committing any practices otherwise violative of the antitrust laws. In the Allen Bradley Co. case[130] the highest court stressed that "when unions participated with a combination of businessmen who had complete power to eliminate all competition among themselves and to prevent all competition from others," it was a situation "not included within the exemption of the Clayton and Norris-LaGuardia Acts." [131]

In addition to the aforesaid statutory exemption for labor, judicial decisions have created a non-statutory exemption for labor based upon national labor policy that protects union activity not specifically addressed by the Clayton Act and the Norris-LaGuardia Acts. When a labor union seeks to attain goals sanctioned by the National Labor Relations Act but not specifically permitted by any statute, for example, the courts have exempted unions from antitrust liability, as illustrated by the U.S. Supreme Court decision in Connell Construction Co. v. Plumbers & Steamfitters Local Union:

The nonstatutory exemption has its source in the strong labor policy favoring the association of employees to eliminate competition over wages and working conditions. Union success in organizing workers and standardizing wages ultimately will affect price competition among employers, but the goals of federal labor law never could be achieved if this effect on business competition were held a violation of the antitrust laws. The Court therefore has acknowledged that labor policy requires tolerance for the lessening of business competition based on differences in wages and working conditions.[132]

Should the labor union activity have an anti-competitive purpose or intention, this exemption may be lost, as illustrated by H. A. Artists & Associates v. Actors Equity Assn.[133] which suggested that the scope of labor's antitrust exemptions be delineated on a case-by-case basis from broad guiding principles derived from the leading labor law decisions of the courts. Here a union representing actors and actresses developed a franchising system that prohibited members from using agents who did not have union franchises. The franchising system required franchised agents to renounce any right to a commission on an employment contract under which the actor or actress received scale wages. While the U.S. Supreme Court acknowledged that the labor exemption does not apply when a labor union combines with a non-labor group to restrain competition, the court delineated the agents as a labor group, reasoning that the particular structure of the legitimate theatre industry made it necessary for performers to secure employment through agents, and that the franchising system was designed to promote the union's legitimate self-interest. Thus, the "combination" or arrangement between the union and the agents did not violate the antitrust laws; but the union's requirement that the agents pay the union a franchise fee was not protected by the legitimate self-interest of the union. In

National Constructors Assn. v. National Electric Contractors Assn.[134] the Fourth U.S. Court of Appeals found the practice or activity of the union requiring all companies contracting with the union to contribute 1 percent of their gross payroll to an industry trust fund to be an interference with market price-setting forces stabilizing prices and therefore a per se illegal price-fixing agreement.[135] Yet earlier the Third U.S. Court of Appeals in Consolidated Express, Inc. v. New York Shipping Assn.[136] had ruled that the recovery of treble damages against a union for an antitrust violation might so burden the collective bargaining relationship that the damage remedy may be withheld even if the union violated the antitrust laws.

Professional sports have almost uniformly sought to defend themselves from antitrust attack under the so-called labor exemption. But in 1976 in Mackey v. National Football League[137] the Eighth U.S. Circuit Court set forth three prerequisites for applying the non-statutory labor exemption, to wit: (1) the restraint primarily affects only the parties to the collective bargaining relationship; (2) the restraint must be concerned with a mandatory subject of collective bargaining; and (3) the restraint must be the product of bona fide, arm's-length negotiation.[138] It would thus appear that since most restraints govern the circumstances of outsiders or non-collective bargaining persons or firms or entities that the labor exemption simply does not apply to the business of professional sports. In Philadelphia World Hockey Club, Inc. v. Philadelphia Hockey Club, Inc.[139] the federal district court in Pennsylvania in 1972 held that even if the NHL Players' Association qualified as a labor organization under Section 2(5) of the National Labor Relations Act,[140] and even if the NHL Players' Association could be certified as the approved collective bargaining representative of the professional hockey players under Section 9 of the National Labor Relations Act,[141] the labor exemption did not apply because, in light of the facts that the reserve system had been in effect for more than 15 years prior to the formation of the NHL Players' Association and that the NHL Players' Association had consistently opposed the reserve system, it could not be said that the reserve system was ever the subject of serious and intensive collective bargaining at arm's length. Even if the reserve system could be the product of collective bargaining the labor exemption still would not apply because (a) all labor union–employer activities are not immune from antitrust attack; (b) the NHL cannot take advantage of the labor exemption to restrain competition and to impair business dealings and transactions of competitors of the NHL; and (c) negotiations by the NHL with the NHL Players' Association would not shield the NFL from liability to outside competitors. The court emphasized that "benefits to organized labor cannot be utilized as a cat's-paw to pull employers' chestnuts out of the antitrust fires."[142] Indeed, only in McCourt v. California Sports, Inc.[143] was the labor exemption successfully utilized to shield the noncompetitive activities of NHL regulations, and then the labor exemption was used over labor's opposition.[144] The majority of the Sixth U.S. Court of Appeals were of the opinion that good faith and arm's-length collective bargaining had brought about the restrictive NHL practices, and therefore the labor exemption would apply. The stinging dissent by Judge Edwards portrayed "the majority's approval of this arrangement" as standing the labor union exemption "squarely on its head."[145] The dissent pointed out that the NHL was not a "labor, agricultural or horticultural organization" within the terms of the Sherman Act, as amended; also the NHL does have capital stock and is organized for profit.[146] In Wood v. National Basketball Assn.[147] the federal district court for the Southern District of New York endorsed the view that the scope of the labor exemption should be defined by the reach of the union's and the employer's right to bargain over employment terms within the relevant unit; here the plaintiff professional basketball player was unable to reach agreement with a team on a suitable contract, and sued the NBA contending, that the labor exemption did not immunize the college draft and the NBA salary ceiling because he was not within the pertinent bargaining unit. The court held, as a matter of law, that the collective bargaining agreement applied to all players who come within the bargaining unit "during the lifetime of the agreement."[148] It is well, however, to note the admonition of the U.S. Supreme Court: "Exemptions from antitrust laws are to be strictly construed."[149]

It should be observed that in a typical industry other than professional sports the availability of the labor exemption is usually tested in a suit brought by an employer or third party who is adversely affected by a union-proposed restriction included within a collective bargaining agreement; the union typically seeks to avoid liability by asserting the labor exemption as a defense. However, in cases involving professional sports the plaintiff is generally a member of the union or the union itself, and the party raising the defense of labor exemption is typically the employer; the defense is raised not for the purpose of seeking immunity for a union-imposed restriction but rather to immunize an employer-devised restraint which may or may not have been approved by the union. This distinction was critical in the court's refusal to apply the labor exemption in Robertson v. National Basketball Assn.[150] The critical question is not whether the labor exemption would protect an exercise of union power, but whether the labor exemption may be utilized by the employer-defendant against the apparent interests of the employee group. Indeed, the courts have bent over backwards to protect the union activity from the onslaught of the antitrust laws, as perhaps logically declared by the court in McCourt v. California Sports, Inc.:

We emphasize today, as we did in Mackey, supra, that the subject of player movement restrictions is a proper one for resolution in the collective bargaining context. When so resolved, as it appears to have been in the current collective bargaining agreement, the labor exemption to antitrust attack applies, and the merits of the bargaining agreement are not an issue for court determination. The bargaining agreement is subject to change from time to time as it expires and is up for renegotiation. The order approving the class action settlements is affirmed.[151]

NOTES

1. See Freedman, Societal Behavior: New and Unique Rights of the Person (1965), at pp. 201 et seq.
2. 259 US 200 (1922). Just a year to two before this celebrated decision the "Black Sox Scandal" broke as gamblers placed their tentacles into the Chicago White Sox professional baseball team owned by Charles A. Comiskey, a penurious gentleman who simply did not pay his players what they believed they deserved, so that the team was torn by cliques and competing interests. In the 1919 World Series against the Cincinnati Reds, a distinct underdog, the Chicago White Sox were favored by 5-1. Chicago's first baseman, "Chick" Gandil, met with an old gambling friend three weeks before the World Series and promised to obtain the cooperation of several of his teammates for $80,000 in "throwing" the games. Gandil recruited six regular players (including two leading pitchers) and one utility infielder. In the first game of the World Series the Chicago pitcher Cicotte who got $10,000 up front, signaled the gamblers that the "deal" was assured by hitting the first Cincinnati batter with a pitched ball; Cincinnati won the first game 9-1. Chicago pitcher Williams the next day displayed uncharacteristic wildness and lost 4-2. The fourth game also went to Cincinnati 2-0 as Cicotte made two errors and Gandil did not drive in a run. Pitcher Williams lost the fifth game 5-0. (Incidentally, Chicago pitcher Dickie Kerr [not in on the "fix"] had won the third game 3-0.) The sixth game went to Chicago in ten innings behind pitcher Kerr; and in the seventh game Cicotte had a change of mind and beat the Reds 4-1. The eighth and decisive game went to Cincinnati, as pitcher Williams was warned by the gamblers to lose or his wife would be hurt. In September 1920 a grand jury in Chicago indicted the Chicago players, but the league and some teams "covered up" the scandal to the best of their abilities and by the time the case went to trial in the summer of 1921 the confessions of Cicotte, Williams, and Jackson had mysteriously disappeared, and so no convictions were obtained. But the Commissioner of Baseball, Judge Kennesaw Mountain Landis, later barred the eight players from baseball for life.
3. Supra note 1 at p. 203.
4. Supra note 2 at pp. 208–209.
5. Salerno v. American League of Professional Baseball Clubs, 429 F2d 1003 (2nd Cir., 1970).
6. See Subcommittee on Study of Monopoly Power of the Subcommittee of the Judiciary, Organized Baseball, H. R. Rep. No. 2002, 82nd Congress, 2nd Session, at pp. 17 and 22. Also see generally 32 Univ of Fla L Rev (1980) at pp. 676 et seq.
7. See Metropolitan Exhibition Co. v. Ewing, 42 F 198 (SDNY, 1890).
8. American League Baseball Club of Chicago v. Chase, 149 NYS 6 (1914).
9. See Gardella v. Chandler, 172 F2d 402 (2nd Cir., 1949).
10. 187 NY Misc 230 (1947).
11. The New York court opined that even if professional baseball were a monopoly, it would not seem to be a combination in restraint of trade or commerce under Section 340 of the New York General Business Law.
12. Supra note 2.
13. 172 F2d 402 (2nd Cir., 1949).
14. 346 US 356 (1953).
15. Supra note 14 at pp. 356–357. The dissent of Mr. Justice Burton read in part:

Whatever may have been the situation when the *Federal Baseball Club* case was decided in 1922, I am not able to join today's decision which, in effect, announces that organized baseball, in 1953, still is not engaged in interstate trade or commerce. In the light of organized baseball's well-known and widely distributed capital investments used in conducting competitions between teams constantly traveling between states, its receipts and expenditures of large sums transmitted between states, its numerous purchases of materials in interstate commerce, the attendance at its local exhibitions of large audiences often traveling across state lines, its radio and television activities which expand its audiences beyond state lines, its sponsorship of interstate advertising, and its highly organized "farm system" of minor league baseball clubs, coupled with restrictive contracts and understandings between individuals and among clubs or leagues playing for profit throughout the United States, and even in Canada, Mexico and Cuba, it is a contradiction in terms to say that the defendants in the cases before us are not now engaged in interstate trade or commerce as those terms are used in the Constitution of the United States and in the Sherman Act. . . .

16. 407 US 258 (1972).
17. Mr. Justice Blackmun opined:

This emphasis and concern are still with us. We continue to loathe, 50 years after *Federal Baseball* and almost two decades after *Toolson*, to overturn those cases judicially when Congress, by its positive inaction, has allowed those decisions to stand for so long and, far beyond mere inference and implication, has clearly evinced a desire not to disapprove them legislatively. Accordingly, we adhere once again to *Federal Baseball* and *Toolson* and to their application to professional baseball. We adhere also to *International Boxing* and *Radovich* and to their respective applications to professional boxing and professional football. If there is any inconsistency or illogic in all this, it is an inconsistency and illogic of long standing that is to be remedied by the Congress and not by this Court. If we were to act otherwise, we would be withdrawing from the conclusion as to congressional intent made in *Toolson* and from the concerns as to retrospectivity therein expressed. Under these circumstances, there is merit in consistency even though some might claim that beneath that consistency is a layer of inconsistency.

18. See State of Wisconsin v. Milwaukee Braves, Inc., 144 NW2d 1 (Wisc., 1966), cert den 385 US 990 (1966), and also 13 Wayne L Rev 417 (1967).
19. See Section 3.8 herein.
20. Supra note 16 at p. 288.
21. National and American Leagues of Professional Baseball Clubs v. Major League Baseball Players' Assn., Grievance Nos. 75-27 and 75-28, Decision No. 29 (Dec. 23, 1975).
22. See 32 Univ of Fla L Rev (1980) at p. 679.
23. 532 F2d 621 (8th Cir., 1977).
24. Note that Mr. Justice Douglas in his dissent in the Flood case, supra note 16, contended that "the only statutory exemption granted by Congress to professional sports concerns broadcasting rights, 15 USC 1291-1295." However, Public Law 93-107 (87 Stat 350), dated September 14, 1973, prohibited the "local blackout" of a game of a

professional football, baseball, basketball, or hockey club, if such game is sold out 72 hours or more before the start of the game. See 18 ALR Fed 489.

25. 569 F2d 527 (7th Cir., 1978), cert den 99 S Ct 214 (1978).
26. See Professional Baseball Schools & Clubs, Inc. v. Kuhn, 693 F2d 1085 (11th Cir., 1982).
27. See generally Insight Magazine (Aug. 25, 1986) at p. 14.
28. 116 F Supp 319 (Pa., 1953).
29. 231 F2d 620 (9th Cir., 1956), reversed 352 US 445 (1957).
30. Supra note 2.
31. See generally 18 ALR Fed 489. Mr. Justice Clark, writing for the majority of the Radovich court, emphasized:

> If this ruling is *unrealistic*, *inconsistent*, or *illogical*, it is sufficient to answer, aside from the distinctions between the businesses, that were we considering the question of baseball for the first time upon a clean slate we would have no doubts. But *Federal Base Ball* held the business of baseball outside the scope of the Act. . . . We, therefore, conclude that the orderly way to eliminate error or discrimination, if any there be, is by legislation and not by court decision. Congressional processes are more accommodative, affording the whole industry hearings and an opportunity to assist in the formulation of new legislation. The resulting project is therefore more likely to protect the industry and the public alike. The whole scope of congressional action would be known long in advance and effective dates for the legislation could be set in the future without the injustices of retroactivity and surprise which might follow court action. (Emphasis added)

32. 196 F Supp 445 (SDNY, 1961).
33. Supra note 1 at p. 211.
34. 348 SW2d 37 (Tex Civ App., 1961).
35. 205 F Supp 60 (Md., 1962), aff. 323 F2d 124 (4th Cir., 1962).
36. 144 AppDC 56, 444 F2d 931 (DC, 1971), cert den 404 US 1047 (1971).
37. 407 F Supp 1000 (Minn., 1975).
38. 543 F2d 606 (8th Cir., 1976); cert dism 434 US 801 (1977).
39. 381 US 676 (1965).
40. Supra note 38 at p. 615, n. 15.
41. Supra note 38 at p. 623.
42. See Section 3.8 herein.
43. Supra note 22 at p. 690.
44. Supra note 38 at p. 621.
45. 390 F Supp 73 (ND Cal., 1974), aff 586 F2d 644 (9th Cir., 1978), cert den 441 US 967 (1979). Joe Kapp had been drafted out of the University of California by the Washington Redskins of the NFL, but he decided to play in the Canadian Football League. The Redskins nevertheless retained their rights to Kapp by keeping his name on their reserve list. At the end of his Canadian Football League career a few years later, Kapp negotiated with and entered into a contract with the Houston Oilers of the American Football League (AFL), but the contract was invalidated on the basis of an agreement between the NFL and the AFL that prohibited players from negotiating during contract periods to change leagues. Kapp was then signed by the Minnesota Vikings

to a two-year contract after he obtained contract releases from both the Canadian Football League and the Redskins. Kapp played for the Vikings for two years, and then the Vikings exercised their option rights to make him play for another year. Other professional football teams in the NFL were then interested in his services, but the Rozelle Rule on "compensation" to the Vikings made it difficult, although Kapp played for the New England Patriots in 1970, and then Kapp refused to sign the Standard Player's Contract for subsequent years, and was dismissed by the Patriots, prior to his law suit.

46. Supra note 45 at p. 81.
47. Supra note 45 at p. 86.
48. 593 F2d 1173 (DC Cir., 1978); for lower court, see 420 F Supp 738 (DC, 1976).
49. 584 F2d 280 (8th Cir., 1978).
50. 15 USC 15.
51. Actually, the case was Alexander v. NFL, filed in the federal district court in Minnesota, but affirmed under the name of Reynolds v. NFL, Supra note 49.
52. Supra note 38.
53. Supra note 49 at pp. 284–285.
54. Tose v. First Pennsylvania Bank et al., 648 F2d 879 (3rd Cir., 1981), cert den 102 S Ct 390 (1981).
55. 550 F Supp 558 (ED Pa., 1982).
56. 519 F Supp 581 (CD Cal., 1981).
57. See NLJ (Aug. 11, 1986) at p. 8; the case is reported as 84 Civ 7484 (SDNY, 1986).
58. *New York Times* (May 13, 1986) at p. B7.
59. Id.
60. Supra note 57.
61. See NLJ (April 25, 1986) at p. 1.

The USFL had its own troubles, as illustrated by Boris v. USFL, decided on February 28, 1984, by the federal district court for Central District of California. Among the findings of the court were the following:

> 1. Plaintiff Boris was a varsity football player at the University of Arizona during the 1980–81 and 1981–82 seasons and for the first three games of the 1982 season.
>
> 2. After the third game of the 1982 season, Boris voluntarily withdrew from the University of Arizona.
>
> 3. Boris is not currently eligible to nor is he playing college football.
>
> 4. Boris will not be eligible to play college football in the fall of 1984 or any time thereafter under the rules and regulations of the NCAA. . . .
>
> 9. The USFL and its member teams have agreed with each other to abide by an "Eligibility Rule" which provides: "No person shall be eligible to play or be selected as a player unless (1) all college football eligibility of such player has expired, or (2) at least five (5) years shall have elapsed since the player first entered or attended a recognized junior college, college or university or (3) such player received a diploma from a recognized college or university."
>
> 10. The USFL and all of the USFL member teams, including defendant Wran-

glers, have agreed among themselves to adhere to and to enforce the Eligibility Rule quoted in the paragraph above.

11. The reasons advanced by the defendants in support of the Eligibility Rule, as it existed relative to the USFL's 1983 football season, are (in summary):
The Eligibility Rule promotes on-field competitive balance among USFL teams: very few college-age athletes are physically, mentally, or emotionally mature enough for professional football; abolition of the Eligibility Rule will not benefit the college athlete; the Eligibility Rule promotes the concept of the importance of a college education; the Eligibility Rule promotes the efficient operation of the USFL by strengthening the sport at the college level so that the USFL does not have to develop players at that level; the Eligibility Rule is not inflexible; since 1983 was the USFL's first season of play, competitive conditions required it to adopt and enforce the same Eligibility Rule previously adopted and enforced by the two powerful and established existent major professional football leagues (the National Football League and the Canadian Football League); if it cannot enforce the Eligibility Rule, its very existence will be threatened, and the best chance that college football players have for increased remuneration (viz., interleague economic competition) will be gone.

12. The Court finds that although the above listed reasons may have varying degrees of merit, the principal reason for the adoption by the USFL and its member teams of the Eligibility Rule was to respond to apparent demands made by college football programs and thereby to gain better access to these programs towards the end of selecting the best college players available.

13. The Eligibility Rule of the USFL, as it existed relative to the USFL's 1983 football season, involved combining for the primary purpose of coercing or excluding third parties, and did in fact have the effect of coercing or excluding those third party individuals deemed ineligible by the Rule. *Joseph E. Seagrams & Sons, Inc. v. Hawaiian Oke and Liquors Ltd.*, 416 F2d 71 (9th Cir. 1969).

14. While in certain areas cooperation and not competition among professional sports teams is required and thus the USFL might in some respects be considered to be an economic entity, as measured against issues presented in this case the Court finds that the USFL teams are economic competitors, *Los Angeles Memorial Coliseum, Inc. v. National Football League*, 468 F. Supp. 154 (C.D. Cal. 1979).

Order re Plaintiff's Motion for Partial Summary Judgment
Plaintiff's motion for partial summary judgment having come on regularly for hearing before this Court on January 30, 1984, the Court having read all of the papers filed by the parties in connection therewith and having considered the oral arguments presented at the hearing,
It is hereby ordered:
1. Plaintiff's motion for partial summary judgment is granted in part in that the Court finds that the "Eligibility Rule" of the United States Football League ("USFL"), as it existed in 1983, and which provided as follows: No person shall be eligible to play or be selected as a player unless (1) all college football eligibility of such player has expired, or (2) at least five (5) years shall have elapsed

since the player first entered or attended a recognized junior college, college or university or (3) such player received a diploma from a recognized college or university.
, as it was applied to plaintiff Robert F. Boris, constituted a "group boycott," and was, therefore, a *per se* violation of section one of the Sherman Act (15 U.S.C. sec 1). Pursuant to 28 U.S.C. sec. 1292(b), the Court is of the opinion that the foregoing order involves a controlling question of law as to which there is a substantial ground for difference of opinion and that an immediate appeal from this order may materially advance the ultimate termination of the litigation. . . .

62. 147 F Supp 154 (SDNY, 1956).
63. 181 NE2d 506 (Ohio, 1961).
64. 389 F Supp 867 (SDNY, 1975), which also held that the NBA draft procedures constituted a group boycott and were illegal per se under Section 1 of the Sherman Act.
65. Supra note 64 at pp. 882–884.
66. Id. at p. 895.
67. As defined in Section 8(d) of the National Labor Relations Act, 29 USC 158(d).
68. Supra note 64.
69. See 556 F2d 682 (2nd Cir., 1976).
70. 349 F Supp 716 (EDNY, 1972), aff 468 F2d 1064 (2nd Cir., 1972).
71. Supra note 22 at p. 686.
72. 401 US 1204 (1971).
73. Denver Rockets v. All-Pro Management, Inc., 325 F Supp 1049 (CD Cal., 1971); also see 25 Baylor L Rev (1973) at p. 10.
74. 401 US 952 (1971).
75. 190 F Supp 241 (SDNY, 1961).
76. Supra note 1 at pp. 215–216:

> With respect to plaintiff's suspension from the league in January of 1954, and the subsequent refusal by the league to reinstate him, plaintiff has patently failed to establish an unreasonable restraint of trade within the meaning of the anti-trust laws. A rule, and a corresponding contract clause, providing for the suspension of those who place wagers on games in which they are participating seems not only reasonable, but necessary for the survival of the league. Every league or association must have some reasonable governing rules, and these rules must necessarily include disciplinary provisions. Surely, every disciplinary rule which a league may invoke, although by its nature it may involve some sort of a restraint, does not run afoul of the anti-trust laws. And, a disciplinary rule invoked against gambling seems about as reasonable a rule as could be imagined. Furthermore, the application of the rule to the plaintiff's conduct is also eminently reasonable. Plaintiff was wagering on games in which he was to play, and some of these bets were made on the basis of a "point spread" system. Plaintiff insists that since he bet only on his own team to win, his conduct, while admittedly improper, was not immoral. But I do not find this distinction to be a meaningful one in the context of the present case. The vice inherent in the plaintiff's conduct is that each time he either placed a bet or refused to place a bet, this operated inevitably to inform bookmakers of an insider's opinion as to the adequacy or

Exemption and Non-exemption 59

> inadequacy of the point-spread or his team's ability to win. Thus, for example, when he chose to place a bet, this would indicate to the bookmakers that a member of the Fort Wayne team believed that his team would exceed its expected performance. Similarly, when he chose not to bet, bookmakers thus would be informed of his opinion that the Pistons would not perform according to expectations. It is certainly reasonable for the league and Mr. Podoloff to conclude that this conduct could not be tolerated and must, therefore, be eliminated. The reasonableness of the league's action is apparent in view of the fact that, at that time, the confidence of the public in basketball had been shattered, due to a series of gambling incidents. Thus, it was absolutely necessary for the sport to exhume gambling from its midst for all times in order to survive.
>
> The same factors justifying the suspension also serve to justify the subsequent refusal to reinstate. The league could reasonably conclude that in order to effectuate its important and legitimate policies against gambling, and to restore and maintain the confidence of the public vital to its existence, it was necessary to enforce its rules strictly, and to apply the most stringent sanctions. One can certainly understand the reluctance to permit an admitted gambler to return to the league, and again to participate in championship games, especially in light of the aura and stigma of gambling which has clouded the sports world in the past few years. Viewed in this context it can be seen that the league was justified in determining that it was absolutely necessary to avoid even the slightest connection with gambling, gamblers, and those who had done business with gamblers, in the future. . . .

See also Molinas v. Podoloff, 133 NYS 2d 743 (1954), for an earlier decision involving the same professional basketball player.

77. See 91 Seton Hall Legis J (1985) at pp. 54–57, which sets forth the NBA Constitution and By-Laws, Article 9A of which deals with franchise relocation:

> A member may transfer its franchise, city of operation, or playing site of any or all of its home games, to a different location, within or outside its existing Territory, as defined in Article 10, only in accordance with and subject to the following provisions:
>
> (a) Application to relocate must be made in writing to the Commissioner. The application shall identify the proposed new location and the arena in which the Member proposes to play its home games, and shall be accompanied by a certified check in the sum of $50,000 to defray the costs of the investigation of the application. Following the disposition of any application the Association shall repay to the applicant the sum of $50,000 less all expenses reasonably incurred in connection with the investigation of the application.
>
> (b) No application to relocate may be made after the first day of March preceding the season in which the proposed relocation is to take effect. Within ten (10) days of the receipt of an application to relocate, the Commissioner shall refer the application to a Committee to investigate the application. The Committee shall be appointed by the Commissioner and shall consist of no fewer than five Governors or Alternate Governors. Within one hundred twenty (120) calendar days from the Commissioner's receipt of the application, the Committee shall report to the Board of Governors with respect to the results of its investigation and its

recommendation of whether the application should be granted or denied. The recommendation of the Committee shall be based solely and exclusively upon the following factors:

(i) Whether the proposed new location can support a franchise in the Association or, if the proposed new location is within the existing Territory of a Member, whether the proposed new location can support another franchise. In evaluating this factor, the Committee shall consider: existing and projected population, income levels and age distribution; existing and projected markets for radio, broadcast television, cable television, and other forms of audio-visual transmission of Association games; the size, quality and location of the arena in which the Member proposes to play its home games; and the presence, history and popularity in the proposed new location of other professional sports teams and major college basketball teams.

(ii) Whether the applicant has demonstrated that it will be able successfully to operate an Association team in the proposed new location. In evaluating this factor, the Committee shall consider the applicant's present and projected financial condition and resources and its past performance in operating a team in the Association.

(iii) Whether the proposed relocation is likely to have an adverse effect upon the Association's ability to market and promote Association Basketball on a nationwide basis in a diverse group of geographic markets.

(iv) Whether the proposed new location presents particular disadvantages for the operation of the Association, such as by creating significant travelling or scheduling difficulties or because of adverse state or local laws or regulations.

(v) Whether other Association Members, in addition to the applicant, are interested in transferring their franchises to the proposed new location, or whether there are persons or entities interested in obtaining an expansion franchise in the proposed new location. In any such event:

(a) Except as otherwise provided herein, all applicants shall follow the procedure set forth in Article 6 of this Article, as the case may be. All additional applications to establish an NBA team in the proposed new location for the season to which the initial application relates shall be made within forty-five (45) days of the Commissioner's receipt of the initial application referred to in subparagraph (a), and the one hundred twenty (120) day period provided for in subparagraph (b) of this Article shall be extended to no longer than forty-five (45) days after the Commissioner's receipt of the initial application.

(b) The Committee appointed pursuant to this Article shall investigate each of the applications and shall recommend which of the applications, if any, should be granted. In reaching its recommendation the Committee shall consider all factors listed in subparagraph (b) (i-iv) of this Article and shall also consider:

(i) which applicant is likely to operate most successfully in the proposed new location, or otherwise best serve the interests of the Association; and

(ii) in the case of the proposed expansion franchise, whether the interests of the Association would best be served by expanding the number of members in the Association.

(c) The Committee is empowered to require from the applicant, and the applicant shall furnish, such information as the Committee deems appropriate for the conduct of this investigation. The Committee may engage consultants or other ex-

perts to assist it in the investigation of the application and may also request such additional information from the Commissioner as the Committee may deem appropriate for the conduct of its investigation. All information supplied to the Committee pursuant to this subparagraph (c) shall be made available to the applicant, and the applicant shall be afforded an opportunity to appear before the Committee to present whatever additional information or arguments the applicant desires. Any other Governor or his representative may also appear before the Committee to present whatever information or arguments such Governor desires.
(d) The report and recommendation of the Committee shall be delivered to each Member of the Board of Governors. The Commissioner shall call a meeting of the Board of Governors to consider the Committee's report and recommendation, which meeting shall be held no sooner than seven (7) days and no later than thirty (30) days after delivery of the Committee's report and recommendation. The applicant shall be afforded an opportunity to appear before the Board of Governors to present whatever information or arguments the applicant desires. The question whether to approve the proposed relocation shall be decided by a majority vote of all of the members, and no vote by proxy shall be permitted. The vote of each Governor on the proposed relocation shall be based solely and exclusively upon the factors listed in subparagraph (b) (i through v) of this Article.''

78. ____F Supp____(SDNY, 1958), aff 384 F2d 682 (2nd Cir.,1958), cert den 390 US 989 (1959), reh den 390 US 1046 (1959).
79. 384 F2d 682 (2nd Cir., 1967), cert den 390 US 989 (1967), reh den 390 US 1046 (1968).
80. 351 F Supp 462 (ED Pa., 1972).
81. See generally 11 Toledo L Rev (1980) at pp. 639–643.
82. 348 F Supp 261 (Mass., 1972), rem 472 F2d 127 (1st Cir., 1972).
83. 355 F Supp 733 (Minn., 1972).
84. See San Francisco Seals, Ltd. v. NHL, 579 F Supp 966 (CD Cal., 1974), holding that professional hockey is subject to the antitrust laws.
85. 600 F2d 1193 (6th Cir., 1979).
86. Supra note 77 for franchise relocation.
87. 460 F Supp 904 (ED Mich., 1978).
According to Judge Engel, who wrote the majority opinion,

> The reserve system, in professional athletics, has been the subject of exhaustive and spirited discussion both in the sports and in the legal world. Its supporters urge that it stimulates athletic competition between the teams of a sports league; its opponents urge that it stifles economic competition among those same teams. We have no doubt that there is a measure of truth in both claims. . . .
>
> Involved in this appeal is the validity, under federal antitrust laws, of the reserve system currently in effect in the National Hockey League. In its present form, the system has been termed a "modified Rozelle Rule" because it closely resembles the rule promulgated for the National Football League by its commissioner, Pete Rozelle, but has been modified to the extent that arbitration is not by the commissioner himself but by a professional and independent arbitrator.
>
> At the heart of the NHL reserve system is By-Law Section 9A. This section provides the rules governing the acquisition of free agents of other clubs in the league and is specifically made applicable to the players in the league by para-

graphs 17 and 18 of the Standard Players Contract, which each player in the NHL is required to sign. Further the Standard Player Contract, expressly including Paragraph 17, was approved by both the NHL team owners and the National Hockey League Players Association (NHLPA) in the current collective bargaining agreement, Sections 9.03(a) and (b).

As can be seen from its terms, By-Law Section 9A mandates that when a player becomes a free agent and signs a contract with a different club in the league, his original club has the right under the By-Law to exact an "equalization payment" from the acquiring club. That payment may be by the assignment of contracts of players, by the assignment of draft choices, or "as a last resort," by the payment of cash. If mutual agreement is not reached, each club submits a proposal to a neutral arbitrator, selected by majority vote of the Board of Governors of the League, who then must select, without change, one of the two proposals submitted. . . .

The trial court and the parties before us in this appeal have all relied upon *Mackey* as properly enunciating the governing principles in determining whether the non-statutory labor exemption applies to the reserve system provisions of a collective bargaining agreement in professional sports. *Mackey v. National Football League*, 543 F.2d 606 (8th Cir. 1976), *cert. dismissed*, 434 U.S. 801, 98 S. Ct. 28, 54 L.Ed.2d 59 (1977). There Judge Lay set forth three broad principles:

> "We find the proper accommodation to be: First, the labor policy favoring collective bargaining may potentially be given pre-eminence over the antitrust laws where the restraint on trade primarily affects only the parties to the collective bargaining relationship.
> . . . Second, federal labor policy is implicated sufficiently to prevail only where the agreement sought to be exempted concerns a mandatory subject of collective bargaining. . . .
> Finally, the policy favoring collective bargaining is furthered to the degree necessary to override the antitrust laws only where the agreement sought to be exempted is the product of bona fide arm's-length bargaining. . . . "

543 F.2d at 614-15 (footnotes omitted).

We see no reason to disagree with the judgment of the district court and of the attorneys on both sides that the proper standards are set out in *Mackey*. In short, it was proper to apply *Mackey's* standards; the issue is whether those standards were properly applied. . . .

We have little difficulty in determining that the first policy considerations favor the exemption. Clearly here the restraint on trade primarily affects the parties to the bargaining relationship. It is the hockey players themselves who are primarily affected by any restraint, reasonable or not.

Second, the agreement concerning the reserve system involves in a very real sense the terms and conditions of employment of the hockey players both in form and in practical effect. As *Mackey* correctly points out, the restriction upon a player's ability to move from one team to another within the league, the financial interest which the hockey players have and their interest in the mechanics of the operation and enforcement of the rule strongly indicate that it is a mandatory bargaining subject within the meaning of the National Labor Relations Act, Section 8(d), 29 U.S.C.§158(d) (1976).

The issue, therefore, in our judgment is narrowed to whether, upon the facts of this case, the agreement sought to be exempted was the product of bona fide arm's-length bargaining. The court in *Mackey* held under the circumstances before it that such arm's-length bargaining was missing. So did the district court here. The underlying facts in the two cases, however, are quite different.

In *Mackey* it was shown that the National Football League Players Association, at least prior to 1974, had stood in a relatively weak position with respect to the clubs. The Rozelle Rule had remained unchanged in form since it was unilaterally promulgated in 1963, even before the Players Association was formed. The Eighth Circuit specifically found that the Rozelle Rule was not bargained over in the negotiations leading to the 1968 or 1970 collective bargaining agreements. . . .

88. Supra note 85 at p. 1212. Interestingly, while the case was pending, the two professional hockey teams agreed upon an alternative compensation and McCourt's contract was reassigned to the Detroit Red Wings.

89. Free Agents and Equalization (Adopted November 27, 1973):

Free Agents

9A. 1. A player who becomes a "free agent" pursuant to subsections 2 or 3 of this By-Law shall have the right to negotiate and contract with any Member Club or with any club in any other league. [Clauses 9A2 thru 9A5 omitted.]

Obligation to make equalization payment

9A. 6. Each time that a player becomes a free agent and the right to his services is subsequently acquired by any Member Club other than the club with which he was last under contract or by any club owned or controlled by any such Member Club, the Member Club first acquiring the right to his services, or owning or controlling the club first acquiring that right, shall make an equalization payment to the Member Club with which such player was previously under contract as prescribed by subsection 8 of this By-Law. Each Member Club may acquire the right to the services of as many free agents as it wishes, subject to the provisions of subsection 9 of this By-Law.

Determination of Equalization Payment Purpose

9A. 7. The purpose of the equalization payment shall be to compensate a player's previous Member Club fairly for loss of the right to his services when that player becomes a free agent and the right to his services is acquired by another Member Club or a club owned or controlled by another Member club.

Procedure

9A. 8.(a) The Member Club acquiring the services of a free agent, or owning or controlling the club acquiring such services, shall immediately notify the player's previous Member Club and the President of that fact by TWX or telegram. The equalization payment shall be determined, if possible, by mutual agreement of the two Member Clubs involved. If no such agreement is reached within three business days after the date on which the player's services are acquired, each of the Member Clubs involved shall within two additional business days submit by TWX or telegram its proposal for an equalization payment to a neutral arbitrator selected from time to time by majority vote of the Board of Governors of the League.

[Clauses 9A8(b), (c), and (d) omitted.]

9A. 8. (e) The cost of the arbitrator shall be borne by the League.

9A. 8. (f) To facilitate a good faith effort to reach agreement on the equalization payment, the acquiring Club shall furnish to the Club entitled to that payment such information as may reasonably be required with respect to any player the assignment of whose contract is proposed by either party as an equalization payment, in whole or in part, including, but not limited to, the salary, bonus, and other compensation of such player, a copy of the player's contract, and any adverse information with respect to the physical, mental, or emotional condition of such player.

9A. 8. (g) The details of the procedure to be followed in the event arbitration is required shall be set forth in the agreement entered into by the League and the arbitrator.

Satisfaction of Equalization Obligation

9A. 9. No Member Club, or any club owned or controlled by such Member Club, shall be entitled to sign or acquire the right to the services of any free agent until it has satisfied in full its equalization obligation under these By-Laws as to each other free agent, the right to whose services it has acquired, by assigning the player contracts and/or draft rights and otherwise consummating the equalization payment required by mutual agreement or by arbitration. It shall be the responsibility of the acquiring Club to notify the President that it has satisfied its equalization obligation.

9A. 10. The President shall disallow the right of any acquiring Member Club to use the services of any signed free agent if he has not received the notice specified in subsection 9 or otherwise previously signed has not been fully satisfied by said Member Club in accordance with this By-Law.

90.

The labor of a human being is not a commodity or article of commerce. Nothing contained in the antitrust laws shall be construed to forbid the existence and operation of labor, agricultural, or horticultural organizations, instituted for the purposes of mutual help, and not having capital stock or conducted for profit, or to forbid or restrain individual members of such organizations from lawfully carrying out the legitimate objects thereof; nor shall such organizations, or the members thereof, be held or construed to be illegal combinations or conspiracies in restraint of trade, under the antitrust laws. [15 U.S.C. #17 (1976)]

91. 504 F Supp 1023 (EDNY, 1980).
92. 476 F Supp 1018 (Mass, 1979).
93. See generally 18 ALR Fed 489.
94. See Section 3.1 hereinbefore.
95. 348 US 236 (1955). Two of boxing's greatest historical moments not involving the huge financial resources of the sport occurred in 1892 and 1908. On September 7, 1892, the first gloved match under the Marquis of Queensberry Rules took place in New Orleans, Louisiana, at the Olympic Club between challenger James J. Corbett of San Francisco and John L. Sullivan of Boston, then champion. The challenger, a quiet bank teller, was unlike Sullivan in that Corbett was the first scientific boxer, who even cho-

Exemption and Non-exemption 65

reographed his evasive footwork. In the 21st round Corbett knocked Sullivan down, and Sullivan was unable to continue the fight after the third knockdown. And on December 26, 1908, Jack Johnson defeated the heavyweight champion from Australia, Tommy Burns, becoming the first black to hold the heavyweight boxing championship title. Johnson held the title until in 1915 Jess Willard knocked him out in the 26th round in Havana, Cuba. (Johnson died in an automobile accident in 1946 at the age of 68.)

96. Note Peller v. International Boxing Club, Inc., 219 F2d 444 (7th Cir., 1955), where a federal district court in Illinois had dismissed an action premised upon the Clayton Act and the Sherman Act on jurisdictional grounds and for failure to state a cause of action; the Seventh U.S. Court of Appeals reversed and remanded for trial consistent with United States v. International Boxing Club, Inc., supra note 95.

97. 150 F Supp 397 (SDNY, 1957).

98. Supra note 1 at pp. 213-214.

99. 358 US 242 (1959).

100. _____ F Supp_____ (Iowa, 1956), aff 325 F2d 768 (8th Cir., 1963).

101. See note 1 at pp. 214-215.

102. 410 F Supp 843 (Pa., 1976).

103. However, it should be noted that in 1976 the original version of World Team Tennis, the draft system, was on its way out, and the particular tennis franchise named as defendant was then defunct. Actually, the defendant here defaulted when it failed to answer the complaint, and it was up to World Team Tennis to defend, which it did by first arguing that plaintiff Cliff Drysdale had no standing to bring his antitrust action under 15 USC 15, for he was not directly damaged by any alleged antitrust violation. But the court ruled that plaintiff's claim fell within the "target area" test, which required the injury to be within the area intended to be protected by Congress since the draft system stifled competition and created limitations on what a player might earn.

It was in 1874 that Major Walter C. Wingfield, a British colonial officer, popularized the sport of lawn tennis, although the game of tennis went back centuries. Wingfield even obtained a British patent for what he called "a portable court for playing tennis." He introduced the oval tennis racket. In March 1874 he published a rule book on tennis and even sold rubber balls, rackets, and nets. It was in 1877 that the All-England Croquet Club at Wimbledon sponsored the first Wimbledon Championship in tennis.

104. 511 F Supp 1103 (Neb., 1981), aff 665 F2d 222 (8th Cir., 1981). See New York Law Journal (March 27, 1987) at p. 5 et seq for article "Tennis Giants Volley for Control under Antitrust Attack."

105. 358 F2d 165 (8th Cir., 1966), cert den 385 US 846 (1966), reh den 385 US 1032 (1966).

106. According to Judge Hamley:

> PGA is an association of some 4,300 golfers, founded in 1916 as a voluntary unincorporated non-profit association. The named individual defendants are persons who were, at the time the complaint was filed on April 23, 1959, officers and employees of PGA and members of its tournament committee. PGA sponsors or co-sponsors substantially all of the professional golf tournaments held in the United States. In order to compete in these golf tournaments, a player must either be a member of PGA, or an approved tournament player, or one of a limited number of participants who may be designated or invited by the local sponsor. Because of the increasing popularity of professional tournament golf, the increas-

ing number of golfers, and the increasing number of persons eligible to enter PGA sponsored tournaments, and because the limitations of time and space make it impossible to play a full tournament with a field of more than 150 or 160 golfers, some means had to be found to limit the number of golfers who could enter these tournaments. PGA rules limiting entry to PGA members, approved tournament players, and a few others, and defining the qualifications necessary for non-member entrants, were intended to accomplish this purpose.

In order to become a PGA member a person must have five years experience, either in the employ of a golf club as a professional or in the employ of a professional, as an assistant at a golf club, or (in recent years) as a tournament player under an agreement with PGA, playing a minimum of twenty-five tournaments per year, or any combination of these methods for a period of five years. Deesen was at all times, and now is unwilling to become employed by a golf club as a professional or as an assistant to a professional at a golf club.

An approved tournament player must be approved first by a local committee of PGA, then by PGA's tournament and executive committees. Approval is given if the applicant has, in the opinion of each of these committees: (1) the ability to play golf and finish in the money in tournaments in which he competes, (2) the financial responsibility to undertake the golf tours, and (3) moral character and integrity. There are no issues herein as to Deesen's financial responsibility or his character and integrity.

There are no exact or definite standards set up to determine ability to play. The nature of golf is such that no precise standard of ability can be established other than by comparison of scores and ability to finish in the money in tournaments. In order to enter PGA sponsored and co-sponsored tournaments, PGA members are not required to meet the standards set for PGA-approved tournament players.

The basic purpose of PGA in requiring persons who seek approved tournament standing to meet certain standards and obtain committee approval appears to be a reasonable one, insofar as the evidence before us indicates. That purpose is to insure that professional golf tournaments are not bogged down with great numbers of players of inferior ability. The purpose is thus not to destroy competition but to foster it by maintaining a high quality of competition. The means PGA has chosen to accomplish this purpose also appear to be reasonable insofar as this record reveals, having in view the national scope of the activity and the practical problems which had to be met. The trial court did not err in holding that, in these respects, Deesen did not establish a violation of section 1 of the Sherman Act.

Deesen also attacks the PGA tournament entry rules on the additional ground that they are not applied uniformly to members and non-members, asserting that the rules are therefore unreasonable on their face. Appellant's specific grievance here is that a PGA member may play in any PGA tournament regardless of his average score, or his ability to finance himself, or the number of tournaments entered, or his ability to finish in the money regularly. Non-PGA members, on the other hand, may not play unless they obtain standing as PGA tournament players. . . .

In *Chicago Board of Trade v. United States*, 246 U.S. 231, 238, 38 S. Ct. 242, 244, 62 L. Ed. 683, the Supreme Court said:

> "The true test of legality is whether the restraint imposed is such as merely regulates and thereby perhaps promotes competition or whether it is such as may suppress or even destroy competition. To determine that question the court must ordinarily consider the facts peculiar

to the business to which the restraint is applied; its condition before and after the restraint was imposed; the nature of the restraint and its effect, actual or probable. The history of the restraint, the evil believed to exist, the reason for adopting the particular remedy, the purpose or end sought to be attained, are all relevant facts."

Measured by the test spelled out in *Chicago Board of Trade v. United States*, the indicated differentiation between PGA and non-PGA members with regard to the right to participate in sponsored tournaments was not, on this record, shown to be for the purpose of suppressing or destroying competition, nor did it have that effect. The trial court did not err in so ruling.

Mere size, unaccompanied by unlawful intent or conduct in the exercise of the power gained through size, does not constitute a violation of section 2 of the Sherman Act. *United States v. Swift & Co.*, 286 U.S. 106, 116, 52 S. Ct. 460, 76 L. Ed. 999. It is the existence of monopoly power coupled with the intent . . . and purposes or with inevitable anticompetitive effects that establishes the offense of monopolization. *United States v. Griffith*, 334 U.S. 100, 197, 68 S. Ct. 941, 92 L. Ed. 1236.

No finding nor evidence has been called to our attention which indicates that PGA has used, or intends to use, its position as the sponsor or co-sponsor of a substantial number of tournaments to preclude sponsorship of tournaments by others, to exclude golfers from access to PGA sponsored tournaments, or to suppress or eliminate competition in professional tournament golf. . . . PGA is entitled to adopt reasonable measures for holding the tournaments to a manageable number. It was required to treat Deesen as well as it treated others in the same category but it was not compelled to give him special treatment merely because he did not wish to accept PGA tournament entry rules and regulations. . . .

107. 359 F Supp 1260 (Ga., 1973). Six years later in 1979 in Weser v. PGA, decided by the federal district court for Northern Illinois, plaintiff challenged the PGA tournament eligibility rules, and the court determined that he had standing to bring suit and that the proper standard to apply was the Rule of Reason. The court stated that the PGA rules may not be reasonable if they permit entry to some golfers who have not proven their competitive ability, or if the regulations are so restrictive that persons who have proven their competitive ability are refused entry in order to favor less qualified members. Whether the PGA rules had this effect was left to be resolved upon the development of a complete factual record, and plaintiff's motion for summary judgment was therefore denied.

108. See Michener, Sports in America (1976) at p. 531, and 15 New England L Rev (1980) at p. 700.

109. North American Soccer League v. NFL, 465 F Supp 665 (SDNY, 1979).

110. Article XI as amended by Section 9.4 read as follows:

(A) No person (1) owning a majority of interest in a member club, or (2) directly or indirectly having substantial operational control, or substantial influence over the operations of a member club, or (3) serving as an officer or director of a member club, nor (4) any spouse or minor child of any such person, may directly or indirectly acquire, retain, or possess any interest in another major team sport (including major league baseball, basketball, hockey and soccer).

(B) The prohibition set forth in subsection (A) hereof shall also apply to relatives of such persons (including siblings, parents, adult children, adult and minor grandchildren, nephews and nieces, and relatives by marriage) (1) if such person directly or indirectly provided or contributed all or any part of the funds used to purchase or operate the other sports league entity or (2) if there exists between such persons and any such relative a significant community of interest in the successful operation of the other sports league entity.

(C) The Commissioner shall investigate, to the extent he deems necessary or appropriate, any reported or apparent violation of this Section and shall report his findings to the Executive Committee prior to imposition of disciplinary action by the Committee.

(D) Beginning on February 1, 1980, any person who, after notice and hearing by the Executive Committee, is found to have violated subsection (A) or (B) above will be subject to fines of up to $25,000 per month for each of the first three months of violations; up to $50,000 per month for the next three months; and up to $75,000 per month thereafter. In addition, violations of more than six months' duration may be dealt with by the Executive Committee pursuant to Article VIII, Section 8.13(B).

(E) If such person does not pay such fine to the League Treasurer within 20 days of its assessment, the unpaid amount thereof may be withheld, in whole or in part, by the Commissioner from available funds in possession of the League Office belonging to the member club with which the person in violation is affiliated.

111. The order stated that the injunction was sought for the purpose of

enjoining and restraining the defendant National Football League ("NFL") and its defendant member teams, and their respective agents and attorneys and all persons acting in concert with them, from entering into, adhering to or enforcing any past, present or future agreement, including any NFL Constitution and/or By-Law provision or amendment thereof, that restricts the ability of any person to maintain, expand or acquire an ownership interest in an NASL franchise. . . .

112. 15 USC 1:

Every contract, combination in the form of trust or otherwise, or conspiracy, in restraint of trade or commerce among the several States, or with foreign nations, is hereby declared to be illegal. Every person who shall make any contract or engage in any combination or conspiracy hereby declared to be illegal shall be deemed guilty of a felony and, on conviction thereof, shall be punished by fine not exceeding one million dollars if a corporation, or if any other person, one hundred thousand dollars, or by imprisonment not exceeding three years, or by both said punishments, in the discretion of the court.

113. 3 WLR 573 (C. A.).
114. 356 F2d 371 (9th Cir., 1966), cert den 384 US 963 (1966).
115. 306 F Supp 1215 (CD Ga., 1969).
116. 286 F Supp 146 (Ind., 1968).
117. _____ F Supp _____ (Ohio, 1960).
118. Supra note 1 at p. 216.
119. 443 US 55 (1979).
120. Id. at pp. 65–67. For a similar holding, see Drolet v. New York State Racing and Wagering Board, 453 NYS2d 361 (1982).
121. See Martinez v. State Racing Commission, 410 NE2d 740 (Mass App., 1980), and Tufariello v. Barry, 401 NYS2d 219 (1978).

Exemption and Non-exemption

122. 445 So2d 58 (La App., 1984).
123. 15 USC 17 and 29 USC 52; also 38 Stat 730 (1914).
124. See Duplex Co. v. Deering, 254 US 443, at p. 484.
125. Id.
126. 29 USC 101–105.
127. See United States v. Hutcheson, 312 US 219 (1941).
128. 325 US 797 (1945).
129. 381 US 657 (1965).
130. Supra note 128.
131. Id. at p. 809.
132. 421 US 616 (1975).
133. 451 US 704 (1981).
134. 689 F2d 1199 (4th Cir., 1982), cert den 104 S Ct 26 (1983).
135. Cf. Larry Moko, Inc. v. Southwestern Pennsylvania B & CT Council, 609 F2d 1368 (3rd Cir., 1979).
136. 602 F2d 494 (3rd Cir., 1979).
137. 543 F2d 606 (8th Cir., 1976).
138. Id. at p. 614.
139. 351 F Supp 462 (Pa., 1972).
140. 29 USC 152(2).
141. 29 USC 159.
142. See generally 18 ALR Red 489.
143. 600 F2d 1193 (6th Cir., 1979).
144. The court was of the opinion that non-labor groups could use the labor exemption as perhaps was done in Meat Cutters v. Jewel Tea Co., Inc., 381 US 676; Scooper Dooper, Inc. v. Kraftco Corp., 494 F2d 840 (3rd Cir., 1974); National Assn. of Broadcast Employees & Technicians v. International Alliance of Theatrical State Employees, 488 F2d 124 (9th Cir., 1973); International Container Transportation Co. v. New York Shipping Assn., 426 F2d 884 (2nd Cir., 1970); and Cordova v. Bache & Co., 321 F Supp 600 (SDNY, 1970).
145. Supra note 143 at p. 1212.
146. See generally 42 Ohio St L J 603 (1981).
147. 602 F Supp 525 (SDNY, 1984).
148. The court cited favorably J. I. Case Co. v. NLRB, 321 US 332 (1944).
149. See Federal Maritime Commission v. Seatrain Lines, Inc., 411 US 726 (1973) at p. 733.
150. 389 F Supp 867 (SDNY, 1975). Here the NBA attempted to argue that any matter which was a mandatory subject of a collective bargaining agreement between an employer and a union was exempt as long as the matter had no substantial effect upon persons outside of the bargaining unit. The court rejected this argument.
151. 460 F Supp 904 (ED Mich., 1978), rev. 600 F2d 1193 (6th Cir., 1979).

4

Aspects of Monopolies and Restraints of Trade in Professional Sports

4.1 INTRODUCTION

It has been said that in every antitrust case there are two routes to a finding of illegality, to wit: "critically analyzing the competitive effects and possible justification of the challenged practice, or subsuming it under one of the per se rules."[1] The per se route is obviously easier to find, for such conduct as price-fixing,[2] market division,[3] tying arrangements,[4] and group boycotts,[5] for example, are illegal, regardless of reasonableness, motive, or effect. In Northern Pacific Railway Co. v. United States[6] the U.S. Supreme Court spoke of the demanding standard in a per se finding of an antitrust violation with respect to restraint of trade: there must be evidence of a "pernicious effect on competition and lack of any redeeming virtue."[7] But, in general, the business of professional sports does not lend itself to the per se violation of antitrust laws. The business of professional sports may better be characterized in terms of the reasonableness or the unreasonableness of the allegedly restrictive practice or activity that may or may not adversely affect competition. This Rule of Reason has been applied historically in a hostile manner if the contract was indeed a restraint of trade or commerce.[8] In 1890 Congress passed the Sherman Antitrust Act[9] in response to public discontent with the predatory practices of large businesses driving or forcing out of the market the smaller competitors; another reason was because the Rule of Reason as then applied was not uniformly respected.[10] The Sherman Act established absolute prohibitions and invoked the equity powers of the federal courts to restrain violations of the act; but it was not until 1911 that the U.S. Supreme Court in Standard Oil Company of New

Jersey v. United States[11] announced that only those restraints in trade or commerce whose character or effect as unreasonably anti-competitive were outlawed by the Sherman Act.[12] Over the years thereafter the Rule of Reason took on subjective and objective character in analyzing such factors as the net economic effect of a restraint,[13] the restraint with which the court had not had "considerable experience"[14] and the redeeming virtues of the restraint itself.[15]

Mr. Justice Oliver Wendell Holmes in Federal Baseball Club of Baltimore v. National League of Professional Baseball Clubs[16] in 1922 raised the ugly spectre that the Rule of Reason might not be applicable to the "professions" as he upheld the immunity of the professional sport of baseball from the antitrust laws: "Personal effort is not a subject of commerce," and professional baseball games "although made for money would not be called trade or commerce in the common or accepted use of those words." He observed that the legal profession was similarly not related to production and was therefore exempt from the antitrust laws. Indeed, it was not until 1975 that the U.S. Supreme Court in Goldfarb v. Virginia State Bar Ass.[17] ruled that the "professions" constituted "trade or commerce." Three years later the highest court in National Society of Professional Engineers v. United States[18] emphasized that the Rule of Reason did not open the field of antitrust inquiry to any argument in favor of a challenged restraint, but the Rule of Reason "focuses directly on the challenged restraint's impact on competitive conditions."

Hereinafter the control of playing facilities, the franchise market, the control of professional athletes, the control of media coverages, and cross-ownership are all delineated in terms of monopolies and restraints of trade. But a brief look at antitrust enforcement is first in order if these and other aspects are to be comprehended. The U.S. Department of Justice and the Federal Trade Commission (FTC), as well as private parties injured by an antitrust violation, are the enforcement vehicles. The criminal provisions of the antitrust laws are exclusively handled by the U.S. Department of Justice, although this federal agency can also obtain civil remedies and may even sue for single (not treble damages in behalf of the United States. Obviously, the liability standard in a criminal case requiring criminal intent is stricter than it is in a civil case.[19] A corporation convicted under a criminal provision of the Sherman Act, for example, may be fined up to $1 million, while a natural person may be fined up to $100,000 and imprisoned up to three years. The Federal Trade Commission has exclusive power to enforce Section 5 of the FTC Act, which condemns unfair methods of competition, and also enforces the Clayton Act; the FTC cannot assess prison terms or damages, for its relief is in the form of an injunction known as a "cease and desist order"; fines up to $10,000 are authorized for violation of a cease and desist order, or a "knowing violation" of the antitrust laws.

Today it would appear that perhaps 90 percent of antitrust enforcement is carried on not by federal government agencies but by private plaintiffs in lawsuits filed in the federal district court. The provision for treble damages under Section 4 of the Clayton Act is a very attractive magnet for the plaintiff, who must first overcome the problem of "standing to sue." Before a person or corporation has standing to sue for antitrust damages, the person or corporation must show injury in "business or property" as a result of another's antitrust violation; even a retail consumer has standing to sue for damages in a price-fixing case,[20] provided that the plaintiff is the immediate victim of the predatory pricing, or a "direct injury" victim.[21] However, in Conference of Studio Unions v. Loew's, Inc.[22] the Ninth U.S. Court of Appeals opined that a plaintiff need only show that he was "within that area of the economy which is endangered by a breakdown of competitive conditions in a particular industry"; but the court concluded here that the labor union and its members had no standing to sue for antitrust injuries sustained by companies that employed members of the union. But purchasers of products or services from a violator or competitors of the violator would appear to have "standing." In Blue Shield of Virginia v. McCready[23] the U.S. Supreme Court in 1982 granted standing to sue status to a user of services of psychologists when the user claimed that she was victimized by a conspiracy between psychiatrists and a health insurer to deny health care coverage on its insurance policy for treatment by psychologists. Although the intended victim of the alleged conspiracy was the psychologist, the court reasoned that the insured patient whose insurance policy excluded psychologists' services was undeniably injured too, and therefore was entitled to sue. But the next year, 1983, the highest court in Associated General Contractors of California, Inc. vs. California State Council of Carpenters[24] denied standing to a labor union which had alleged that the defendant employers had coerced various union members into dealing with nonunion companies and thereby "restrained the business activities of the unions."

It should be apparent that not all forms of injury caused by antitrust violations are reprehensible, as was evident in Brunswick Corp. v. Pueblo Bowl-O-Mat, Inc.,[25] decided by the U.S. Supreme Court in 1977. The competitor of a bowling corporation sued following a merger with a small bowling alley that was in poor financial condition and likely to go out of business; the plaintiff competitor argued that, as a result of the merger or acquisition by the defendant, a large operator of bowling alleys, the acquired firm remained in competition with the plaintiff. The court found no antitrust injury, for the plaintiff was simply complaining that the market had become more competitive after the merger.

A private plaintiff is also entitled to obtain an injunction against the continuation of an antitrust violation or even against a threatened antitrust violation. Under Section 4B of the Clayton Act private antitrust damage actions must be brought within four years from the time the cause of action accrued, i.e., when damages are ascertainable.

Aside from the labor exemption, delineated in Section 3.8 of Chapter 3 herein, there are other exemptions from the antitrust laws, such as the insurance industry; The McCarran-Ferguson Act[26] authorizes the states to regulate the business of insurance but exempts the insurance business from the antitrust laws insofar as such state regulation exists. In Union Labor Life Insurance Co. v. Pireno[27] the U.S. Supreme Court identified three criteria for "the business of insurance" that qualify for the antitrust exemption, to wit: "first, whether the practice has the effect of transferring or spreading a policyholder's risk; second, whether the practice is an integral part of the policy relationship between the insurer and the insured; and third, whether the practice is limited to entities within the insurance industry." But it should be observed that the McCarran-Ferguson Act does not provide exemption for such illegal insurance practices as boycotts, coercion, or intimidation.

Another exemption from the antitrust laws is found in Section 6 of the Clayton Act, which gives an exemption to agricultural cooperatives; together with the Capper-Volstead Act this legislation encourages farmers to create cooperatives for marketing of their agricultural products even to the extent of combining and setting prices. But these agricultural cooperatives cannot engage in exclusionary practices or restraints of trade against competitors. The Fisheries Cooperative Marketing Act of 1976 provided an antitrust exemption for fishermen similar in scope to the exemption for agricultural cooperatives. Export associations under the Webb-Pomerene Act are also exempt from antitrust attack so as to permit exporters to compete with similar foreign associations; but such export associations cannot engage in activities that restrain trade within the United States, nor can the export association participate in a foreign cartel. The Export Trading Company Act of 1982 authorizes the U.S. Department of Justice to certify properly qualified export trading companies that are exempt from public prosecution under the antitrust laws.

Where the antitrust laws are not applicable, the authority of a federal regulatory agency protects competition, as perhaps illustrated by the role of the Civil Aeronautics Board, which had exclusive jurisdiction over the airline industry.[28] (Today the airline industry finds itself within the jurisdiction of the antitrust laws after the Civil Aeronautics Board was abolished, however.) Courts generally defer to agency regulation except where the agency actually does not effectively regulate in the antitrust area, as demonstrated by the Seventh U.S. Court of Appeal's determination in MCI Communications Corp. v. AT&T Co.[29] that the Federal Communications Commission had not considered the competitive consequences of its ruling on a rate or service change. But a state that regulates effectively will not subject the regulated industry to the federal or state antitrust laws, according to the U.S. Supreme Court's 1943 pronouncement in Parker v. Brown[30] that the framers of the U.S. Constitution and the legislators of antitrust laws did not intend to interfere with the ability of individual states to regulate in the public interest. In its 1985 decision, Southern Motor Carriers Rate Conference v. United States,[31] the highest court decided that the activities of the state rating bureau, i.e., a legal cartel setting prices proposed by common carriers, qualified for "state action" exemption. The court opined that state compulsion is required before the "state action" exemption applies unless there is evidence that permissive rather than compulsory action would be substantially more competitive. However, in California Retail Liquor Dealers' Association v. Midcal Aluminum Co.[32] the same court ruled that the California state legislative scheme permitting wine producers and wine distributors to establish retail prices for wine in California did not qualify for the "state action" exemption from the antitrust laws because the scheme was not actively supervised by the state of California. Towns, cities, and counties may have the benefit of the "state action" exemption from the antitrust laws if their regulatory schemes are expressly and particularly authorized by the state, as shown in Town of Hallie v. Eau Claire,[33] where the Wisconsin statute authorized the municipality to regulate a specific market and where displacement of competition was a foreseeable result of that state delegation of authority to regulate.

4.2 CONTROL OF PLAYING FACILITIES

The case of United States v. International Boxing Club, Inc.,[34] or International Boxing Club, Inc. v. United States,[35] presents an eminent example of control over playing facilities which merited condemnation under the antitrust laws. Here International Boxing Club (IBC) acquired joint control with Joe Louis of the key boxing arenas and stadiums in the United States, guaranteeing that a professional boxing championship could not be successfully staged without IBC involvement and consent. Similarly, in Hecht v. Pro-Football, Inc.[36] the plaintiff owner of a professional football team who wished to obtain playing facilities in the Washington, D.C., area convinced the court that the exclusive lease of Robert F. Kennedy Stadium to the Washington Redskins was a restraint of the business of professional football and violative of Sections 1 and 3 of the Sherman Act. It appeared that the lease contained a covenant which granted the Washington Redskins of the NFL exclusive use of the stadium, the only facility in the area for the presentation of professional football.

The most striking example of control of playing facilities is seen in the efforts of the city of Oakland, California, to use its eminent domain power[37] over the playing facilities of the Oakland Raiders professional football team so as to maintain the team in Oakland. It was in 1980 that the team announced its intention to move to Los Angeles.[38] The trial court dismissed the action by the city of Oakland because (a) the property or playing facility is not located entirely within the boundaries of the city of Oakland; (b) there is no reasonable probability that the city will devote the property or playing facilities to a public use within seven years; (c) the property or playing facility is not subject to acquisition by eminent domain "for the stated purpose"; (d) the city of Oakland did not adopt a resolution of necessity that conclusively established the matters set forth in Section 1240.030 of the California Civil Procedure Code, and furthermore did not adopt a resolution of necessity prior to commencement of the eminent domain action here, nor did the city provide the Oakland Raiders professional football team with the requisite notice and opportunity to be heard as required by law; and (e) the public interest and necessity required neither the proposed project nor the acquisition by the city of the Oakland Raiders professional football team.[39] On appeal, the California appellate court affirmed,[40] holding that there was no statutory authority for the "condemnation of diverse contract rights necessary to operation of the Raiders' business enterprise." However, the California Supreme Court[41] found that there was a basis in law for the taking of intangible property by eminent domain because neither the Fifth Amendment of the U.S. Constitution, nor Article I, Section 19, of the California Constitution, nor Section 1235.170 of the California Civil Procedure Code (defining property subject to eminent domain as including "real and personal property and any interest therein") distinguished between real or personal property and tangible or intangible property. The highest California court agreed that "the acquisition and . . . operation of a sports franchise may be an appropriate municipal function," but remanded the case to the trial court to determine whether there was a valid public use to justify the city's eminent domain action. The trial court, in a bifurcated trial,[42] rendered a decision in favor of the Oakland Raiders professional football team; but the appellate court reversed[43] and remanded to the trial court to rule whether the stated purpose for the condemnation constituted a public use.[44] Thereupon the California Superior Court of Monterey County dismissed the action,[45] holding that the constitutional and statutory requisites of "public use" had not been met, and furthermore there could be no public use because the NFL Constitution and Bylaws prohibited a city from ownership and operation of an NFL franchise.

4.3 THE FRANCHISE MARKET

Professional sports leagues hold vast powers over their team owners and the professional athletes who are members of those teams by virtue of the "franchise market," i.e., the power to control the admission of new franchises and the power to regulate the movement of existing franchises. This power to control the admission of new franchises is fortified by a rule of the professional sports leagues that requires a franchise applicant to obtain first permission from three-fourths of the team owners of the particular league.[46] If the franchise applicant seeks to locate its team within an existing team's territory, it must pay an indemnity to the existing team, which resulted, for example, in the New York Nets paying $4 million to the New York Knickerbockers for invasion of Knickerbocker territory, even though the new team heightened fan interest in professional basketball in the New York metropolitan area![47] Franchise applicants are also discouraged by an unusually high "expansion fee," which money is shared by existing teams in the league.[48] These and other restrictive practices on franchise applicants have generally been upheld by the courts, as shown in Levin v. NBA,[49] where the court granted summary judgment in favor of the National Basketball Association league:

Here the plaintiffs wanted to join with those unwilling to accept them, not to compete with them, but to be partners in the operation of a sports league for plaintiffs' profit. Further, no matter which reason one credits for the rejection, it was not an anti-competitive reason. . . . the exclusion from membership in the league did not have an anti-competitive effect nor an effect upon the public interest.

The same reasoning prevailed in Mid-South Grizzlies v. NFL[50] in 1982:

"They do not want to compete with the NFL. They tried that and failed. Now they seek to join the asserted antitrust violators and share all the advantages of an established organization. Plaintiffs try to eschew this obvious conclusion by emphasizing that a franchise's revenue does not come solely from jointly earned profits; some money is earned by individual promotion, for example, of team paraphernalia and from local broadcast revenues. This does not change the obvious fact that the ability to earn these individual profits is an indirect benefit of being a member of the league."[51]

The professional sports leagues also argue that, since a league is a single entity and a combination in restraint of trade under Section 1 of the Sherman Act requires at least two independent actors, there can be no illegal conspiracy in restraint of trade.[52] But many courts have rejected this argument since the conspiracy is among competing teams that make up the league.[53] Nevertheless, courts continue to find bars on franchise acquisition to have no anti-competitive effect.[54] It is also perfectly reasonable to assume that any franchise applicant will have the necessary financial abilities and capacities, will have no connection with gambling or crime, and will hold no ownership interests in other clubs in the same league.[55]

Undoubtedly, the most important judicial pronouncement on franchises of professional sports teams was the 1984 decision of the Ninth U.S. Court of Appeals in the case of the Oakland Raiders professional football team.[56] In short, the team was permitted to move its franchise from Oakland, California, to Los Angeles, where the team became the Los Angeles Raiders of the NFL. The decision here in Los Angeles Memorial Coliseum Commission v. National Football League ran contrary to such mistaken beliefs that the league had authority to prohibit the relocation of existing franchises,[57] that the league could deny transfers of ownership of NFL franchises,[58] that the league could decline to add new clubs or teams,[59] that the league could assess "compensation" when one club or team was allowed to invade another's territory,[60] that the league could compel the sharing of gate receipts and telecast revenues,[61] and that the league could compel collective financial support for an individual member franchisee.[62] Yet the Commissioner of Baseball in 1978 had successfully blocked the trade or sale of several key players of the pennant-winning Oakland Athletics professional baseball team because it was an action detrimental to the best interests of professional baseball.[63] Indeed, in the Oakland Raiders professional football team case, the Ninth U.S. Court of Appeals was perfectly convinced that a move to Los Angeles would promote competition between the Raiders and the Los Angeles Rams and also produce lower ticket prices and enhance consumer choice.[64] And this prospect of increased competition provided the court's justification for invoking the antitrust laws to condemn the NFL's efforts to block the Raiders' move to Los Angeles.[65]

Movement or relocation of franchises in professional sports leagues may also be viewed in the context of the right to travel, and any restraint upon such movement or travel could have constitutional implications. The U.S. Supreme Court in Shapiro v. Thompson[66] in 1969 had occasion to note that "the nature of our Federal Union and our constitutional concepts of personal liberty unite to require that all citizens be free to travel throughout . . . the land uninhibited by regulations which unnecessarily burden or restrict this movement."[67] An 1867 decision of the highest court in Crandall v. State of Nevada[68] had echoed this sentiment in terms of the right of a citizen "to come to the seat of the government to assert any claim he may have upon the government, or to transact any business he may have with it. . . . This right is in its nature independent of the will of any state over whose soil he must pass in the exercise of it." Under the Commerce Clause the right to travel is afforded business entities,[69] but Congress has the power to regulate interstate commerce and could conceivably restrict the exercise of the right to travel.[70]

League rules prohibiting gambling and ownership of other professional sports teams can be overbearing, although in Molinas v. National Basketball Assn.[71] the court recognized that fan confidence demanded that anti-gambling rules were "necessary for the survival of the league." But in North American Soccer League v. NFL[72] the cross-ownership ban of the NFL[73] prohibiting owners from owning teams in another league was held to lack a legitimate business purpose and had in effect an anti-competitive effect upon the professional sport of soccer. A rule prohibiting corporations, for example, from owning professional teams would appear to be an unreasonable restriction and subject to antitrust attack.[74]

The issue of franchise movement or franchise relocation in professional team sports is tinged with deep emotional as well as monetary ties to the cities or states where the professional teams are located. According to the *New York Times* (Sept. 29, 1983) the relocation of the New York Jets of the NFL to the Meadowlands Complex in New Jersey cost New York City's economy approximately $33.3 million, including direct revenues of $1.2 million in taxes, at least $500,000 in rental at Shea stadium, and millions in transit fares, in addition to the deep emotional loss of New York City fans. The New York City business community was also adversely affected by the franchise relocation.[75] It is no wonder that professional sports leagues are obsessed with the need to control franchise movement or franchise relocation. There is a high degree of financial interdependence, but the stability of each franchise is important to the overall financial success. If franchises were permitted to move freely, such as a move into an existing franchise market or to a distant franchise market, the franchise movement or relocation could jeopardize the existing financial security of all professional teams in that league. Stability of franchise operations is also important to cities and states which support those franchises; public bonds are often utilized to construct stadiums and arenas for use of professional sports teams. It was in 1966 in State of Wisconsin v. Milwaukee Braves, Inc.[76] that league-imposed restrictions on franchise movement were attacked unsuccessfully. It appears that the defendant professional baseball team had moved in 1953 from Boston to Milwaukee with league approval; but decreasing revenues and poor attendance at games contributed to the request by the new owners of the defendant to move the franchise to Atlanta, and the league approved that move. The state of Wisconsin thereupon brought suit to prevent relocation of the franchise, and Major League Baseball argued that its system of regulation was "necessary and reasonable to promote and preserve the quality of playing skills among member clubs" on a national basis. The Wisconsin lower court, however, ruled that baseball was subject to Wisconsin antitrust law, despite the U.S. Supreme Court cases to the contrary.[77] The Wisconsin lower court also held that professional baseball was an illegal monopoly and had engaged in an illegal boycott under Wisconsin law: "Even if the shutdown of baseball in Milwaukee was not intended to restrain trade, the decisions to transfer, not to expand, and to refuse to deal with the Milwaukee market would nevertheless be illegal efforts to protect and extend the power of an existing monopoly." Accordingly, that Wisconsin trial court granted injunctive relief requiring the league to facilitate the organization and operation of a major league baseball team in Milwaukee. But the Wisconsin Supreme Court by a 4-3 vote reversed, refusing to apply the state's antitrust laws to major league baseball because state regulation of the operations of major league baseball would conflict with Congressional policy and unreasonably burden interstate commerce. Thus, the interests of the league and the franchise owner prevailed over the interest of the community in retaining the major league baseball team. In other professional sports the courts have similarly denied transfers of team ownership,[78] approved the decision not to add a new club or team to the league,[79] acquiesced in the league decision to discipline a team owner,[80] and subsequently agreed to an expansion into other cities at a time of inter-league rivalry.[81] On the other hand, courts have struck down as illegal efforts of teams to sequester players[82] and a stadium lease agreement that prevented use of the facility by a potential rival to the NFL leasee.[83] Between 1950 and 1984 there have been 11 baseball team transfers by the league,[84] 15 football team transfers by the league,[85] 28 basketball team transfers by the league,[86] and 14 hockey team transfers by the league.[87] This total of 68 franchise moves in baseball, football, basketball, and hockey professional sports attests to the power of the leagues to accomplish what they deem beneficial to the business of professional sports. But the three-fourths rule by the NFL for removal or relocation of a team was deemed in Los Angeles Memorial Coliseum Commission v. National Football League[88] to be in violation of Section 1 of the Sherman Act. The Oakland Raiders professional football team became the Los Angeles Raiders professional football team within the NFL. But rules limiting transfers and expansion teams freely to select their home cities is not per se illegal under Section 1 of the Sherman Act.

Interestingly, the federal tax laws have been a key factor in stimulating franchise acquisitions, for the Internal Revenue Code allows depreciation of player contracts,[89] capital gains,[90] carryover losses,[91] and the formation of Subchapter S corporations.[92] Professional athletes have also benefitted from favorable tax treatment of deferred income,[93] capital gains,[94] income-averaging,[95] income-splitting,[96] and other tax-saving devices.

4.4 CONTROL OF PROFESSIONAL ATHLETES

Still another aspect of monopolies and restraints of trade in professional sports is seen in the control exercised over professional athletes. Aside from the many restraints or restrictive practices hereinbefore delineated, there are the instances of restraints under the National Labor Relations Act[97] and restraints geared to discrimination based upon skin color and sex.[98] In the first place, it is clear that all professional sports fall within the coverage of the National Labor Relations Act,[99] which gives rise to the continuing conflict between the antitrust laws and collective bargaining agreements. But collective bargaining agreements are given immunity from the antitrust laws under the doctrine of the non-statutory labor exemption, delineated hereinbefore in Section 3.8 of Chapter 3 herein. In NFL v. NLRB[100] the Eighth U.S. Court of Appeals determined that the NFL had committed an unfair labor practice by its rule that "any player leaving the bench area while a fight is in progress on the field will be fined $200." In effect, the Commissioner of Football could not promulgate such a rule unilaterally without consultation with the players' union under the collective bargaining process. A similar result for professional soccer occured in Morio v. North American Soccer League.[101] But the applicability of the labor exemption from the antitrust laws rests upon the existence of a good faith, arm's-length collective bargaining process; and, if the restriction or restraint imposed by the team owners or the league falls outside those dimensions, the restriction or restraint may be attacked under the antitrust laws. Obviously, the examination of the collective bargaining process must be made with great care if the labor exemption is to have any meaning whatsoever. In McCourt v. California Sports, Inc.[102] the majority opinion found that there had been bona fide arm's-length bargaining because the National Hockey League according to the court, had been willing to discuss the by-law during the course of contract negotiations, even though the NHL did not intend to change its position. But the players' association itself is not immune from other liability as shown in Chuy v. NFL Players' Assn.,[103] where the professional football player sued the union for alleged breach of its statutory duty of fair representation, to wit: the union had refused to investigate and pursue his grievance against his team, the

Philadelphia Eagles professional football team, which grievance Chuy subsequently won. The federal district court in Pennsylvania held that the refusal of the union to engage an attorney for Chuy and to process the grievance against his team was motivated by bad faith and was a violation of the statutory duty of fair representation by the union. This duty of fair representation requires a union to serve as the sole spokesman of employee interests; as the U.S. Supreme Court in Steele v. Louisville & Nashville Railroad Co.[104] expressed it, "The organization chosen to represent a craft is to represent all its members, the majority as well as the minority, and is to act for and not against those whom it represents." It should be observed that federal labor laws make arbitration rather than the courts the favored mechanism for dispute resolution because arbitration is generally more efficient in handling such matters; indeed, the duty to arbitrate under a collective bargaining arrangement is compulsory, but cannot precede the judicial determination that the agreement actually created such a duty to arbitrate.[105]

Discrimination based on skin color or sex is another control over the professional athlete exercised by the league or the professional team owners. In baseball it was not until 1946 that Jackie Robinson became a Brooklyn Dodger and broke the color barrier in the major leagues of professional baseball.[106] But there is still a dearth of black persons in the managerial roles in professional sports. Discrimination based on sex is still rampant, even though Title VII of the Civil Rights Act[107] permits jobs to be reserved to one sex or the other if such a restriction is based upon "bona fide occupational qualifications."[108] Discrimination of the handicapped is also an important issue, and much remains to be done in that field.[109]

Another interesting restraint or control of the professional athlete is seen in the league by-laws which prohibit a club from "tampering" with players on other teams.[110] It is improper for another team or outsider to "negotiate with or make an offer to" a player whose rights are held by another club or team.[111] Discussions may be held with a player only if the prospective employer first secures the permission of the club with which the player is connected.[112] "Tampering" may result in a team losing a draft choice or being required to pay "compensation" to the offended club or team. The leagues justify the "tampering" rule as necessary to preserve the image of the professional game as involving honest athletic competition. Judge Sweigert in the Kapp case[113] opined that "the tampering rule . . . [is] patently unreasonable insofar as [it is] used to enforce other NFL rules." Split or divided loyalties of the player is another reason the NFL offered in support of its "tampering" rule.

Another restraint imposed upon ticket-purchasers for professional sports contests is the ticket-tying arrangement which was upheld in Coniglio v. Highwood Services, Inc.[114] Here the Buffalo Bills professional football team required an individual who desired to purchase a season ticket for all regular season games to buy, in addition, tickets for one or more exhibition, preseason games. This ticket-tying arrangement was held not to violate the Sherman Act, as similar tying arrangements were upheld in Driskill v. Dallas Cowboys Football Club, Inc.[115] because the practices had no anti-competitive effect. In Laing v. Minnesota Vikings Football Club, Inc.[116] the ticket-tying restraints were upheld because the availability of a substantial number of tickets for individual games during the season indicated that the professional football team here lacked the requisite compulsion over consumers to support the antitrust violation. And in Pfeiffer v. New England Patriots Football Club, Inc.[117] the federal district court in Massachusetts found nothing wrong with the Patriots' ticket-tying arrangements since no one was coerced into buying a ten-game season ticket package because single-game tickets were available for every home game played in 1971.

4.5 CONTROL OF MEDIA COVERAGES

In 1961 Congress granted limited exemption from antitrust liability to allow professional sports leagues to enter into television pooling arrangements with broadcasters.[118] Section 1291 of Title 15 of U.S. Code specifically provides antitrust exemption for joint agreements under which a professional sports league sells or transfers to a purchaser pooled television rights to the games of its member clubs. But Section 1292 specifically denies antitrust exemption to an agreement which prohibits the televising of any games within any area, except within the home territory of a member club on the day when such club is playing a home game. Section 1293 prohibits any agreement for the telecasting of any professional football game on Friday evenings or any Saturday during the period of time beginning on the second Friday in September and ending on the second Saturday of December in any year, from any telecasting station located within 75 miles of the game site of any intercollegiate or interscholastic football contest to be played on such a date, the purpose of Section 1293 being the protection of the substantial revenues which colleges, high schools, and other schools derive from gate receipts of their football contests. In 1973 Congress proscribed agreements which would prevent the broadcasting of a professional football, baseball, basketball, or hockey club in the local area, if such game is sold out 72 hours or more before the start of the game.[119]

But the baseball exemption from the antitrust laws is not broad enough to encompass broadcasting and television, which media activities are not central enough to baseball, according to Henderson Broadcasting Corp. v. Houston Sports Assn.[120] Here there was an alleged conspiracy with another radio station in Texas to divide and allocate advertising in audience territories and to eliminate competition for advertising revenue and listening audiences. The "blackout rule"[121] delineated in Public Law 93-107 since 1973, has repeatedly been vindicated as a reasonable restraint rationally related to the operation of a profitable stadium for a legitimate public purpose.[122] In WTWV, Inc. v. NFL[123] the Eleventh U.S. Court of Appeals held that the "blackout" of the station was permissible under Section 2 of the Sports Broadcasting Act of 1961 because the station broadcast with sufficient power that its telecasts were viewable with the 75-mile zone; "home territory" was defined by signal penetration, not by station location.

Of more than passing interest is the fact that the first sports report to appear in any newspaper was in 1779 when the *Whitehall Evening Post* of London, England, published a story of a sporting event.[124] The first radio broadcast of a professional sporting event in the United States was in October 1921 when radio station WJZ, then in Newark, New Jersey, broadcast the 1921 World Series in professional baseball as the New York Giants beat the New York Yankees 5 games to 3.[125]

4.6 CROSS-OWNERSHIP

In January 1982 in North American Soccer League v. NFL[126] the Second U.S. Court of Appeals ruled that an NFL rule banning persons owning or controlling NFL clubs from having a financial interest in any other professional sports league team violated the Rule of Reason under Section 1 of the Sherman Act. The trial court[127] had found that the purpose and intent of the cross-ownership ban (which came into force in the 1950s) was to suppress competition in interstate commerce on the part of the North American Soccer League (NASL), but the court denied the plaintiff a permanent injunction because the NFL and its member clubs are a "single economic entity," to which Section 1 of the Sherman Act did not apply. But the federal appellate court reversed:

The characterization of NFL as a single economic entity does not exempt from the Sherman Act an agreement between its members to restrain competition. To tolerate such a loophole would permit league members to escape antitrust responsibility for any restraint entered into by them that would benefit their league or enhance their ability to compete even though the benefit would be outweighed by its anticompetitive effects. . . . The sound and more just procedure is to judge the legality of such restraints according to well-recognized standards of our antitrust laws. . . .

The cross-ownership ban was not a "group boycott" nor a "concerted refusal to deal," according to the court: "Circumstances could exist that might justify a ban by a weak league as necessary to protect it against serious competitive harm by a cross-owner who threatened to misuse his position in that league to favor a stronger competing league and its members." According to one note writer the three economic justifications for the cross-ownership ban are (1) commercial confidentiality; (2) preservation of good will; and (3) avoiding conflicting interests.[128] Elimination of the cross-ownership ban could afford the team owners a mechanism by which they can acquire a significant interest in established competing leagues and thereby limit competition between leagues. As a result the existing team owners could enjoy an even greater market concentration and exert even greater economic leverage over players, cities and states, and fans.[129]

NOTES

1. See generally 66 Columbia L Rev 625 (1966) at p. 627.
2. See United States v. Trenton Potteries Co., 273 US 392 (1927), and Kiefer-Stewart Co. v. Joseph E. Seagram & Sons, 340 US 211 (1951).
3. See Timken Roller Bearing Co. v. United States, 341 US 593 (1951).
4. See International Salt Co. v. United States, 332 US 392 (1947).
5. See Silver v. New York Stock Exchange, 373 US 341 (1963), and generally 46 Missouri L Rev (1980) at pp. 813 to 815.
6. 356 US 1 (1958).
7. Id. at p. 5.
8. See 15 New Eng L Rev 3 (1980).
9. 15 USC 1 to 7.
10. See 41 Virginia L Rev 159 (1955).
11. 221 US 1 (1911).
12. Chief Justice White opined:

> Let us consider the language of the first and second sections [of the Sherman Act], guided by the principle that where words are employed in a statute which had at the time a well-known meaning at common law or in the law of this country they are presumed to have been used in that sense unless the context compels to the contrary. . . . [T]he statute was drawn in the light of the existing practical conception of the law of restraint of trade, because it groups as within that class, not only contracts which were in restraint of trade in the subjective sense, or act, but all contracts which theoretically were attempts to monopolize, yet which in practice had come to be considered as in restraint of trade in a broad sense . . . The statute under this view evidenced the intent not to restrain the right to make and enforce contracts, whether resulting from combination or otherwise, which did not unduly restrain interstate or foreign commerce, but to protect that commerce from being restrained by methods, whether old or new, which would constitute an interference that is an undue restraint. . . . [I]t follows that it was intended that the standard of reason which had been applied at the common law and in this country in dealing with subjects of the character embraced by this statute, was intended to be the measure used for the purpose of determining whether in a given case a particular act had or had not brought about the wrong against which the statute provided.

13. See National Society of Professional Engineers v. United States, 435 US 679 (1978).
14. See Broadcast Music Inc. v. Columbia Broadcasting System, 441 US 1 (1979).
15. See Continental Television, Inc. v. GTE Sylvania, Inc., 433 US 36 (1977).
16. 259 US 200 (1922).
17. 421 US 773 (1975).
18. Supra note 13.
19. See United States v. United States Gypsum Co., 438 US 422 (1978).
20. See Reiter v. Sonotone Corp., 442 US 330 (1979).
21. See Loeb v. Eastman Kodak Co., 183 F 704 (3rd Cir., 1910).
22. 193 F2d 51 (9th Cir., 1951), cert den 342 US 919 (1952).
23. 457 US 465 (1982).

24. 459 US 519 (1983).
25. 429 US 477 (1977).
26. Public Law 15 of 79th Cong. (Ch 20-lst Sess, S. 340), delineated in Warren Freedman, Richards On Insurance, 5th ed. (1952) at pp. 178 et seq.
27. 458 US 119 (1982).
28. See Pan American World Airways, Inc. v. United States, 371 IS 296 (1963).
29. 708 F2d 1081 (7th Cir., 1983).
30. 317 US 341 (1943).
31. 105 S Ct 1721 (1985).
32. 445 US 97 (1980).
33. 105 S Ct 1713 (1985).
34. See Section 3.5 of Chapter 3 herein.
35. 358 US 242 (1959).
36. 444 F2d 931 (DC, 1971), cert den 404 US 1047 (1971).
37. See generally 13 Fordham L Rev 553 (1985). Note that eminent domain is a governmental power that may be utilized to acquire property or facility for public use from an unconsenting owner provided that the owner receives compensation for the loss. See 1 Nichols On Eminent Domain, 3rd ed. (1981) at Section 1.11.
38. City of Oakland v. Oakland Raiders, 32 Cal3d 60, 646 P2d 835 (1982).
39. Supra note 37.
40. 123 Cal App3d 422 (1981).
41. Supra note 38.
42. 150 Cal App3d 267 (1983).
43. Id.
44. Id.
45. No. 76044, Judgment at 1-2 (Cal Super Ct, Monterey County, Aug. 10, 1984).
46. Note Section 3.1(b) of NFL Constitution and By-laws, described in Los Angeles Memorial Coliseum Commission v. National Football League, 468 F Supp 154 (CD Cal., 1979), aff 726 F2d 1381 (9th Cir., 1979), cert den 105 S Ct 397 (1984). Also see Section 4.2 of the NHL Constitution and By-laws, delineated in San Francisco Seals, Ltd. v. NHL, 379 F Supp 966 (CD Cal., 1974).
47. See New York Times (July 7, 1977) at p. Al.
48. See 60 NYU L Rev 925 (Nov. 1985).
49. 385 F Supp 149 (SDNY, 1974).
50. 550 F Supp 558 (Ed Pa., 1982).
51. See generally 25 Ariz L Rev (1983) at pp. 1012 et seq.
52. See Copperweld Corp. v. Independence Tube Corp., 104 S Ct 2731 (1984).
53. For example, North American Soccer League v. NFL, 670 F2d 1249 (2nd Cir., 1982), cert den 459 US 1074 (1982).
54. See Seattle Totems Hockey Club v. NHL, F Supp (WD Wash., 1983), aff. 783 F2d 1347 (9th Cir, 1983).
55. Supra note 48 at p. 951. Also note Section 4.6 herein.
56. 726 F2d 1881 (9th Cir, 1984).
57. See San Francisco Seals, Ltd. v. NHL, 379 F Supp 966 (CD Cal., 1974).
58. See Levin v. NBA, 385 F Supp 149 (SDNY, 1974).
59. See Mid-South Grizzlies v. NFL, 550 F Supp 558 (ED Pa., 1982).
60. See New York Times (July 27, 1977) at p. Al.

61. See Markham and Teplitz, Baseball Economics and Public Policy (1981) at pp. 89-93.
62. See *New York Times* (June 16, 1977) at p. 29.
63. Charles O Finley & Co. v. Kuhn, 569 F2d 527 (7th Cir., 1978).
64. Supra note 56 at pp. 1392 and 1395.
65. But note the view of Markham and Teplitz in their book, supra note 61 at pp. 23-24:

> While clubs constituting a league compete with one another for league standing, they do not, because of the geographical nature of the "market," compete for customers. . . . This is not meant to imply that absolutely no competition for customers exists among major-league clubs. The four large metropolitan areas supporting two or more clubs may be characterized by a certain amount of interclub competition for patronage and fan loyalty. Moreover, the network telecast of a major-league game may compete with a hometown game played on the same day. The essential point, however, is that such fringe competition is not likely to affect the decision making of individual clubs in such matters as ticket prices. Thus, ticket prices are likely to be determined not by competition with other clubs but by competition with alternate uses of people's leisure time, such as television, going to the beach, or puttering around the yard. The revenues earned by a club with any given home game are determined much more by its own league standing and its relative standing with the visiting team than by an independent competitive commercial strategy it may adopt against other teams in its league. . . . In economic terms, the price cross-elasticity of demand among games played in different home parks is extremely low—in fact, in most cases it is virtually zero.

66. 394 US 618 (1969).
67. Id. at p. 629.
68. 73 US 35 (1867).
69. See United States v. Guest, 383 US 745 (1966).
70. See generally 55 Neb L Rev 117 (1975).
71. 190 F Supp 241 (SDNY, 1961).
72. 670 F2d 1249 (2nd Cir., 1982), cert den 459 US 1074 (1982).
73. Section 4.6 herein.
74. See generally 81 Harv L Rev 418 (1967) at p. 428.
75. At *New York Times* (Sept. 29, 1983), p. B 19.
76. 144 NW2d 1 (Wis., 1966), cert den 385 US 990 (1966).
77. See Federal Baseball Club of Baltimore v. National League of Professional Baseball Clubs, 259 US 200 (1922), and Toolson v. New York Yankees, 346 US 356 (1953).
78. See Levin v. NBA, 385 F Supp 149 (SDNY, 1974).
79. See Mid-South Grizzlies v. NFL, 550 F Supp 558 (ED Pa., 1982), aff 720 F2d 772 (3rd Cir., 1983).
80. See Charles O. Finley & Co. v. Kuhn, 569 F2d 527 (7th Cir., 1978), cert den 439 US 876 (1978).
81. See American Football League v. National Football League, 323 F2d 124 (4th Cir., 1963).
82. See Robertson v. National Basketball Assn., 404 F Supp 832 (SDNY, 1975).
83. See Hecht v. Pro-Football, Inc., 570 F2d 982 (4th Cir., 1977).

84. See Johnson, Municipal Administration and the Sports Franchise Relocation Issue (Pub Adm Rev., Nov-Dec 1983):

Baseball (11); 1953—Boston to Milwaukee (Braves); 1954—St. Louis (Browns) to Baltimore; 1955—Philadelphia to Kansas City (Athletics); 1958—Brooklyn to Los Angeles (Dodgers); 1958—New York to San Francisco (Giants); 1961— Washington (Senators) to Minnesota (Twins); 1966—Milwaukee to Atlanta (Braves); 1966—Los Angeles to Anaheim (Angels); 1968—Kansas City to Oakland (Athletics); 1970—Seattle (Pilots) to Milwaukee (Brewers); 1972—Washington (Senators) to Arlington, Texas (Rangers).

85. Id.:

Football (15): 1952—Brooklyn to Dallas; 1953—Dallas (Texans) to Baltimore (Colts); 1960—Chicago to St. Louis (Cardinals); 1961—Los Angeles to San Diego (Chargers); 1963—Dallas (Texans) to Kansas City (Chiefs); 1971—Boston to Foxboro, Mass. (Patriots); 1971—Dallas to Irvine (Cowboys); 1973—Buffalo to Orchard Park (Bills); 1975—Detroit to Pontiac, Mich. (Lions); 1976—New York to Rutherford, N.J. (Giants); 1980—Los Angeles to Anaheim (Rams); 1982— Bloomington to Minneapolis (Vikings); 1982—Oakland to Los Angeles (Raiders); 1984—New York to Rutherford, N.J. (Jets); 1984—Baltimore to Indianapolis (Colts).

86. Id.:

Basketball (26): Since 1950 there have been 26 shifts in pro basketball: 1952— Tri-Cities to Milwaukee (Blackhawks); 1956—Milwaukee (Blackhawks) to St. Louis (Hawks); 1958—Ft. Wayne to Detroit (Pistons); 1958—Rochester to Cincinnati (Royals); 1961—Minneapolis to Los Angeles (Lakers); 1963—Philadelphia to San Francisco (Warriors); 1964—Chicago (Zephyrs) to Baltimore (Bullets); 1964—Syracuse (Nationals) to Philadelphia (76er's); 1969—St. Louis to Atlanta (Hawks); 1969—Anaheim (Amigos) to Los Angeles (Stars); 1969—Teaneck, N.J. (Americans) to Commach, L.I. (Nets); 1969—Minneapolis (Muskies) to Washington (Caps); 1970—Houston (Mavericks) to Charlotte (Cougars); 1970— Minneapolis (Muskies) to Pittsburgh (Pipers); 1971—New Orleans (Buccaneers) to Memphis (Pro's); 1971—Los Angeles to Salt Lake City (Stars); 1971—Washington (Caps) to Norfolk (Squires); 1972—San Diego to Houston (Rockets); 1973— Cincinnati (Royals) to Kansas City (Kings); 1974—Baltimore to Landover, Md. (Bullets); 1975—Charlotte (Cougars) to St. Louis (Stars); 1976—Memphis (Tams) to Baltimore (Claws); 1978—Commach, L.I., to Rutgers, N.J. (Nets); 1979— Buffalo (Braves) to San Diego (Clippers); 1980—New Orleans to Salt Lake City (Jazz); 1983—San Diego to Los Angeles (Clippers).

87. Id.:

Hockey (14): 1973—Philadelphia to Vancouver (Blazers); 1973—Ottawa (Nationals) to Toronto (Toros); 1973—New York (Raiders) to Cherry Hill, N.J. (Knights); 1973—Boston to Hartford (Whalers); 1974—Detroit (Stags) to Baltimore (Blades); 1974—Cherry Hill (Knights) to San Diego (Mariners); 1975— Denver to Ottawa (67's); 1975—Oakland (Seals) to Cleveland (Barons); 1975— Kansas City (Scouts) to Denver (Rockies); 1976—Cleveland (Barons) to Minneapolis (North Stars); 1976—Toronto (Toros) to Birmingham (Bulls); 1978—Houston (Aeros) to Winnipeg (Jets); 1980—Atlanta to Calgary (Flames); 1982—Denver (Rockies) to Rutherford, N.J. (Devils).

88. 726 F2d 1381 (9th Cir., 1984), cert den 105 S Ct. 397 (1984).
89. Section 167(a) of Internal Revenue Code.
90. Sections 1201 and 1202 of Internal Revenue Code.
91. Sections 1211 and 1212 of Internal Revenue Code.
92. Sections 1371 to 1379 of Internal Revenue Code.
93. Sections 404m 1348(b)(1), and 83(c)(1) of Internal Revenue Code.
94. Sections 1201(b), 1348(b), and 56(a) of Internal Revenue Code.
95. Sections 1301 et seq. of Internal Revenue Code.
96. See United States v. Hundley, Jr., 48 TC 339 (1958).
97. See generally 8 Ohio North L Rev (1981) at pp. 459 et seq.
98. Id. at pp. 444 et seq.
99. See North American Soccer League v. NLRB, 613 F2d 1379 (5th Cir., 1980).
100. 503 F2d 12 (8th Cir., 1974).
101. 501 F Supp 633 (SDNY, 1980).
102. 600 F2d 1193 (6th Cir., 1979).
103. 495 F Supp 137 (ED Pa., 1980), and 595 F2d 1265 (3rd Cir., 1979), for his case against the Philadelphia Eagles where Chuy won substantial damages for salary and for emotional distress after the team physician told Chuy that he had a fatal disease!
104. 323 US 192 (1944).
105. See, for example, Kansas City Royals Baseball Corp. v. Major League Baseball Players' Assn., 409 F Supp 233 (WD Mo., 1976), aff 532 F2d 615 (8th Cir., 1976).
106. See Broom and Selznick, The Jackie Robinson Case, Sport and Society: An Anthology (1973), at pp. 235-238.
107. 42 USC 2000.
108. See generally 66 ALR3d 1262 (1975) on application of state law to sex discrimination in sports.
109. See generally 44 ALR3d 148 (1979).
110. See Kapp v. National Football League, 390 F Supp 73 (ND Cal., 1974).
111. Article 9.2 of the NFL Constitution and By-laws read as follows:

> If a member Club, or any officer, shareholder, director, partner, employee, agent or representative thereof, or any person holding an interest in said Club shall tamper, negotiate with, or make an offer to a player on the Active, Reserve or Selection List of another member Club, then unless the offending Club shall clearly prove to the Commissioner that such action was unintentional, the offending Club, in addition to being subject to all other penalties provided in the Constitution and By-laws, shall lose its selection choice in the next succeeding Selection Meeting in the same round in which the affected player was originally chosen. If such affected player was never selected in any Selection Meeting, the Commissioner shall determine the round in which the offending Club shall lose its selection choice. Additionally, if the Commissioner decides such offense was intentional, the Commissioner shall have the power to fine the offending Club and may award the offended Club 50% of the amount of the fine imposed by the Commissioner. In all such cases the offended Club must first certify to the Commissioner that such an offense has been committed.

Aspects of Monopolies and Restraints of Trade

112. The "tampering" rule in professional baseball allows negotiation only if the club holding rights in the player "shall have, in writing, expressly authorized such negotiation or dealing prior to their commencement." See Flood v. Kuhn, 407 US 258(1972) at p. 259.

113. Supra note 110 at p. 82.

114. 495 F2d 1286 (2nd Cir., 1974), cert den 419 US 1022 (1975).

115. 498 F2d 321 (5th Cir., 1974).

116. 372 F Supp 59 (Minn., 1973), aff 492 F2d 1381 (8th Cir., 1974), cert den 419 US 832 (1974).

117. —F Supp—(Mass., 1973).

118. Pub L 87-331, 75 Stat 732 (1961), 15 USC 1291-1295.

119. Pub L 93-107, 87 Stat 350 (1973). See generally 18 ALR Fed 489.

120. 541 F Supp 263 (SD Tex., 1982).

121. Supra note 115.

122. See Hertel v. City of Pontiac, 470 F Supp 603 (Mich., 1979). See also Blaich v. NFL, 212 F Supp 319 (SDNY, 1962).

123. 678 F2d 142 (11th Cir., 1982).

124. See Wallechinsky and Wallace, The People's Almanac 2 (1978), Chapter 8.

125. Id. at p. 730.

126. 670 F2d 1249 (2nd Cir., 1982), cert den 103 S Ct 499 (1982).

127. 505 F Supp 659 (SDNY, 1981).

128. See 15 New Eng L Rev 3 (1980) at pp. 735-737.

129. See 25 Ariz L Rev (1981) at p. 1010.

5

Other Anti-Competitive Practices Against the Professional Athlete

5.1 ELIGIBILITY RULES

Of the innumerable anti-competitive practices aimed at the professional athlete, rules on eligibility and on discipline are probably the most common. In Greenleaf v. Brunswick-Balke-Collender Co.[1] the plaintiff, a professional billiards player, was denied entrance to a particular tournament conducted by the Billiard Association of America, a promotion vehicle of the defendant manufacturer of billiards equipment. It was alleged by the plaintiff that in return for the right to play in the tournament the defendant required players to grant permission for one year for the association to use their names for testimonial purposes related to the business activities of the defendant. Apparently plaintiff was allied with a billiards products wholesaler who did not deal in defendant's products. The federal district court in Massachusetts in 1947 denied defendant's motion for summary judgment on the ground that defendant, assuming it to be an illegal monopoly, cannot legally discriminate against or refuse to deal with plaintiff without sufficient cause. Eligibility rules were attacked also in Kapp v. National Football League,[2] where the court ruled that the so-called Rozelle Rule[3] imposed restraints virtually unlimited in time and extent and went far beyond any possible need of the NFL for fair protection of interests of the professional football teams; indeed, the restraint on eligibility imposed such undue hardship as to be unreasonable under any legal test. In 1967 the Bowling Proprietors' Association was ordered to revoke its rules that rendered ineligible for its bowling tournaments those bowlers who had bowled in establishments whose operators were not members of the Bowling Proprietors' Association.[4] The year previous in Washington State Bowling Proprietors' Assn. v. Pacific Lanes, Inc.[5] the Ninth U.S. Court of Appeals opined that the defendant, who had set rules for its bowling tournaments that barred bowlers who had done any organized bowling in establishments not affiliated with defendant, was guilty of antitrust violation. The court declared the ban on eligibility to be a group boycott, a per se violation of the Sherman Act, regardless of its possible reasonableness.

On the other hand, some bans on eligibility have been deemed not violative of the antitrust laws because the restraints were not so arbitrary nor unreasonable, as illustrated by Heldman v. U.S. Lawn Tennis Assn[6] (USLTA). Here the USLTA threatened to bar from its tennis tournaments players who had signed contracts with plaintiff to play in the circuit of non-USLTA tournaments; the court observed that there were sound reasons for USLTA's eligibility rules which were not anti-competitive, to wit: assurance of uniformity of play, encouragement of tennis competition of the highest ethical standards, and orderly scheduling of tournaments to accommodate the reasonable needs of all professional tennis players. The USLTA rules, the court noted, provided barred players with a full hearing including the right to counsel and appeal to the courts. The court found no evidence that the USLTA intended to monopolize women's professional tennis, nor was there evidence of any group boycott.

In professional golf, Deesen v. Professional Golfer's Association[7] also approved in 1966 the eligibility rules of the PGA as fostering high competitive standards because non-PGA members could compete in PGA tournaments; plaintiff here, a professional golfer, was denied entrance to a PGA tournament because of his prolonged lack of adequate performance. The court concluded that, while PGA was required to treat the plaintiff as well as it treats other professional golfers in the same category, PGA was not compelled to give plaintiff special treatment because plaintiff did not wish to accept PGA tournament entry rules and regulations. About nine years later in Abendroth v. PGA[8] the federal district court for the Northern District of California considered a similar issue of eligibility after the defendant PGA had changed its rules to introduce somewhat more rational selection criteria: any golfer could qualify after a period of 32 months if certain performance requirements were met; and the method of selecting nonmember approved tournament players was changed to require a specified level of performance at an annual qualifying school. If a nonmember who so qualified failed thereafter to maintain the requisite standard of performance in actual tournament play, he would have to return to the qualifying school. But PGA rules provided that its officials could grant extensions of eligibility to certain golfers and thus relieve them of the burden of requalifying. Plaintiff Abendroth qualified in 1974, but his performance deteriorated subsequently due to a family crisis; at the 1975 qualifying school he failed, and received no extension of eligibility. The court refused to grant him an injunction against PGA even though he would suffer irreparable harm from the PGA eligibility rule, which plaintiff argued was unreasonable and without standards. However, the federal district court in Georgia in 1973 in Blalock v. Ladies' Professional Golf Assn.[9] reversed the disciplinary action against plaintiff on the grounds that the tribunal which heard the case was composed of persons who were her competitors! That court felt that the competitors would gain by Blalock's exclusion, and that fact constituted a potential for abuse.

Eligibility determinations, for the most part, are deemed by the courts to be the prerogative of the enterprise in the regulation of its own affairs. The pertinent issue for antitrust purposes is whether the enterprise has exercised its regulatory powers consistent with the conditions which justify self-regulation. In STP Corp. v. United States Auto Club, Inc.[10] the court opined that the actions of a private governing body should be interfered with by the judiciary "*only* if it finds that the powers were exercised in an unlawful, arbitrary or malicious fashion and in such manner as to affect the property rights of one who complains.[11] This federal district court in Indiana rejected plaintiff's complaint that its turbine cars were unreasonably precluded from competing effectively in the Indianapolis 500 race; defendant's rules were geared to safety and did not come "within the proscription of the antitrust laws."[12] Indeed, the *purpose* of the rule is the keystone to the determination whether the court will sanction or reject the rule, as shown in United States v. U.S. Trotting Assn.[13] which decision followed the action of the federal government in attacking the rules of the USTA approving certain tracks, registering certain horses, and licensing certain drivers. The court sustained these USTA rules:

The defendant contends that the main purposes of the U.S.T.A. are lawful and that restraints, if any, incidental to its activities are reasonable and reasonably related to the attainment of those purposes. Defendant alleges that the main purpose behind the organization of U.S.T.A. was to provide a voluntary association open to all persons and organizations interested in the betterment of harness racing; that this main general purpose was implemented by the adoption of U.S.T.A. By-Laws, Rules and Regulations which set forth the expressed main purposes of U.S.T.A., i.e. the registration and identification of horses, rules of racing "within the fence," and the preservation of the integrity of harness racing.

Plaintiff has failed to establish that the main purpose of U.S.T.A. is an unlawful or hidden one different from its expressed purposes just mentioned. To determine whether the manner or means utilized by a defendant to attain its purposes are unlawful, the rule to be applied is whether the restraint imposed, if any, is such as "merely regulates and perhaps thereby promotes competition or whether it is such as may suppress or even destroy competition." *Chicago Board of Trade v. United States*, 246 U.S. 231, 238. The Court cannot find upon this record that the activities of U.S.T.A. in maintaining and enforcing its Rules and Regulations are unlawful as unreasonable and undue restraints upon competition in interstate commerce. Nor can the Court find that such activities are anything more than reasonable restraints that merely regulate and standardize harness racing, promote competition in harness racing, and generally enable U.S.T.A. to attain its main and not unlawful purposes as contended by defendant.

Other aspects of the eligibility rules may be seen in Bowman v. NFL,[14] where the plaintiffs were former professional football players of the World

Football League who sought employment in the NFL after their league had gone out of business. The NFL resolution had stated that "for 1975 only . . . any player who has been under a 1975 contract as a player or coach in another major professional football league may not sign with any NFL club for 1975. . . . " The court saw the NFL rule as prohibiting new acquisitions of players and thereby denying those players the opportunity to contract with a NFL club which might be willing to compensate the player for contributing his efforts in a close league race. It would appear that the above restriction was deemed to be distinct and separate from rules governing on-the-field competition, which properly fall within the prerogative of the NFL.[15] A rule of the National Hockey League on noneligibility of a player with one eye was upheld in Neeld v. NHL[16] as a safety requirement and not a rule anti-competitive in nature.

5.2 DISCIPLINARY RULES

Disciplinary rules frequently are successfully attacked for their illegal restraints, as was demonstrated in Blalock v. Ladies' Professional Golf Assn.[17] Plaintiff was suspended from membership in the defendant association for allegedly moving her golf ball in tournament play; she was initially fined, put on probation, then suspended without a hearing. The federal district court in Georgia termed defendant's conduct a group boycott, illegal under Section 1 of the Sherman Act; it was a "naked restraint of trade" committed by her professional golf competitors, who comprised the executive board of the defendant association.[18] On the other hand, disciplinary rules may serve purposes beyond stifling of competition, as illustrated by Brenner v. World Boxing Council.[19] Here a boxing promoter failed to honor his agreement with the World Boxing Council (WBC) and was suspended from promoting WBC world title contests of professional boxers. The court found that the plaintiff promoter was given sufficient notice of his suspension and had failed to demonstrate that the executive committee of the WBC that suspended him was composed of competitors who stood to gain from his suspension. The Second U.S. Court of Appeals concluded that the discipline imposed by the WBC was aimed at achieving aims and objectives other than participant parity, safety, and league integrity. In Molinas v. National Basketball Assn.[20] the plaintiff professional basketball player was barred from playing professional basketball after his criminal conviction for betting; the NBA rules providing for the suspension of players who place wagers on games in which they are participating was found by the court to be reasonable and necessary for the survival of the NBA. The court observed that each time Molinas either placed a bet or refused to place a bet on his team, his actions operated to inform bookmakers of an insider's calculated opinion as to the adequacy or inadequacy of the "pointspread" or his team's ability or inability to win in a particular game. Thus, the NBA rule against wagering was mandatory if NBA was to avoid even the slightest connection with gamblers and gambling. And in professional bowling the court upheld the discipline meted out to the plaintiff in Manok v. Southeast District Bowling Assn.[21] Plaintiff was suspended from the American Bowling Congress for knowingly bowling with a person whom he knew to be using an alias for purposes of fraudulently obtaining a higher handicap in bowling and for sharing in the ill-gotten prize money. The federal district court in California found no evidence of a conspiracy in restraint of trade, and no evidence of a discriminatory application of the disciplinary rules. The court also indicated that it was loathe to review suspensions from voluntary associations absent a clear showing of bad faith.

The "reserve system," delineated at length here in Chapters 3 and 4, has been described in terms of its anti-competitive character, in that it operates to remove a professional player from his free choice of teams, thereby having a restraining effect on the interstate market of professional players. The Standard Player's Contract in use in 1972 in the National Hockey League,[22] for example, was not only a restraint upon the right of the professional player to sell his services in an unfettered market, but it was a self-enforcing contract in that a player knew that if he violated the "reserve clause" of his contract with one team, he would be boycotted by the other teams of the NHL.[23] Indeed, nearly all league or team disciplinary actions against players take on the appearance of a group boycott,[24] for when an athlete is disciplined and denied the right to continue playing, it is because there is a joint agreement among the member clubs or teams that they will refuse to deal with the player for the period of his discipline or the time of his suspension as a player. This joint action produces an injury since the professional athlete is precluded from selling his or her services to the league member teams, and thus is denied a livelihood. And concerted refusals to deal are per se unreasonable under the antitrust laws;[25] but professional sports must have the means to protect itself against actions of participants who might seriously injure, if not destroy, the professional sports enterprise. The success of the professional sports enterprise is dependent upon the fans' belief that the games and matches represent honest and fair competition, a true test of skills, conditioning, and even coaching and managing. It would be hazardous if professional sports could not protect itself against wrongful acts or omissions of its professional players.

5.3 DISCRIMINATION BASED ON SEX, COLOR, OR NATIONAL ORIGIN

Discrimination based on sex, color, or national origin, for example, has also found its way into professional sports, but in general there have been very few, if any, cases involving professional sports enterprises whose activities for the most part are public and in the public spotlight. In Ludtke v. Kuhn[26] the court invalidated the Commissioner of Baseball's total exclusion of female sports writers from locker rooms at Yankee Stadium, and in Maclean v. First Northwest Industries of America, Inc.[27] the court in Washington ruled that ladies' promotions conducted by a professional basketball team violated the state equal rights amendment (ERA) laws. In Richards v. U.S. Tennis Assn.[28] it was held "grossly unfair, discriminatory and inequitable," as well as violative of his-her rights under the New York Human Rights Law, for the defendant to determine the sex of a transsexual (Dr. Renee Richards) by the use of a so-called sex-chromatin test. In April 1987 various civil rights groups have organized to make a national effort to influence minority hiring policies "in the front offices" of professional sports[29]: "The ranks of managers, coaches, and front-office personnel remain virtually all-white preserves," according to the NAACP.[30]

NOTES

1. 79 F Supp 362 (Pa., 1947).
2. 390 F Supp 73 (ND Cal., 1974); aff 586 F2d 644 (9th Cir., 1974), cert den 441 US 907 (1974).
3. See Section 3.2 of Chapter 3 herein.
4. United States v. Bowling Proprietors' Assn.,_____F Supp_____(SDNY, 1967).
5. 356 F2d 371 (9th Cir., 1966), cert den 384 US 963 (1966).
6. 354 F Supp 1241 (SDNY, 1973).
7. 358 F2d 165 (9th Cir., 1966), cert den 385 US 846 (1966), reh den 385 US 1032 (1966).
8. No. 75-2358 (ND Cal., 1975).
9. 359 F Supp 1260 (ND Ga., 1973).
10. 286 F Supp 146 (SD Ind., 1968).
11. Id. at p. 151.
12. Id. at p. 171.
13. 1960 Trade Cas 69,671 (SD Ohio, 1960).
14. 402 F Supp 754 (Minn., 1975).
15. See generally 81 Harv L Rev 418 (1967).
16. 594 F2d 1297 (9th Cir., 1979).
17. 359 F Supp 1260 (Ga., 1973).
18. It should be noted that in a preliminary action in 1972 the same federal district court in Georgia had found that plaintiff had demonstrated substantial probability of success on the merits of her claim that her suspension was an illegal restraint on interstate commerce.
19. 675 F2d 445 (2nd Cir., 1982).
20. 190 F Supp 241 (SDNY, 1961).
21. 306 F Supp 1215 (Cal., 1969).
22.

> Clause 6. The Player represents and agrees that he has exceptional and unique knowledge, skill and ability as a hockey player, the loss of which cannot be estimated with certainty and cannot be fairly or adequately compensated by damages. The Player therefore agrees that the Club may possess, to enjoin him by appropriate injunction proceedings from playing hockey for any other team and or for any breach of any of the other provisions of this contract.
>
> Clause 17. The Club agrees that it will on or before September 1st next following the season covered by this contract tender to the Player personally or by mail

directed to the Player at his address set out below his signature hereto a contract upon the same terms as this contract save as to salary. The Player hereby undertakes that he will at the request of the Club enter into a contract for the following playing season upon the same terms and conditions as this contract save as to salary which shall be determined by mutual agreement.

Clause 18. The club and the player severally and mutually promise and agree to be legally bound by the Constitution and By-Laws of the league and by all the terms and provisions thereof, a copy of which shall be open and available for inspection by club . . . and the player at the main office of the league and at the main office of the club.

23. See Boston Professional Hockey Assn. v. Cheevers, 348 F Supp 261 (Mass., 1972), remanded 472 F2d 127 (1st Cir., 1972).
24. Cf. Silver v. New York Stock Exchange, 373 US 292 (1963).
25. See Klor's Inc. v. Broadway-Hale Stores, Inc., 359 US 207 (1959).
26. 461 F Supp 86 (SDNY, 1978).
27. 600 P2d 1027, (Wash., 1979).
28. 400 NYS2d 267 (1977).
29. New York Times (April 16, 1987) at p. B12.
30. Id.

6

State Regulation of Professional Sports

6.1 STATE ANTITRUST STATUTES

Most states have constitutional or statutory antitrust provisions[1] which are similar to the federal Sherman Act,[2] denouncing monopolies and restraints of trade on the ground of public policy.[3] In theory, state antitrust provisions were enacted to reach agreements and combinations in restraint of trade (as well as monopolies) that were beyond the scope of federal power.[4] State antitrust statutes are not designed to regulate the public market or to control the price of goods offered for sale in the public market; state antitrust statutes primarily seek to suppress monopolies tyranny and oppression of combined wealth.[5] State antitrust statutes generally go into more detail than federal antitrust laws about the reasons for condemning a particular combination or monopoly,[6] as illustrated in Twin Falls Farm & Dairy Distributing, Inc. v. D & B Supply Co.,[7] where the Idaho statute governing combinations in restraint of trade spelled out the prerequisite of "concerted action" between two or more individuals. State antitrust statutes have no retroactive or ex post facto operation, and generally apply only to offenses occurring after enactment;[8] but if such an offense continues to exist after enactment of the statute, the statute will apply.[9]

Where the antitrust offense goes beyond the parameters of the state, the state may still exercise its antitrust powers, for, as stated in Tober Foreign Motors, Inc. v. Reiter Oldsmobile, Inc.,[10] Congress did not intend the Sherman Act or other federal antitrust legislation to withdraw from states their traditional regulatory powers and market-shaping acts. In this Massachusetts case the state statute dealing with unfair methods of competition and unfair or deceptive acts or practices, and dealing with grants by motor vehicle manufacturers of new dealership franchises which would compete with established franchises in the same markets, was not void as conflicting with the federal statute. Indeed, the Sherman Act did not preempt the field, and, as the New Jersey court observed in State of New Jersey v. Lawn King, Inc.,[11] no state antitrust statute has even been declared unconstitutional for being in conflict with the Sherman Act! Furthermore, a state regulatory scheme is not preempted by the federal antitrust laws simply because in a hypothetical situation a private party's compliance with the state statute might cause him to violate the antitrust laws of the federal government; a party may enjoin the enforcement of a state statute only if the state statute, on its face, is patently irreconcilable with federal antitrust policy.[12] This is particularly the case where there exists sufficient local significance and impact to justify the exercise of the state's policy powers.[13] But if there is a clear conflict between state and federal antitrust laws (and interstate commerce is involved), the federal statute would control.[14] If the persons doing business in interstate commerce are exempt from federal antitrust laws, these persons are also exempt from state antitrust laws.[15] In Partee v. San Diego Chargers Football Co.[16] the California court ruled that the professional football player did not have an antitrust claim against the defendant team or the NFL for violation of Section 16700 of the California Business and Professional Code (the Cartwright Act) because application of the Cartwright Act to the interstate activities of professional football would impermissibly burden interstate commerce. Professional football was seen by the court as a nationwide business to which the California antitrust laws were inapplicable: there is a need for a nationwide league structure and a nationally uniform set of rules. Fragmentation of the NFL structure on the basis of state lines would adversely affect the success of the competitive business enterprise, and different state antitrust decisions would likely compel all member teams to comply with the laws of the strictest state, to the detriment of all states and the business of professional football. And in Matuszak v. Houston Oilers, Inc.[17] the Texas Court of Civil Appeals opined that the Texas trial court did not abuse its discretion in granting temporary injunctive relief against the professional football player despite allegations that the contract between the player and the defendant team was in violation of Texas antitrust laws; the federal antitrust law had preempted state antitrust laws here with respect to professional sports.

It is obvious that professional baseball's exemption from the federal antitrust laws, as delineated herein Section 3.1 of Chapter 3, means that state antitrust laws are similarly inapplicable to the professional sport of baseball.[18] Indeed, in Flood v. Kuhn[19] the federal district court for the Southern District of New York expressly stated that defendant's restrictive practices do not constitute violations of the antitrust laws of New York, California, or any other states where professional baseball is played. Both the Second U.S. Court of Appeals[20] and the U.S. Supreme Court[21] affirmed that holding that state antitrust laws do not apply to professional baseball because state antitrust statutes would conflict with the federal policy exempting professional baseball from the impact of the federal antitrust laws. National uniformity and the burden on interstate commerce are cited as reasons that outweigh the state's interest in regulating professional baseball. Earlier in 1966 in State of Wisconsin v. Milwaukee Braves, Inc.[22] the Wisconsin Supreme Court had pointed out that Congresional silence demonstrated that professional baseball was not subject to state antitrust laws as well as the federal antitrust laws. Enforcement of a state antitrust law against decisions of the league as to the location of baseball franchises and membership in the league, for example, would conflict with national policy in this segment of interstate commerce.

But all professional sports other than baseball would appear to be prime targets for state antitrust law enforcement, unless the "trade or commerce" was exclusively transacted in interstate commerce. Where the "trade or commerce" occurred primarily and substantially within the state, however, the state antitrust laws would be applicable. Little FTC Acts modeled after the Federal Trade Commission Act,[23] for example, have emerged since the 1960s in the various states to overcome some of the inadequacies of the FTC Act, as amended, particularly the recognition of a private cause of action by consumers or business entities seeking to curb unfair trade practices, deceptive acts, and unfair methods of competition. While perhaps one-half of the states have enacted such Little FTC Acts, most of these states have exempted from application of the state antitrust acts advertising and broadcasting, the conduct of learned professionals, employer-employee disputes, and securities transactions.[24] If a professional basketball team in North Carolina responded to an advertisement of a commercial employment agency offering the services of an experienced bookkeeper, and the agency represented that it screened all candidates, and the team hired the bookkeeper, and the bookkeeper embezzled huge sums of money, the professional basketball team would sue the employment agency under the North Carolina Little FTC Act, as was successfully done in Winston Realty Co. v. G.H.G., Inc.[25] The jury awarded treble damages to the plaintiff, even discounting plaintiff's contributory negligence because the North Carolina statute was intended to fight unfair and deceptive trade practices. Indeed, state antitrust law enforcement is generally directed toward outlawing those restraints of trade which were invalid at common law; courts today forbid those restraints which are unreasonable or injurious to the public welfare.[26] State antitrust laws affect only intrastate commerce, while federal antitrust laws affect interstate commerce which may or may not include intrastate commerce.[27] In HMC Management Corp. v. New Orleans Basketball Club[28] the Louisiana court was troubled by the complexity of the suit by plaintiff management corporation, authorized to operate the state's stadium facility, against the defendant professional basketball team and the NBA. Plaintiff alleged breach of the stadium lease and conspiracy to violate the state's antitrust laws. The court was asked to determine which of two leases between the parties was valid, and whether the terms of the leases had in fact been violated; if a violation was found, then the court had to decide whether the violation had occurred as a result of the violation of state antitrust laws or whether the federal antitrust laws were applicable and had preempted the issue.

6.2 RIGHTS OF ATHLETES AND THE STATE

In Arlosoroff v. NCAA[29] the Fourth U.S. Court of Appeals examined a rule of the National Collegiate Athletic Association which deemed that an athlete used up a year of eligibility for each year he had participated in any organized competition that occurred after the student's twentieth birthday and before he enrolled in college. Arlosoroff complained that the NCAA rule had a significantly disproportionate impact on foreign students since in many foreign countries military service is mandatory after high school, a fact that rendered it more likely that foreign students would be over the age of 20 before enrolling in college in the United States. Plaintiff also raised the constitutional issue of a rule that was applicable to years of competition completed *before* the NCAA adopted the rule. The court vacated the preliminary injunction which plaintiff had secured in the federal district court, holding that NCAA action did not involve "state action" so that the constitutional challenges to the NCAA eligibility rule could not be entertained. The court presented two conditions, either of which must be present if a private enterprise could be made accountable under the U.S. Constitution: (1) the activity must be found to involve a traditional public function; or (2) the state through its involvement with the enterprise must have caused or procured the action complained about.[30] The court construed the first requisite very narrowly in holding that the "public function" must be one "traditionally reserved exclusively to the state"; it was perfectly obvious that the regulation of college athletics had no tradition of state exclusivity. The court found that the state of Louisiana did not direct the offending NCAA action; mere subsidization of athletics through scholarships was insufficient to make the state a procurer of the NCAA activity: "There is no suggestion in this case that representatives of the state institutions joined together to vote as a bloc to effect adoption of the Bylaw over the objections of private institutions.[31] Thus, it is self-evident that the athlete does not have a protectible interest in participating in intercollegiate athletics, and moreover the equal protection challenge is unavailing in face of the rational relation standard typically applied that defers to the regulatory agency.[32]

The professional athlete, on the other hand, may have greater constitutional protection by the very nature of the fact that professional sports is a business, even though the professional sports leagues do not partake of state authority. In the leading case of Ludtke v. Kuhn,[33] the federal district court for the Southern District of New York ruled that "state action" was present in connection with the Commissioner of Baseball's decision to exclude a female sports reporter[34] from the locker rooms at Yankee Stadium, which was owned by the City of New York. The court opined that "state action" is present where the direct

State Regulation

perpetrator of the discriminatory act is, though a private entity, "so entwined" with an agency of the state that the state agency must be responsible for the private entity's act in violation of the Fourteenth Amendment. Clearly, the city of New York had also subsidized the professional team's use of the stadium, the use of the stadium was a "public use," and that act in question involved unabashed sex discrimination! The five factors taken from Jackson v. Statler Foundation[35] (decided by the Second U.S. Court of Appeals), to wit:

(1) the private entity's degree of dependence on government aid; (2) the extent and intrusiveness of governmental regulation involved; (3) whether or not aid is given to all similar institutions or is suggestive of government's approval of the activity challenged in the particular case; (4) whether or not the institution under attack performs a public function; and (5) the legitimacy of the organization's claim to be regarded as private in character, in associational or constitutional terms

were deemed to be relevant to that conclusion of the federal district court. Furthermore:

The undisputed facts show that the Yankees' interest in protecting ballplayer privacy may be fully served by much less sweeping means than that implemented here. The court holds that the state action complained of unreasonably interferes with plaintiff Ludtke's fundamental right to pursue her profession in violation of the due process clause of the Fourteenth Amendment.[36]

In sharp contrast to the Ludtke v. Kuhn decision[37] is the federal district court in the District of Columbia's holding in DeFrantz v. United States Olympic Committee,[38] (USOC), where no "state action" was found, even though the private corporation was federally chartered:

The USOC is an independent body, and nothing in its chartering statute gives the federal government the right to control that body or its officers. Furthermore, the facts here do not indicate that the federal government was able to exercise any type of "*de facto*" control over the USOC. The USOC decided by a secret ballot of its House of Delegates. The federal government may have had the power to prevent the athletes from participating in the Olympics even if the USOC had voted to allow them to participate, but it did not have the power to make them vote in a certain way. All it had was the power of persuasion. We cannot equate this with control. To do so in cases of this type would be to open the door and usher the courts into what we believe is a largely nonjusticiable realm, where they would find themselves in the untenable position of determining whether a certain level, intensity, or type of "Presidential" or "Administration" or "political" pressure amounts to sufficient control over a private entity so as to invoke federal jurisdiction. We accordingly find that the decision of the USOC not to send an American team to the summer Olympics was not state action, and therefore, does not give rise to an actionable claim for the infringements of the constitutional rights alleged.

The court here found no violation of any supposed right of amateur athletes to compete in the Olympic Games in Moscow:

> Plaintiffs have been unable to draw our attention to any court decision which finds that the rights allegedly violated here enjoy constitutional protection, and we can find none. Plaintiffs would expand the constitutionally-protected scope of liberty and self-expression to include the denial of an amateur athlete's right to compete in an Olympic contest when that denial was the result of a decision by a supervisory athletic organization acting well within the limits of its authority. Defendant has not denied plaintiffs the right to engage in every amateur athletic competition. Defendant has not denied plaintiffs the right to engage in their chosen occupation. Defendant has not even denied plaintiffs the right to travel, only the right to travel for one specific purpose. We can find no justification and no authority for the expansive reading of the Constitution which plaintiffs urge. To find as plaintiffs recommend would be to open the floodgates to a torrent of lawsuits. . . .[39]

6.3 ANTI-COMPETITIVE RESTRAINTS

State antitrust laws, like the federal statutes, deal with such anti-competitive restraints as refusals to deal, exclusive franchising, and price-fixing. Absent conspiracy or combination in restraint of trade or commerce and absent monopoly, a person or league or company engaged in private business may normally refuse to deal with a buyer for any reason or for no reason.[40] But a "concerted" refusal to deal, or a group boycott, is illegal per se under every state antitrust law, even if it has no adverse effect on competition.[41] A businessmen's association's refusal to deal with nonmembers is illegal at common law;[42] but it is not illegal for the association to forbid its members to trade with persons suspended or expelled from the association for violating its reasonable rules.[43] An association whose members boycott those who deal with nonmembers will violate a state antitrust statute even though any person may become a member of the association.[44] A combination or conspiracy among manufacturers not to sell to discounters may be unlawful under most state antitrust laws.[45] Exclusive franchising is generally regulated by state franchising laws, but a franchise agreement requiring the franchisee to buy only from persons approved by the franchisor is an unlawful restraint under state antitrust laws.[46] Price-fixing combinations are unlawful both at common law and under nearly every state antitrust law.[47]

A person or company who seeks to set aside a state antitrust law as repugnant to the U.S. Constitution must show "standing to sue," i.e., that he is within the class with respect to whom the state law is unconstitutional, and that the alleged unconstitutional feature of the state law injured him.[48] In HMC Management Corp. v. New Orleans Basketball Club[49] the Louisiana appellate court ruled that the corporate manager of the Superdome or stadium, the State of Louisiana, the city of New Orleans, the Louisiana Stadium and Exposition District, and the Attorney General of Louisiana all had standing to sue on the lease of Superdome with the defendant professional basketball team. The court concluded that all the parties "have a real and actual interest in the action brought. The extent of that interest and the relief afforded may very well vary considerably dependent upon which contract is determined to be applicable to all the parties after a hearing on the merits of the case. However, whatever the ultimate result may be, these parties cannot be prevented from asserting their interests through use of the exception of no right of action." It should be noted that all the plaintiffs alleged "as a concurrent cause of action that the various defendants are presently conspiring to violate the antitrust laws of the State of Louisiana," although the court readily admitted that

most of the violations that are alleged cannot be subject to the Louisiana Anti-Trust Laws. Indeed the State finds itself in a rather peculiar position where under the types of relief sought it would prohibit Jazz and NBA from conducting its business with players, scheduling of events, etc. as being violations of the law, yet insist that the games be plaed in Louisiana. We also recognize the chaos that would result should this court seek to enforce by specific performance or injunctive relief the requirement that the Jazz play its games in the Superdome, inasmuch as such an order must consistently require that some other member team be made to appear and play that game. Clearly the vast majority of the anti-trust allegations have interstate commerce application and lie within the field of federal regulation. Yet, at the same time we conclude that there is an area . . . not pre-empted by federal law. We refer to the contract of lease between the parties and the alleged violations of that lease. The determination of which lease is valid between the parties and whether its terms have been violated is a state question. None of the parties seriously contend that it is not. It should then follow that if the violation of that lease has occurred as a result of a violation of the state anti-trust law, the issue would remain a state matter unless it is shown that federal law is applicable and pre-empts that issue.

To put it in terms of this suit, plaintiffs have alleged a violation of the lease contract. Presuming that plaintiffs are able to establish proof of violation of the contract provisions, then plaintiffs would be entitled to damages for that violation (without considering at this time the availability of other types of relief). Whatever the amount of damages that may pertain under the contractual obligations, if the proven violation was also proven to be the result of a conspiracy or overt action of the defendants within the prohibition of the state antitrust law, treble damages may be awarded instead of the contractual damage. R.S. 51-137. . . .

Because it is possible that some allegations of specific activity could be made to state a cause of action, we conclude that the trial judge should not have dismissed the defendants from suit but should have permitted plaintiffs an opportunity to amend the petition under C.C.P. Art. 934. We amend the judgment to permit amendment and remand this issue to the trial court to fix the delay for amendment in accordance with C.C.P. Art. 934.

NOTES

1. See Commonwealth of Massachusetts v. McHugh, 93 NE2d 751 (Mass., 1950).
2. Id.

3. See Fox Film Corp. v. Ogden Theatre Co., 17 P2d 294 (Utah, 1932).
4. See State of Minnesota v. Duluth Board of Trade, 121 NW 395 (Minn., 1909).
5. See Cumberland Telephone and Telegraph Co. v. State of Mississippi, 54 So 670 (Miss., 1911).
6. Supra note 4.
7. 528 P2d 1286 (Ida., 1982).
8. See generally 54 Am Jur2d Section 454.
9. See In Re Davies, 61 NE 118 (NY, 1901).
10. 381 NE2d 908 (Mass., 1978).
11. 375 A2d 295 (N.J., 1977).
12. See Rice v. Norman Williams Co., 102 S Ct 3294 (1982).
13. See State of Washington v. Sterling Theatres Co., 394 P2d 226 (Wash., 1964).
14. Supra note 1.
15. See State of Wisconsin v. Milwaukee Braves, Inc., 144 NW2d 1 (Wis., 1966), cert den 385 US 990 and 1044 (1966).
16. 34 Cal3d 378 (1983).
17. 515 SW2d 725 (Tex Civ App, 1974).
18. See State of Wisconsin v. Milwaukee Braves, Inc., 144 NW2d 1 (Wis., 1966), cert den 385 US 990 (1966), reh den 385 US 1044 (1966).
19. 316 F Supp 271 (SDNY, 1970).
20. 443 F2d 264 (2nd Cir., 1970).
21. 407 US 258 (1970).
22. Supra note 18. See generally ABAJ (May 1, 1986) at pp. 58 et seq.
23. 15 USC 45 et seq.
24. See, for example, Manning v. Zuckerman, 444 NE2d 1262 (Mass., 1983), and State of Rhode Island v. Piedmont Funding Co., 382 A2d 819 (R.I., 1978).
25. 331 SE 2d 677 (N.C., 1985).
26. See generally 54 Am Jur2d 457 et seq.
27. See generally 54 Am Jur2d 461 et seq.
28. 375 So2d 700 (La App., 1979), cert den 378 So2d 1384 and 379 So2d 11 (1979).
29. 746 F2d 1019 (4th Cir., 1984).
30. Id. at p. 1021.
31. Id. at p. 1022.
32. See 10 JC & Univ L 167 (1983-1984).
33. 461 F Supp 86 (SDNY, 1978).
34. Among the findings of fact by the court were the following:

> In March, 1978, at the Yankees' spring training camp in Fort Lauderdale, Florida, the Yankees' manager gave one or more women journalists access to the Yankees' locker room. Shortly thereafter the Yankees were instructed that they were to comply with the Commssioner's policy, and the Yankees' manager stated that women reporters would be excluded from the clubhouse once the regular season began.

The Annual Notice issued to all major league baseball teams by the Office of the Commissioner of Baseball has, since at least 1974, stated that access to clubhouses "should" be granted to accredited members of the media. The World Series Manual issued by the Commissioner's Office for the World Series provides that the clubhouses will be opened to the press within five minutes of the close of each game except after the final game when they will be opened immediately. . . .

Professional hockey teams began to admit accredited female reporters to their locker rooms at the National Hockey League All Star Game in the winter of 1975.

Professional basketball teams began to admit accredited female reporters to their locker rooms in the spring of 1975.

As of today, of the 22 teams in the National Basketball Association, all but two or three admit accredited female reporters, including both New York area teams.

As of today, approximately 14 of the 18 teams in the National Hockey League, including the New York Rangers, give female reporters access to their locker rooms. The Office of the Commissioner was informed by an official of the National Hockey League in January 1978 that "about half" of the NHL teams allowed women reporters into their locker rooms.

Accredited female reporters have also been given access to the locker rooms of, for example, the New York Cosmos professional soccer team, the Minnesota Vikings professional football team and the University of San Francisco basketball team.

Women reporters who have been given access to locker rooms in other sports have found a substantial portion of their material comes from the locker room and thus that access to the locker room is an important part of their job. They are able to compete fully with the male reporters on their beat because they are given equal access to the news and the newsmakers. . . . The New York Yankees clubhouse is divided into nine separate rooms, i.e. the office; the players' lounge; the trainer's room; a doctor's office; a sauna; a washroom which contains several individual sinks; a room containing the toilets; and the shower room which includes adjoining drying areas.

Male reporters have traditionally been granted access only to the central locker room area and the manager's office.

The shower and toilet facilities are completely hidden from any view from the locker room. Swinging doors could easily be placed in the doorway which leads into the adjacent washroom.

The individual player cubicles in the central locker room area are approximately four feet wide and three feet deep and a player can comfortably dress in the cubicle. A curtain could be hung across the cubicle's one open side.

35. 496 F2d 623 (2nd Cir., 1974).
36. The court also remarked that

> the other two interests asserted by the defendants, maintaining the status of baseball as a family sport and conforming to traditional notions of decency and propriety, are clearly too insubstantial to merit serious consideration. Weighed against plaintiff's right to be free of discrimination based upon her sex, and her fundamental right to pursue her profession, such objectives cannot justify the defendants' policy under the equal protection or due process clauses of the Fourteenth Amendment.
>
> Since plaintiff Ludtke has been deprived, under color of the authority of the state, of rights secured to her by both the due process and equal protection clauses of the Fourteenth Amendment to the Federal Constitution, 42 U.S.C. § 1983, she is entitled to the injunctive relief sought and to an award of counsel fees. 42 U.S.C. § 1988.

> Having ruled for plaintiffs on Ludtke's § 1983 claim, the court finds it unnecessary to rule on any other federal or state law claim in order to afford plaintiffs all of the relief to which they are presently entitled.

37. Supra note 33.
38. 492 F Supp 1181 (D.C., 1980).
39. The court concluded with this last paragraph:

> At this point, we find it appropriate to note that we have respect and admiration for the discipline, sacrifice, and perseverance which earns young men and women the opportunity to compete in the Olympic Games. Ordinarily, talent alone has determined whether an American would have the privilege of participating in the Olympics. This year, unexpectedly, things are different. We express no view on the merits of the decision made. We do express our understanding of the deep disappointment and frustrations felt by thousands of American athletes. In doing so, we also recognize that the responsibilities of citizenship often fall more heavily on some than on others. Some are called to military duty. Others never serve. Some return from military service unscathed. Others never return. These are the simple, although harsh, facts of life, and they are immutable.

40. See McElhenney Co. v. Western Auto Supply Co., 269 F2d 332 (4th Cir., 1959).
41. See People of California v. Santa Clara Valley Bowling Proprietors' Assn., 238 Cal App2d 225 (1965).
42. Note Harelson v. Tyler, 219 SW 908 (Mo., 1920).
43. Id.
44. See State of Missouri ex rel Hadley v. Kansas City Live Stock Exchange, 109 SW 675 (Mo., 1908).
45. See Reeves v. Decorah Farmers Cooperative, 140 NW 844 (Iowa, 1913).
46. Note Temperato v. Horstman, 321 SW2d 657 (Mo., 1959).
47. See Endicott v. Rosenthal, 16 P2d 673 (Cal., 1931), and Commonwealth of Massachusetts v. McHugh, 93 NE2d 751 (Mass., 1950).
48. See Mallinkrodt Chemical Works v. Missouri, 238 US 41 (1917).
49. 375 So 2nd 700 (La App, 1979).

7

Aspects of Tort and Contract Liability in Professional Sports

7.1 INJURIES TO PLAYERS, SPECTATORS, OR OFFICIALS

Tort and contract liability arising in professional sports are no different than in any other context except for the added fact that the public is always involved in the public exhibition of professional sports. For example, when the professional basketball player Rudy Tomjanovich was assaulted on the court by Kermit Washington, the injured player successfully sued the offender and his basketball team, for the assault was deemed reckless and unprovoked.[1] But spectators at professional sporting events who are injured during the course of the event by the ball or even by a player will generally be held to have assumed the risk of injury unless the "assault" was reckless and perhaps deliberate. The Uniform Player Contract for the National Basketball Association[2] gives the club or team and the league full control over the conduct of the professional player at all times, as does the NFL Player Contract.[3] Violence indeed in professional sports reached the point where the Sports Violence Act of 1980 was introduced[4] making it a federal crime for a player in a professional sports event to knowingly use excessive physical force and thereby cause a risk of significant bodily injury to another person; but Congress never enacted the bill. It was the 1979 case of Hackbart v. Cincinnati Bengals, Inc.[5] that probably was responsible for such proposed legislation: here the plaintiff's neck was fractured during a professional football game with the Denver Broncos in 1973. It appears that Charles "Booby" Clark of the Denver Broncos had run an unsuccessful pass play when a Cincinnati Bengal player intercepted the pass; plaintiff had been blocking Clark by throwing himself in front of Clark. Clark was so angry and frustrated that he clubbed plaintiff's neck from the rear with his forearm, and the blow knocked both players to the ground. The Tenth U.S. Court of Appeals adopted the standard of reckless misconduct for determining liability in professional football games: "[There are] no principles of law which allow a court to rule out certain tortious conduct by reason of general roughness of the game or difficulty of administering it."[6] The court found that there were specific rules prohibiting the type of blow which seriously injured Hackbart, and furthermore the testimony of players demonstrated that intentionally striking a player from the rear was also prohibited by the customs of the game.[7] The court held Clark and the defendant team liable under the reckless misconduct standard, which was subject to the six-year statute of limitations.[8] Thus, the Hackbart decision allows a civil cause of action for injuries suffered during the course of a professional sports event, based upon the following: (1) the intentional act; (2) the violation of the rules and customs of the professional game; and (3) the actor of tortfeasor was aware of the probability of injury to another person or persons. Indeed, a higher standard of conduct is required for the professional player: in Tope v. Waterford Hills Road Racing Corp.[9] the Michigan appellate court ruled that professional race car drivers should be held to that higher standard of care; and in Heldman v. Uniroyal, Inc.[10] the Ohio appellate court echoed: "A higher degree of knowledge and awareness is imputed to professional tennis players than to average non-professional tennis players."

Professional athletes have won several interesting cases brought to recompense them for injuries, as illustrated by Chuy v. Philadelphia Eagles Football Club,[11] where the evidence was found to support a jury verdict that the disclosure of erroneous information by the team physician about the plaintiff player constituted an intentional infliction of mental distress. Liability for failure to detect a cancerous mole was upheld in Wilson v. Vancouver Hockey Club.[12] And in Fischer v. United States[13] a member of the U.S. Air Force Academy football team was allowed to sue the federal government under the Federal Tort Claims Act for injuries allegedly suffered by plaintiff as a result of prescribed drug medication. But often such injuries suffered by the professional player are included within the workers' compensation laws, and, if exclusive, any remedy against others is barred, as illustrated by Ellis V. Rocky Mountain Empire Sports, Inc.:[14] here a professional football player injured his knee in a basketball game shortly before his trade to a new team; the knee was operated on after the trade, and was reinjured in preseason contact drill practice. After plaintiff was placed on waivers, he brought suit against the team, the coach, the team doctor, and the medical clinic, alleging that he had been required to practice before his knee had healed. The Colorado appellate court in rejecting the claim held that an employment relationship made workers' compensation the exclusive remedy. But Rowe v. Baltimore Colts[15] raises an important caveat:

> Whenever a person engages in an occupation requiring violent physical contact with others similarly inclined, he must expect that injury may arise therefrom. The injury is neither unusual nor extraordinary. Therefore, we hold that an injury sustained by a professional football player as the result of legitimate and usual physical contact with

other players, whether under actual or simulated game conditions, cannot be said to be an "accidental injury" within the meaning of the Maryland Workmen's Compensation Law.[16]

The New York Court of Appeals on November 25, 1986, had occasion to deal with the case of jockey Ron Turcotte who was thrown from a horse during a race at Aqueduct, sustaining severe injuries that caused paraplegia and the end of his career. Suit was brought against the New York Racing Association, the track operator, for its alleged failure to groom and water the track surface safely and properly; another defendant was the employer of another jockey whose allegedly foul tactics during the race caused the Turcotte horse to trip, fall, and injure Turcotte. The highest New York court held that the doctrine of Assumption of Risk was a valid defense to all defendants:

The complaint should be dismissed as to all defendants because by participating in the race, the plaintiff consented that the duty of care owed him by defendants was no more than a duty to avoid reckless or intentional harmful conduct. . . . It is fundamental that to recover in a negligence action a plaintiff must establish that the defendant owed him a duty to use reasonable care and that it breached that duty.

The court observed that plaintiff himself had testified before trial to "facts establishing that horse racing is a dangerous activity," i.e., bumping of horses is a common and dangerous occurrence, all of which the court held to be an assumed risk. Indeed, the professional athlete is, as a matter of law, held to have assumed the risk of such known dangers that are inherent in the professional sport.

While questions as to liability of professional sports teams or leagues for injury or death of a participant in or a spectator at a professional athletic game or contest properly belong in a treatise on the law of torts,[17] there is an interesting parallel question with respect to the liability of the professional team or league for injury or death of an umpire, referee, or judge of the particular professional athletic game or contest. In Toone v. Adams[18] an umpire at a professional baseball game was assaulted by a fan while leaving the game, and the injured umpire sued the professional baseball club, its manager, and the fan. The North Carolina court found no breach of any legal duty by the team or its manager, nor any causal relationship between the assault by the fan and the conduct of the manager or the team. Similarly, in Davis v. Jones,[19] a timekeeper appointed by the Georgia State Athletic Commission was not entitled to recover for his injuries sustained when a professional wrestler dove through the ropes and hurled himself upon the plaintiff timekeeper; the Georgia court ruled that it was common knowledge that professional wrestlers are pushed or fall through the ropes during a wrestling match, and since the plaintiff was an experienced timekeeper, he was charged with knowledge of the danger involved to any person sitting close to the ring during the professional wrestling bout. Even a volunteer umpire at a Little League baseball game is deemed to assume the risk of injury sustained when he was hit in the groin by a baseball pitched after he had called time out and while his attention was diverted from the playing field.[20]

7.2 MUNICIPAL LIABILITY

Another interesting facet of tort liability in professional sports relates to the liability of the municipality for maintenance of the city auditorium or community recreational center building, or the like. Generally, in the absence of a statute, a municipality is exempt from tort liability in connection with the exercise of its governmental functions, but may be found liable in connection with the exercise of its proprietary or private functions.[21] But in recent years the prime attention of municipalities has been directed toward the issue of taxpayers' suits seeking to enjoin the municipality from making any expenditures in connection with professional sports. For example, in Bazell v. City of Cincinnati[22] the Ohio court decided that the defendant city, by undertaking jointly with a county to erect a stadium in accordance with an agreement under which the county was to issue revenue bonds and the city was to cause the stadium to be erected with funds generated by the issuance of the revenue bonds (the stadium was to be owned by the city), did not exceed its authority on the theory that the stadium was not designed to benefit the public at large, but was intended to benefit private persons for their own profit. The court, in affirming a dismissal of the taxpayer's suit seeking to enjoin the city, opined that in large cities like Cincinnati, the opportunities for open-air athletes are limited and the need therefore is greater than in less congested communities; that with the development of professional baseball and professional football as national pastimes providing the public with a great source of relaxation and entertainment, no one could question the extent of public interest in a local professional baseball or local professional football team; and that it was common practice for municipalities to lease auditoriums to private organizations sponsoring public concerts, public exhibitions, public conventions, and other public-involved activities. And in Martin v. City of Philadelphia[23] the Pennsylvania court similarly found that the city was empowered under the state constitution to secure a loan in the amount of $25 million to build a sports stadium; the possible use of the stadium by professional athletic teams did not convert the project into a private enterprise so as to render the loan invalid under the "public purpose" requirement of the state constitution. The court opined that if the city chose to lease the stadium to one or two professional football clubs having a major league franchise and to one or two professional baseball clubs having a major league franchise, such a lease would be legally and constitutionally permissible. (It should be noted that then in 1966 the city of Philadelphia had three large stadiums!) In Ginsberg v. City of Denver[24] the Colorado court had its doubts about the public purpose in the city purchasing the stadium for leasing to the owner of a professional football team and the owner of a minor league professional baseball club; but the court stated that it was unwilling to nullify the action of the city of Denver, which appeared to be in tune with the trend of the times, as most large cities were constructing or had constructed large sports stadiums.

On the other hand, the Florida court in Brandes v. Deerfield Beach[25] held that a Florida constitutional prohibition against municipal taxation for nonmunicipal purposes was violated in 1966 by the city's issuance of improvement bonds, secured by certain tax revenue, for the purpose of constructing a 5,000-seat stadium and for the purpose of acquiring several other facilities to be used by a professional baseball team during summer-training camp. In conjunction with the bond issuance, the city promised to lease the spring training facility to a corporation which in turn would sublease the training facility to a professional baseball club; in return for the rental of the stadium and training facility, the city agreed to assume responsibility for maintaining the properties and for providing utilities and police protection during games. The court viewed these arrangements as not consonant with "public purpose" because the advantage to the public resulting from public aid in promoting the private enterprise was merely incidental.[26] Furthermore, the municipal bond issuance violated the municipality's charter, which prohibited the city from lending its credit for nonpublic purposes. Indeed, restrictions are generally placed upon the power of cities and states to incur indebtedness as a means of protecting taxpayers from the consequences of unchecked governmental deficit spending. These restrictions frequently prohibit the local or state government from exceeding a defined limit of indebtedness in any given year or require the local or state government to obtain approval of the taxpayers or their elected representatives prior to creating debts or prior to exceeding a fixed limit of indebtedness.[27] In Alan v. County of Wayne[28] a lower court's decision invalidating the county's issuance of bonds to finance construction of a multimillion dollar stadium to be used primarily by a professional baseball team was affirmed by the Michigan court. Here the circumstances surrounding the issuance of the bonds were that the county of Wayne, after establishing an Authority to issue the bonds and to sublease the stadium, entered into a lease with the Authority in which lease the county unconditionally pledged its full faith and credit to pay a fixed rental equivalent to the debt service on the bonds, irrespective of whether the stadium was actually completed or used for any purpose; furthermore, the county agreed that the bondholders would be able to enforce covenants of the lease against the county, including the full faith and credit obligation, although the bonds issued by the Authority stated that the bonds were self-liquidating and did not constitute a general obligation of the county but declared that the county regarded the payment of rent to be a general obligation for which ad valorem taxes could be levied without limitation. The Michigan appellate court, while agreeing that the use by a private sports organization was a "public purpose" for which the issuance of public improvement bonds was constitutionally permissible, nevertheless concluded that the type of bonds actually issued was legislatively and constitutionally unauthorized and therefore illegal, because the bonds had to be repaid solely from revenues derived from operation of the fiananced facility, which was not the case here since it was the Authority that would operate the stadium!

In professional football, the city of Pittsburgh promised prior to 1966 to make expenditures, if necessary, to discharge bonded indebtedness resulting from construction of a stadium to be used by the Pittsburgh Steelers professional football team. The Pennsylvania court in Conrad v. City of Pittsburgh[29] upheld the agreement whereby in accordance with an enabling act the city established a Stadium Authority to issue bonds for construction of the multipurpose stadium to be sublet to the Steelers, and subsequently the city contracted with the Stadium Authority to make an annual grant to it in the event and to the extent any deficiency between income derived from the tenants of the stadium and the amount required to service the debt and to maintain the stadium, provided that the deficiency was to be paid only from current revenues of the city. The court here opined that contracts or obligations creating obligations not exceeding current revenues did not create debts within the ban of the state constitution prohibiting any city from increasing its indebtedness by more than 2 percent of assessed valuation without voter approval.

7.3 OTHER BUSINESS PRACTICES

Another contract liability example in the field of professional sports is found in Topps Chewing Gum, Inc. v. Major League Baseball Players' Association.[30] Here plaintiff manufacturer and distributor of baseball cards contended that the defendant's recommendation to its members not to renew the individual license agreements with the plaintiff and for the defendant itself to negotiate with plaintiff on behalf of all professional baseball players in the major leagues, constituted a "group boycott" which was illegal per se under Section 1 of the Sherman Act. But the federal district court for the Southern District of New York did not agree with the plaintiff, pointing out that per se violations had to involve agreements directed against competitors, and plaintiff and defendant were simply not competitors! Applying the Rule of Reason, the court found that factual conditions existed as to the monopolization claim, the definition of the applicable market, and the competitive impact, if any, of defendant's action in inducing players not to renew individual contracts with the plaintiff, and so summary judgment was not in order.

A disconcerting word about the business liability practices of the owners of teams in the NFL can be found in the 1986 book by one David Harris entitled *The League*.[31] The author opined that the heroics of NFL athletes on the field have been overshadowed by the off-field shenanigans of its team owners, who have devised hidden-asset plays, double-hocked collateral laterals, end runs around NFL By-laws, and astonishing double reverses on signed agreements! The author's rogues' gallery of team owners emphasizes the callous business tactics such as betting heavily on their teams and seeking revenue from the installation of hugely profitable "luxury boxes" in their stadiums.

The professional athlete as a business person has also indulged in questionable business practices, as witness the tax liabilities of certain players. For example, the professional athlete who plays in Canada and foreign countries as well as in the United States, will generally be able to allocate income to U.S. sources on a "time basis."[32] But the Canadian professional player in the United States may have a more difficult problem, as illustrated by Stemkowski v. Commissioner,[33] where the court held that the standard professional hockey contract covered the preseason, regular season, and playoff periods, and so the allocation of income would be made on the basis of the proportion that the number of days played in the United States bore to the total number of days in the period.[34]

NOTES

1. See generally 8 Ohio North L Rev (1981) at pp. 450 et seq.
2. Note paragraphs 4, 16, and 17, in particular, of the NBA Uniform Player Contract found in the Appendix.
3. NFL Player Contract, found in the Appendix.
4. 96th Cong., H.R. 7903 (1980).
5. 601 F2d 516 (10th Cir., 1979), cert den 444 US 931 (1979).
6. Id. at p. 520.
7. Id. at p. 521.
8. Id. at p. 525.
9. 265 NW2d 761 (Mich App., 1978).
10. 371 NE2d 557 (Ohio App., 1977).
11. 431 F Supp 254 (ED Pa., 1977).
12. 5 D L R 4th 282 (Canada, 1984).
13. 451 F Supp 918 (EDNY, 1978).
14. 602 P2d 895 (Colo App., 1979).
15. 454 A2d 872 (Md App., 1983).
16. Id. at p. 878.
17. See Freedman, Prime Defenses to Negligence (Hanrow Press, 1986), and also 7 ALR2d 704, 149 ALR 1174, and 142 ALR 868.
18. 137 SE2d 132 (N.C., 1964).
19. 112 SE2d 3 (Ga., 1959).
20. See Dillard v. Little League Baseball, Inc., 390 NYS2d 735 (1985).
21. See generally 120 ALR 1376 and 142 ALR 1340.
22. 233 NE2d 864 (Ohio, 1968), cert den 391 US 601 (1968).
23. 215 A2d 894 (Pa., 1966).
24. 436 P2d 685 (Colo., 1968).
25. 186 So2d 6 (Fla., 1966).
26. See generally 67 ALR3d 1186 at pp. 1197 et seq.
27. See generally 56 Am Jur2d Sections 592 et seq.
28. 200 NW2d 628 (Mich., 1972).

29. 218 A2d 906 (Pa., 1966).
30. ___F Supp___(SDNY, 1985); cf. 547F Supp 102 (Del., 1985).
31. Bantam Books, 1986.
32. See U.S. Treasury Regulations § 1.861-4(b).
33. 690 F2d 40 (2nd Cir., 1982).
34. See also Linseman v. Commissioner, 82 TC No. 39 (1984).

8

Professional Sports As First Amendment Expression

8.1 COMMERCIAL SPEECH

Freedom of speech is explicitly covered by the First Amendment to the U.S. Constitution, and there are forms of speech that have been raised in the context of professional sports, as illustrated by Savin v. Butz,[1] where a professional ski instructor was denied a permit to give lessons by the National Forest Service. This federal agency had a policy of not authorizing ski schools in locations where one ski school already existed under permit. Plaintiff contended that the denial of a permit was an unlawful abridgement of his freedom of speech in violation of the First Amendment. But the Tenth U.S. Court of Appeals in 1975 classified the nonverbal activities of the plaintiff as "commercial speech" precluding any First Amendment protection. This exception to the First Amendment freedom of speech had been developed in Valentine v. Christensen,[2] where the U.S. Supreme Court in 1942 upheld a New York City law prohibiting distribution of commercial advertising material on public streets: "The Constitution imposes no restraint on government [regulation] as respects purely commercial advertising." The highest court reiterated this "commercial speech" exception in its 1951 decision in Breard v. Alexandria[3] by holding that an ordinance prohibiting door-to-door solicitations did not violate the First Amendment because of the commercial feature of the selling involved. But the next year in 1952 in Burstyn, Inc. v. Wilson,[4] the highest court repudiated this entire rationale and held that large-scale business orientation of motion picture production, distribution, and exhibition did *not* prevent that medium from being accorded First Amendment protection. And in 1975 in Bigelow v. Virginia[5] the Court held that advertisements for abortion were entitled to First Amendment protection, and that the commercial nature of the activity or transaction was insufficient to justify denial of that freedom of speech protection. The next year the highest court in Virginia Pharmacy Board v. Virginia Consumer Council[6] pontificated:

> It is clear that speech does not lose its First Amendment protection because money is spent to project it, as in a paid advertisement of one form or another. . . . Speech likewise is protected even though it is carried in a form that "sold" for profit . . . and even though it may involve a solicitation to purchase or otherwise pay or contribute money. . . . If there is a kind of commercial speech that lacks all First Amendment protection, therefore, it must be distinguished by its content. Yet speech whose content deprives it of protection cannot simply be speech on a commercial subject.[7]

Thus, professional sporting events cannot carte blanche be denied First Amendment protection. But in MacDonald v. Newsome[8] it was held that a county ordinance in North Carolina prohibiting the sport of professional surfing in certain specified areas did not violate plaintiff's right to freedom of expression. There must be some intention to communicate some idea or proposition before an act can be classified as "expression," according to the court, which found that plaintiff here did not "endeavor to make a public declaration or statement" through his actions of professional surfing.

Nude bathing has similarly not been sanctioned by the First Amendment. In People v. Hollman, the New York Court of Appeals on October 21, 1986, had occasion to opine:

> While there may be contexts in which a public display of nudity would reasonably be understood as a means of communicating an idea, it cannot be said that nude sunbathing on a beach is a form of expression likely to be understood by the viewer as an attempt to convey a particular point of view. Although defendant apparently has a specific philosophy regarding nudism, his mere nude appearance did not create a great likelihood that his philosophy would be imparted to the public. Rather, the likely message to viewers was that defendant, like many others on the beach, had doffed his clothing to enhance his comfort, acquire an even tan, or simply display his body to others. Such conduct cannot be considered sufficiently expressive to invoke the protection of the First Amendment and Article I §8 of the New York Constitution merely because its setting was a beach where nudity is commonplace.

8.2 PERFORMATIVE AND SYMBOLIC SPEECH

Free speech can take many forms, including "performative speech,"[9] which does not rest upon its persuasiveness or upon the information it imparts, but upon the performance which results from the meaning of the words conveyed by such speech. For example, "performative speech" would embrace the words "I bet you a dollar that it won't rain tomorrow" because the uttering of the speech is indeed the doing of an action. The First Amendment, it should be observed, inhibits governmental restriction on speech, not on conduct or actions, so that "performative speech" is generally outside the First Amendment protection. In Giboney v. Empire Storage and Ice Co.[10] the U.S. Supreme Court stated that "it has never been deemed an abridgement of freedom of speech or press to make a course of conduct illegal merely because the conduct was in part initiated, evidenced, or carried out by means of language, either spoken, written or printed." And Mr. Justice Douglas in his dissent in Roth v. United States[11] expressed the view that speech is not entitled to First Amendment protection if it is "so closely brigaded with illegal action as to be an inseparable part of it." In 1975 in United States v. Quinn[12] the Fifth U.S. Court of Appeals observed that "it may categorically be stated that extortionate speech has no more constitutional protection than that uttered by a robber while ordering his victim to hand over the money, which is no protection at all." In People v. Rubin[13] the California court deemed the defendant's violent words to be "performative speech" or a solicitation of murder, whether or not the defendant was serious or jestful or merely publicity-seeking, and therefore his words were not entitled to the protection of the First Amendment.

Another form of speech may be delineated as "symbolic speech" or the reverse of "performative speech," in the sense that conduct may be deemed "speech" and therefore be protected under the First Amendment. Justice William Brennan of the U.S. Supreme Court in 1980 remarked that "some behavior is so intimately connected with expression that for practical purposes it partakes of the same transcendental constitutional value as pure speech."[14] First Amendment protection has been applied to nonverbal conduct in many instances including public display of a flag,[15] a silent sit-in in a public library,[16] picketing,[17] and even nude dancing.[18] In Tinker v. Des Moines Independent Community School District[19] the right of high school students to wear black armbands as a protest to the Vietnam War was upheld as "the type of symbolic act that is within the Free Speech Clause of the First Amendment." In Post Newsweek Station-Conn, Inc. v. Travelers Insurance Co.[20] the federal district court in Connecticut held that athletic exercise lies "on the periphery of protected speech," but ruled against the plaintiff as having no special right of access to the skating exhibition which plaintiff wanted to televise. The restrictive activities of the municipal proprietor of the arena where the skating exhibition would take place were not arbitrary nor capricious, for unrestricted televising of the skating exhibition would have had an adverse effect on the financial returns of the skating exhibition. The court opined that the skating exhibition did not constitute an "exchange of ideas, at least in the sense that there was no political speech involved"; but even if the arena constituted a First Amendment forum because it was a public meeting place, it was not so because the forum was used for entertainment purposes and not for "expression of ideas." It should be observed that an entertainer or performer has an exclusive right of publicity over his or her performance, and that a telecaster that televises the entire performance without permission of the entertainer or performer could be held liable in tort for damaging the economic value of the entertainer's or performer's investment in his work or performance.[21] The U.S. Supreme Court concluded in the Zacchini case[22] that "there is no doubt that entertainment, as well as news enjoys First Amendment protection. It is also true that entertainment itself can be important news. . . . But it is important to note that neither the public nor respondent will be deprived of the benefit of petitioner's performance as long as his commercial stake in his act is appropriately recognized." Earlier in 1973 a federal district court in Florida held that a professional wrestling match or exhibition was a form of entertainment and therefore not within the free speech protection; in Murdock v. City of Jacksonville[23] the defendant city had granted another wrestling promoter the exclusive right to use a city-owned arena for wrestling exhibitions. The court here ruled that wrestling did not convey any "symbolic speech" that would be protected by the First Amendment, for it lacked the element of communication in the sense that there was no effort to convey a meaning or give vent to ideas by plaintiff's conduct. In Wooley v. Maynard[24] the court observed that Maynard had covered up that portion of his New Hampshire automobile license plates which contained the state motto "Live Free or Die"; and the district federal court deemed this conduct to be protected "speech" because his act was done with "intent to communicate affirmative opposition to the motto." The U.S. Supreme Court upheld Maynard's claim to First Amendment grounds, although the court opined that Maynard's subsequent act in applying for special license plates which did not bear the state motto "undermined" the symbolic speech claim because it negated the contention that he intended to communicate affirmative opposition to the state motto.

Hair styles which convey something in the nature of a message, in contrast to merely expressing one's lifestyle, are another example of symbolic speech which might be protected by the First Amendment. For example, in Kelley v. Johnson[25] the hair regulations of a police department were attacked as violative of a "patrolman's right of free expression under the First Amendment." But the U.S. Supreme Court in 1976 preferred to decide the issue as implicating "only the more general contours of the substantive liberty interest protected by the Fourteenth Amendment."[26] The dissent of Justice Thurgood Marshall observed that "the parties did not address any First Amendment issues in any detail in this Court."[27] In upholding the police regulations on hair length the highest court concluded that "the constitutional issue to be decided . . . is whether petitioner's determination that such regulations should be enacted is so irrational that it may be branded 'arbitrary' and therefore a deprivation of respondent's 'liberty' in freedom to choose his own hairstyle."[28] The federal district court in Colorado in Brick v. Board of Education[29] perhaps best expressed this rule of law: "Plaintiff has acknowledged that his hair style does not symbolize any political, religious, sociological, or moral point of view, stating that the length of hair was an expression of his individuality. Such symbolic expressions of individuality are not within the First Amendment. . . . It protects expressions of ideas and points of view which make a significant contribution to the 'marketplace of ideas.'" In both Corley v. Daunhauer[30] and in Church v. Board of Education[31] the federal district courts in Arkansas and Michigan respectively found that the hair was grown in a particular manner precisely to convey a given political or cultural message, and therefore was protected by the freedom of speech guarantees of the First Amendment.

Clothing or dress regulations are also protected by the First Amendment if they carry a message or express a political or cultural viewpoint. Nude dancing, for example, has been recognized as commanding First Amendment protection;[32] but in East Hartford Education Assn. v. Board of Education[33] a challenge by a high school teacher to the defendant's dress code requiring teachers to wear ties was unsuccessful.[34] The Second U.S. Court of Appeals stated that

> even though intended as an expression, symbolic speech remains conduct subject to regulation by the state. . . . As conduct becomes less and less like "pure speech" the showing of governmental interest required for its regulation is progressively lessened. . . . The teacher's message is sufficiently vague to place it close to the "conduct" end of the speech-conduct continuum. . . . While the regulation of the school board must still pass constitutional muster, the showing required to uphold it is significantly less than if the teacher had been punished, for example, for publicly speaking out on an issue concerning school administration.[35]

8.3 PROFESSIONAL SPORTS AS SPEECH

A prime example of First Amendment rights involved the professional sport of rugby in a scheduled match between a South African team and a group of American rugby players in Albany, New York, in 1981. In Selfridge v. Carey[36] the president of the Eastern Rugby Union of America, Inc., and other American rugby players sought preliminary and permanent injunctive relief to enjoin the Governor of New York from cancelling the scheduled rugby match, contending violation of their First Amendment rights. At the outset of his opinion Chief Judge Munson of the federal district court for the Northern District of New York stated: "This court recognizes, in all candor, that this particular match has attracted extraordinary political prejudice, reflecting current global awareness of South Africa's apartheid policies. . . . [But] the plaintiffs here are members of a representative sports organization being thwarted in their plan to schedule an event on public land." Indeed, "a denial of a safe public forum would place the plaintiffs in stymied silence, and deprive them of their right to withstand political criticism by pursuing an activity which they choose to view as apolitical. Plaintiffs' intentional ignorance of the racial syntax involved here deserves First Amendment protections. . . . " The court then pointed out that the First Amendment "insures protection of political or apolitical views through right of association." The court criticized the New York governor for banning "a lawful public assembly," "a constitutionally protected activity":

By enjoining the scheduled sporting event, the Governor of the State of New York seeks to destroy the very constitutional freedoms that have ennobled the more than century long struggle to ensure racial equality in this country. The benefits of such a constitutional heritage must not be commanded by executive fiat, and extended or withheld on the basis of changing popular demand.

The Second U.S. Court of Appeals, on appeal, denied the stay of the district court's order, and stressed the following in its affirmance:

We understand the Court's order to place no restriction upon any proper governmental authorities of the City of Albany or the State of New York to cancel the game or halt its progress in the event that episodes occurring, or which they have probable cause to believe are imminent, at or near the site, pose a danger to the public safety beyond the control of reasonably available local and state resources. In short, the game may be played, but the defendants are not prevented from taking steps, including cancellation or termination of the game, to prevent any dangerous situation from getting out of control.[37]

Thus, the state government's restraint on the rugby players' freedom of speech was affirmed. In 1968 in United States v. O'Brien[38] the U.S. Supreme Court had summed up the extent of governmental control allowed in regulating "speech" mixed with "conduct":

We think it clear that a government regulation is sufficiently justified if it is within the constitutional power of the Government; if it furthers an important or substantial governmental interest; if the governmental interest is unrelated to the suppression of free expression, and if the incidental restriction on the alleged First Amendment freedoms is no greater than is essential to the furtherance of that interest.[39]

Three years later the highest court in Cohen v. California[40] refused to sanction the view that the Constitution, "while solicitous of the cognitive content of individual speech, has little or no regard for that emotive function which, practically speaking, may often be the more important element of the overall message sought to be communicated."[41] Professor Nimmer, in his article "The Meaning of Symbolic Speech under the First Amendment,"[42] pointed out that "even if a communication is substantially devoid of all cognitive content, its emotive content is surely protectable. It would be shocking to conclude that symphonic compositions or nonrepresentational art could be the subject of governmental censorship. Both are fully within the ambit of the First Amendment notwithstanding their lack of both verbal and cognitive content."[43]

In the sports field is the 1980 decision of the New York courts in Ren-Guey v. Lake Placid 1980 Olympic Games, Inc.[44] The plaintiff in the action was a Taiwanese athlete who had entered the United States to compete in the 1980 Winter Olympics; he sought to enjoin enforcement of a 1979 International Olympic Committee resolution stipulating that Taiwanese participants in Olympic Games must use a flag and national anthem not of the Republic of China but of the Chinese Taipei Olympic Committee. The lower New York court granted an injunction, reasoning that the committee's decision constituted "state action" unsupported by sufficient governmental interest, thus violating the alien plaintiff's Fourteenth Amendment rights. The lower New York court also recognized the significance of flags and anthems as national symbols within the running of the Olympic Games; and it concluded that depriving the plaintiff use of his rightful national symbols, while granting this privilege to every other delegation, amounted to denial of due process and equal protection of the laws:

> This Court now determines that the [IOC] resolution discriminates against this plaintiff in violation of his Fourteenth Amendment rights. No foreign visitor in the State of New York may be discriminated against because of his national origin by any organization being supported by public funds. The Court also finds that to deny this plaintiff the right to display his national flag is contrary to the public policy of the United States and of the State of New York. Discrimination is abhorred by the people of this country and that abhorrence has been reflected by a multitude of cases and statutes.[45]

But the New York Appellate Division[46] reversed, treating the issue as a political question and therefore unjusticiable; the appellate court observed that the President of the United States had "the sole power to recognize foreign governments" as more particularly set forth in a Statement of Interest filed by the U.S. Attorney General in behalf of the U.S. Department of State. The New York Court of Appeals subsequently affirmed.[47]

It must be emphasized that the First Amendment protection is only against governmental action, federal, state, or local; as the U.S. Supreme Court in 1976 expressed it, the First Amendment does not "provide redress against a private corporation or person who seeks to abridge the free expression of others."[48] But in a defamation context, for example, judicial enforcement of a tort cause of action in a civil lawsuit between private parties may constitute "state action" for freedom of speech purposes.[49] A private property owner who objects to an ideological message by speakers assembling in his private shopping center has no recourse to the First Amendment, although he would be otherwise protected if the presence of demonstrators blocks ingress and egress "essential to the use or economic value of the property."[50] But to require access by outsiders to media channels of communication, for example, constitutes an abridgement of First Amendment rights of broadcasters[51] and newspaper owners.[52] To confer that right upon an outsider that his message be broadcast or written up in a newspaper is an abridgement of freedom of the press also.[53]

Free speech is more readily recognized and protected when the speech takes place in a "public forum" such as public parks and perhaps public stadiums. Justice Owen Roberts in the 1939 U.S. Supreme Court decision in Hague v. C.I.O.[54] spelled out the conditions surrounding First Amendment access to public places:

Wherever the title of streets and parks may rest, they have immemorially been held in trust for the use of the public and, time out of mind, have been used for purposes of assembly, communicating thoughts between citizens, and discussing public questions. Such use of the streets and public places has, from ancient times, been a part of the privileges, immunities, rights, and liberties of citizens. The privilege of a citizen of the United States to use the streets and parks for communication of views on national questions may be regulated in the interest of all; it is not absolute, but relative, and must be exercised in subordination to the general comfort and convenience, and in consonance with peach and good order; but it must not, in the guise of regulation, be abridged or denied.[55]

Note that the First Amendment rights must be exercised in subordination to the general comfort and convenience, and in consonance with peace and good order.

A variation on the theme of the First Amendment protection is seen in Central Telecommunications, Inc. v. TCI Cablevision, Inc.[56] Here on October 17, 1986, the Eighth U.S. Court of Appeals affirmed a $57 million jury award against a cable television franchisee that used coercive tactics in an attempt to retain its de facto exclusive franchise (televising professional sporting events). The court rejected the franchisee's argument that the First Amendment entitled it to use coercive tactics; the court observed that threats to competitors and city officials did not merit First Amendment protection.

A defense related to the First Amendment defense concerns the exercise of the constitutional right to petition the government. In Eastern Railroad Presidents Conference v. Noerr Motor Freight, Inc.[57] and in United Mine Workers of America v. Pennington[58] the U.S. Supreme Court held that the antitrust laws do not prohibit people from associating together or even conspiring, in order to convince the legislature or executive branch of government to take some action, whether or not the action sought would be anti-competitive. But the activity must not be a sham to cover price-fixing or other violation of the antitrust laws.[59]

It should be observed that professional sports also encounter other constitutional issues such as due process of law and equal protection of the laws, as perhaps seen in Dryer v. Los Angeles Rams Football Co.,[60] where a professional football player challenged the arbitration procedure in his standard player's contract, mandated by the collective bargaining agreement, to wit: the NFL Commissioner can remove a matter from the arbitration process. The California court held that the provision was so unfair as to be unenforceable:

Unquestionably, the NFL Commissioner's interests are closely allied with those of management. He is appointed and paid by team owners; he functions as something of a managerial overseer. In that role, the assessment and discipline of certain types of player misconduct is confided to him. In the dichotomy of player versus management, it is difficult to conceive of a close alliance between the Commissioner's interests and those of management. Given the Commissioner's management bias, the removal power conferred on him by section 8 clearly would, if exercised, deprive a player of the fair opportunity to present his position. Therefore, if the instant dispute falls within the ambit of the Commissioner's removal power, the existence of a fair and impartial arbitration mechanism would be purely illusory; to subject plaintiff to such an illusion of neutral dispute resolution would be unconscionable.

Inasmuch as the Commissioner's discretion in exercising the removal power is broad enough to encompass any dispute, including that at issue here, the grievance and arbitration procedures incorporated from the collective bargaining agreement into the arbitration clause of plaintiff's contract must be deemed so unfair as to be unenforceable.

Notwithstanding the strong public policy favoring arbitration as a means of dispute resolution and the corollary maxim that every intendment must be indulged to give effect to an agreement to arbitrate . . . that policy cannot displace the necessity that minimal standards of due process attend the curtailment of the sacrosanct right to trial by jury. . . . A provision permitting one individual, with interests so allied to one of the parties, to designate himself the sole arbiter of any dispute does not achieve the "minimum levels of integrity" which we must demand of a contractually structured substitute for judicial proceedings.[61]

The decision of a referee or umpire or official in a professional sports contest may be based upon honest judgment or upon misapplication of a rule; the result in either case can be catastrophic, for frequently the financial security of a professional sports team (and indeed the league itself) can turn upon a favorable or unfavorable decision by a referee or umpire or official. Whether a court of law should sit in judgment on the validity of the decision of a referee or umpire or official is open to question: in Bain v. Gillespie[62] an Iowa trial judge was faced with a fatal judgment call by the plaintiff basketball referee in an important collegiate basketball game: "Heaven knows what unchartered morass a court would find itself in if it were to hold that an athletic official subjects himself to liability everytime he might make a questionable call. The possibilities are mind boggling." In Shapiro v. Queens County Jockey Club[63] the New York court stated:

It has been found of great practical importance to have umpires, referees, timekeepers, and other officials . . . who are experienced, mentally alert, fair and otherwise well-qualified to make immediate decisions and those decisions must be final and binding. In more than one sense, such officials are truly judges of facts, since they are closer to the actual situation and characters involved, at the time, as well as when under circumstances in which the events occurred. Surely, their immediate reactions and decisions of the questions which arose during the conduct of the sport should receive greater credence and consideration than possibly the remote, subsequent matter-of-fact observation by a court in litigation.

NOTES

1. 515 F2d 1061 (10th Cir., 1975); see generally 46 Albany L Rev (1982) at pp. 962 et seq.

2. 316 US 52 (1942).
3. 341 US 622 (1951).
4. 343 US 495 (1952).
5. 421 US 809 (1975).
6. 425 US 748 (1976).
7. Id. at p. 761.
8. 437 F Supp 796 (EDNC, 1977).
9. See generally Nimmer, On Freedom of Speech (1984) and Freedman, Freedom of Expression on Private Property (Westport, Conn.: Quorum Books, forthcoming).
10. 336 US 490 (1949).
11. 354 US 476 (1957).
12. 514 F2d 1250 (5th Cir., 1975).
13. 96 Cal App3d 968 (1979).
14. See Richmond Newspapers, Inc. v. Virginia, 448 US 555 (1980) at p. 588.
15. See Stromberg v. California, 283 US 359 (1931).
16. See Brown v. Louisiana, 383 US 131 (1966).
17. See Thornhill v. Alabama, 310 US 88 (1940).
18. See Doran v. Salem Inn, Inc., 422 US 922 (1975). Earlier in 1972 the highest court in State of California v. LaRue, 409 US 109 (1972), had acknowledged in dicta that some public dances or performances of a sexual nature are "within the limits of constitutional protection of freedom of expression" (p. 118).
19. 393 US 503 (1969).
20. 510 F Supp 81 (Conn., 1981).
21. See Zacchini v. Scripps-Howard Broadcasting Co., 433 US 562 (1977).
22. Id. at p. 578.
23. 361 F Supp 1083 (MD Fla., 1973).
24. 430 US 705 (1977).
25. 425 US 238 (1976).
26. Id. at p. 245.
27. Id. at p. 251.
28. Id. at pp. 247-248.
29. 305 F Supp 1316 (Colo., 1969).
30. 312 F Supp 811 (ED Ark., 1970).
31. 339 F Supp 538 (ED Mich., 1972).
32. Supra note 18.
33. 562 F2d 838 (2nd Cir., 1977).
34. The appellant contended the following benefits would accrue from his "tielessness":

- (a) He wishes to present himself to his students as a person who is not tied to "establishment conformity."
- (b) He wishes to symbolically indicate to his students his association with the ideas of the generation to which those students belong, including the rejection of many of the customs and values, and of the social outlook, of the older generation.
- (c) He feels that dress of this type enables him to achieve closer rapport with his students, and thus enhance his ability teach. (P. 857)

35. Id. at p. 858.
36. 522 F Supp 693 (NDNY, 1981), aff 660 F2d 516 (2nd Cir., 1981).
37. See generally 46 Albany L Rev 937 (1982).
38. 391 US 367 (1968).
39. Id at p. 377.
40. 403 US 15 (1971).
41. Id. at p. 26.
42. 21 UCLA L Rev 29 (1973).
43. Id. at pp. 34-35.
44. New York Supreme Court, Essex County, No. 50-80 (Feb. 7, 1980); rev 424 NYS2d 535 (1980), aff 403 NE2d 178 (1980).
45. Id.
46. Id.
47. Id.
48. See Hudgens v. N.L.R.B., 424 US 507 (1976).
49. See New York Times v. Sullivan, 376 US 254 (1964).
50. See Prune Yard Shopping Center v. Robins, 447 US 74 (1980).
51. See Columbia Broadcasting System, Inc. v. Democratic National Committee, 412 US 94 (1973).
52. See Miami Herald Publishing Co. v. Tornillo, 418 US 241 (1974).
53. Supra notes 51 and 52.
54. 307 US 496 (1939).
55. Id. at pp. 515-516.
56. 800 F2d 711 (8th Cir., 1986).
57. 365 US 127 (1961).
58. 381 US 657 (1965).
59. See California Motor Transport Co. v. Trucking Unlimited, 404 US 508 (1972).
60. 151 Cal App3d 266 (1984).
61. Id. at p. 271.
62. 357 NW2d 47 (Ia Ct App., 1984).
63. 53 NYS2d 135 (1945). See generally NLJ (Sept. 29, 1986) at p. 24.

APPENDIX

NATIONAL BASKETBALL ASSOCIATION

UNIFORM PLAYER CONTRACT
(Rookie or Veteran—Two or More Seasons)

THIS AGREEMENT made this .... day of ...., 19...... by and between .... (hereinafter called the "Club"), a member of the National Basketball Association (hereinafter called the "Association") and .... whose address is shown below (hereinafter called the "Player").

WITNESSETH:

In consideration of the mutual promises hereinafter contained, the parties hereto promise and agree as follows:

1. The Club hereby employs the Player as a skilled basketball player for a term of .... year(s) from the 1st day of September 19....... The Player's employment during each year covered by this contract shall include attendance at each training camp, playing the games scheduled for the Club's team during each schedule season of the Association, playing all exhibition games scheduled by the Club during and prior to each schedule season, playing (if invited to participate) in each of the Association's All-Star Games and attending every event (including, but not limited to, the All-Star Game luncheon and/or banquet) conducted in association with such All-Star Games, and playing the playoff games subsequent to each schedule season. Players other than rookies will not be required to attend training camp earlier than twenty-eight days prior to the first game of each of the Club's schedule seasons. Rookies may be required to attend training camp at an earlier date. Exhibition games shall not be played on the three days prior to the opening of the Club's regular season schedule, nor on the day prior to a regularly scheduled game, nor on the day prior to and the day following the All-Star Game. Exhibition games prior to each schedule season shall not exceed eight (including intra-squad games for which admission is charged) and exhibition games during each regularly scheduled season shall not exceed three.

2. The Club agrees to pay the Player for rendering services described herein the sum of $........, per year, (less all amounts required to be withheld from salary by Federal, State and local authorities and exclusive of any amount which the Player shall be entitled to receive from the Player Playoff Pool) in twelve equal semi-monthly payments beginning with the first of said payments on November 1st of each season above described and continuing with such payments on the first and fifteenth of each month until said sum is paid in full; provided, however, if the Club does not qualify for the playoffs, the payments for the year involved which would otherwise be due subsequent to the conclusion of the schedule season shall become due and payable immediately after the conclusion of the schedule season.

3. The Club agrees to pay all proper and necessary expenses of the Player, including the reasonable board and lodging expenses of the Player while playing for the Club "on the road" and during training camp if the Player is not then living at home. The Player, while "on the road" (and at training camp only if the Club does not pay for meals directly), shall be paid a meal expense allowance as set forth in the Agreement currently in effect between the National Basketball Association and National Basketball Players Association. No deductions from such meal expense allowance shall be made for meals served on an airplane. While the Player is at training camp (and if the Club does not pay for meals directly), the meal expense allowance shall be paid in weekly installments commencing with the first week of

training camp. For the purposes of this paragraph, the Player shall be considered to be "on the road" from the time the Club leaves its home city until the time the Club arrives back at its home city. In addition, the Club agrees to pay $50.00 per week to the Player for the four weeks prior to the first game of each of the Club's schedule seasons that the Player is either in attendance at training camp or engaged in playing the exhibition schedule.

4. The Player agrees to observe and comply with all requirements of the Club respecting conduct of its team and its players, at all times whether on or off the playing floor. The Club may, from time to time during the continuance of this contract, establish reasonable rules for the government of its players "at home" and "on the road," and such rules shall be part of this contract as fully as if herein written and shall be binding upon the Player. For any violation of such rules or for any conduct impairing the faithful and thorough discharge of the duties incumbent upon the Player, the Club may impose reasonable fines upon the Player and deduct the amount thereof from any money due or to become due to the Player during the season in which such violation and/or conduct occurred. The Club may also suspend the Player for violation of any rules so established, and, upon such suspension, the compensation payable to the Player under this contract may be reduced in the manner provided in the Agreement currently in effect between the National Basketball Association and National Basketball Players Association. When the Player is fined or suspended, he shall be given notice in writing, stating the amount of the fine or the duration of the suspension and the reason therefor.

5. The Player agrees (a) to report at the time and place fixed by the Club in good physical condition; (b) to keep himself throughout each season in good physical condition; (c) to give his best services, as well as his loyalty to the Club, and to play basketball only for the Club and its assignees; (d) to be neatly and fully attired in public and always to conduct himself on and off the court according to the highest standards of honesty, morality, fair play and sportsmanship; and (e) not to do anything which is detrimental to the best interests of the Club or of the Association.

6. (a) If the Player, in the judgment of the Club's physician, is not in good physical condition at the date of his first scheduled game for the Club, or if, at the beginning of or during any season, he fails to remain in good physical condition (unless such condition results directly from an injury sustained by the Player as a direct result of participating in any basketball practice or game played for the Club during such season), so as to render the Player, in the judgment of the Club's physician, unfit to play skilled basketball, the Club shall have the right to suspend such Player until such time as, in the judgment of the Club's physician, the Player is in sufficiently good physical condition to play skilled basketball. In the event of such suspension, the annual sum payable to the Player for each season during such suspension shall be reduced in the same proportion as the length of the period during which, in the judgment of the Club's physician, the Player is unfit to play skilled basketball, bears to the length of such season.

(b) If the Player is injured as a direct result of participating in any basketball practice or game played for the Club, the Club will pay the Player's reasonable hospitalization and medical expenses (including doctor's bills), provided that the hospital and doctor are selected by the Club, and provided further that the Club shall be obligated to pay only those expenses incurred as a result of continuous medical treatment caused solely by and relating directly to the injury sustained by the Player. If, in the judgment of the Club's physician, the Player's injuries resulted directly from playing for the Club and render him unfit to play skilled basketball, then, so long as such unfitness continues, but in no event after the Player has received his full salary for the season in which the injury was sustained, the Club shall pay to the Player the compensation prescribed in paragraph 2 of this contract for such season. The Club's obligations hereunder shall be reduced by any workmen's compensation benefits (which, to the extent permitted by law, the Player hereby assigns to the Club) and any insurance provided for by the Club whether paid or payable to the Player, and the Player hereby releases the Club from any and every other obligation or liability arising out of any such injuries.

(c) The Player hereby releases and waives every claim he may have against the Association and every member of the Association, and against every director, officer, stockholder, trustee, partner, and employee of the Association and/or any member of the Association (excluding persons employed as players by any such member), arising out of or in connection with any fighting or other form of violent and/or unsportsmanlike conduct occurring (on or adjacent to the playing floor or any facility used for practices or games) during the course of any practice and/or any exhibition, championship season, and/or play-off game.

7. The Player agrees to give to the Club's coach, or to the Club's physician, immediate notice of any injury suffered by him, including the time, place, cause and nature of such injury.

8. Should the Player suffer an injury as provided in the preceding section, he will submit himself to a medical examination and treatment by a physician designated by the Club. Such examination when made at the request of the Club shall be at its expense, unless made necessary by some act or conduct of the Player contrary to the terms of this contract.

9. The Player represents and agrees that he has extraordinary and unique skill and ability as a basketball player, that the services to be rendered by him hereunder cannot be replaced or the loss thereof adequately compensated for in money damages, and that any breach by the Player of this contract will cause irreparable injury to the Club and to its assignees. Therefore, it is agreed that in the event it is alleged by the Club that the Player is playing, attempting or threatening to play, or negotiating for the purpose of playing, during the term of this contract, for any other person, firm, corporation or organization, the Club and its assignees (in addition to any other remedies that may be available to them judicially or by way of arbitration) shall have the right to obtain from any court or arbitrator having jurisdiction, such equitable relief as may be appropriate, including a decree enjoining the Player from any further such breach of this contract, and enjoining the Player from playing basketball for any other person, firm, corporation or organization during the term of this contract. In any suit, action or arbitration proceeding brought to obtain such relief, the Player does hereby waive his right, if any, to trial by jury, and does hereby waive his right, if any, to interpose any counterclaim or set-off for any cause whatever.

10. The Club shall have the right to sell, exchange, assign or transfer this contract to any other professional basketball club and the Player agrees to accept such sale, exchange, assignment or transfer and to faithfully perform and carry out this contract with the same force and effect as if it had been entered into by the Player with the assignee club instead of with this Club. The Player further agrees that, should the Club contemplate the sale, exchange, assignment or transfer of this contract to another professional basketball club or clubs, the Club's physician may furnish to the physicians and officials of such other club or clubs all relevant medical information relating to the Player.

11. In the event that the Player's contract is sold, exchanged, assigned or transferred to any other professional basketball club, all reasonable expenses incurred by the Player in moving himself and his family from the home city of the Club to the home city of the club to which such sale, exchange, assignment or transfer is made, as a result thereof, shall be paid by the assignee club. Such assignee club hereby agrees that its acceptance of the assignment of this contract constitutes agreement on its part to make such payment.

12. In the event that the Player's contract is assigned to another club the Player shall forthwith be notified orally or by a notice in writing, delivered to the Player personally or delivered or mailed to his last known address, and the Player shall report to the assignee club within forty-eight hours after said notice has been received or within such longer time for reporting as may be specified in said notice. If the Player does not report to the club to which his contract has been assigned within the aforesaid time, the Player may be suspended by such club and he shall lose the sums which would otherwise be payable to him as long as the suspension lasts.

13. The Club will not pay and the Player will not accept any bonus or anything of value for winning any particular Association game or series of games or for attaining a certain position by the Club's team in the standing of the league operated by the Association as of a certain date, other than the final standing of the team.

Appendix

14. This contract shall be valid and binding upon the Club and the Player immediately upon its execution. The Club agrees to file a copy of this contract with the Commissioner of the Association prior to the first game of the schedule season or within forty-eight (48) hours of its execution, whichever is later; provided, however, the Club agrees that if the contract is executed prior to the start of the schedule season and if the Player so requests, it will file a copy of this contract with the Commissioner of the Association within thirty (30) days of its execution, but not later than the date hereinabove specified. If pursuant to the Constitution and By-Laws of the Association, the Commissioner disapproves this contract within ten (10) days after the filing thereof in his office, this contract shall thereupon terminate and be of no further force or effect and the Club and the Player shall thereupon be relieved of their respective rights and liabilities thereunder.

15. The Player and the Club acknowledge that they have read and are familiar with Section 35 of the Constitution of the Association, a copy of which, as in effect on the date of this Agreement, is attached hereto. Such section provides that the Commissioner and the Board of Governors of the Association are empowered to impose fines upon the Player and/or upon the Club for causes and in the manner provided in such section. The Player and the Club, each for himself and itself, promises promptly to pay to the said Association each and every fine imposed upon him or it in accordance with the provisions of said section and not permit any such fine to be paid on his or its behalf by anyone other than the person or club fined. The Player authorizes the Club to deduct from his salary payments any fines imposed on or assessed against him.

16. Notwithstanding any provisions of the Constitution or of the By-Laws of the Association, it is agreed that if the Commissioner of the Association shall, in his sole judgment, find that the Player has bet, or has offered or attempted to bet, money or anything of value on the outcome of any game participated in by any club which is a member of the Association, the Commissioner shall have the power in his sole discretion to suspend the Player indefinitely or to expel him as a player for any member of the Association and the Commissioner's finding and decision shall be final, binding, conclusive and unappealable. The Player hereby releases the Commissioner and waives every claim he may have against the Commissioner and/or the Association, and against every member of the Association, and against every director, officer, stockholder, trustee and partner of every member of the Association, for damages and for all claims and demands whatsoever arising out of or in connection with the decision of the Commissioner.

17. The Player and the Club acknowledge and agree that the Player's participation in other sports may impair or destroy his ability and skill as a basketball player. The Player and the Club recognize and agree that the Player's participation in basketball out of season may result in injury to him. Accordingly, the Player agrees that he will not engage in sports endangering his health or safety (including, but not limited to, professional boxing or wrestling, motorcycling, moped-riding, auto racing, sky-diving, and hang-gliding); and that, except with the written consent of the Club, he will not engage in any game or exhibition of basketball, football, baseball, hockey, lacrosse, or other athletic sport, under penalty of such fine and suspension as may be imposed by the Club and/or the Commissioner of the Association. Nothing contained herein shall be intended to require the Player to obtain the written consent of the Club in order to enable the Player to participate in, as an amateur, the sport of golf, tennis, handball, swimming, hiking, softball or volleyball.

18. The Player agrees to allow the Club or the Association to take pictures of the Player, alone or together with others, for still photographs, motion pictures or television, at such times as the Club or the Association may designate, and no matter by whom taken may be used in any manner desired by either of them for publicity or promotional purposes. The rights in any such pictures taken by the Club or by the Association shall belong to the Club or to the Association, as their interests may appear. The Player agrees that, during each playing season, he will not make public appearances, participate in radio or television programs or permit his picture to be taken or write or sponsor newspaper or magazine articles or sponsor commercial products without the written consent of the Club, which shall not be withheld except in the reasonable interests of the Club or professional basketball. Upon request, the Player shall consent to and make himself available for interviews by representatives of the media conducted at reasonable times. In addition to the foregoing, the Player agrees to participate, upon request, in all other reasonable promotional activities of the Club and the Association.

19. The Player agrees that he will not, during the term of this contract, directly or indirectly entice, induce, persuade or attempt to entice, induce or persuade any player or coach who is under contract to any member of the Association to enter into negotiations for or relating to his services as a basketball player or coach, nor shall he negotiate for or contract for such services, except with the prior written consent of such member of the Association. Breach of this paragraph, in addition to the remedies available to the Club, shall be punishable by fine to be imposed by the Commissioner of the Association and to be payable to the Association out of any compensation due or to become due to the Player hereunder or out of any other moneys payable to him as a basketball player. The Player agrees that the amount of such fine may be withheld by the Club and paid over to the Association.

20. (a) In the event of an alleged default by the Club in the payments to the Player provided for by this contract, or in the event of an alleged failure by the Club to perform any other material obligation agreed to be performed by the Club hereunder, the Player shall notify both the Club and the Association in writing of the facts constituting such alleged default or alleged failure. If neither the Club nor the Association shall cause such alleged default or alleged failure to be remedied within five (5) days after receipt of such written notice, the National Basketball Players Association shall, on behalf of the Player, have the right to request that the dispute concerning such alleged default or alleged failure be referred immediately to the Impartial Arbitrator in accordance with Article XXI, Section 2(h), of the Agreement currently in effect between the National Basketball Association and National Basketball Players Association. If, as a result of such arbitration, an award issues in favor of the Player, and if neither the Club nor the Association complies with such award within ten (10) days after the service thereof, the Player shall have the right, by a further written notice to the Club and the Association, to terminate this contract.

(b) The Club may terminate this contract upon written notice to the Player (but only after complying with the waiver procedure provided for in subparagraph (f) of this paragraph (20) if the Player shall do any of the following:

(1) at any time, fail, refuse or neglect to conform his personal conduct to standards of good citizenship, good moral character and good sportsmanship, to keep himself in first class physical condition or to obey the Club's training rules; or

(2) at any time, fail, in the sole opinion of the Club's management, to exhibit sufficient skill or competitive ability to qualify to continue as a member of the Club's team (provided, however, that if this contract is terminated by the Club, in accordance with the provisions of this subparagraph, during the period from the fifty-sixth day after the first game of any schedule season of the Association through the end of such schedule season, the Player shall be entitled to receive his full salary for said season); or

(3) at any time, fail, refuse or neglect to render his services hereunder or in any other manner materially breach this contract.

(c) If this contract is terminated by the Club by reason of the Player's failure to render his services hereunder due to disability caused by an injury to the Player resulting directly from his playing for the Club and rendering him unfit to play skilled basketball, and notice of such injury is given by the Player as provided herein, the Player shall be entitled to receive his full salary for the season in which the injury was sustained, less all workmen's compensation benefits (which, to the extent permitted by law, the Player hereby assigns to the Club) and any insurance provided for by the Club paid or payable to the Player by reason of said injury.

(d) If this contract is terminated by the Club during the period designated by the Club for attendance at training camp, payment by the Club of the Player's board, lodging and expense allowance during such period to the date of termination and of the reasonable travelling expenses of the Player to his home city and the expert training and coaching provided by the Club to the Player during the training season shall be full payment to the Player.

Appendix

(e) If this contract is terminated by the Club during any playing season, except in the case provided for in subparagraph (c) of this paragraph 20, the Player shall be entitled to receive as full payment hereunder a sum of money which, when added to the salary which he has already received during such season, will represent the same proportionate amount of the annual sum set forth in paragraph 2 hereof as the number of days of such season then past bears to the total number of days of such schedule season, plus the reasonable travelling expenses of the Player to his home.

(f) If the Club proposes to terminate this contract in accordance with subparagraph (b) of this paragraph 20, the applicable waiver procedure shall be as follows:

(1) The Club shall request the Association Commissioner to request waivers from all other clubs. Such waiver request must state that it is for the purpose of terminating this contract and it may not be withdrawn.

(2) Upon receipt of the waiver request, any other club may claim assignment of this contract at such waiver price as may be fixed by the Association, the priority of claims to be determined in accordance with the Association's Constitution or By-Laws.

(3) If this contract is so claimed, the Club agrees that it shall, upon the assignment of this contract to the claiming club, notify the Player of such assignment as provided in paragraph 12 hereof, and the Player agrees he shall report to the assignee club as provided in said paragraph 12.

(4) If the contract is not claimed, the Club shall promptly deliver written notice of termination to the Player at the expiration of the waiver period.

(5) To the extent not inconsistent with the foregoing provisions of this subparagraph (f) the waiver procedures set forth in the Constitution and By-Laws of the Association, a copy of which, as in effect on the date of this agreement, is attached hereto, shall govern.

(g) Upon any termination of this contract by the Player, all obligations of the Club to pay compensation shall cease on the date of termination, except the obligation of the Club to pay the Player's compensation to said date.

21. In the event of any dispute arising between the Player and the Club relating to any matter arising under this contract, or concerning the performance or interpretation thereof (except for a dispute arising under paragraph 9 hereof), such dispute shall be resolved in accordance with the Grievance and Arbitration Procedure set forth in the Agreement currently in effect between the National Basketball Association and the National Basketball Players Association.

22. Nothing contained in this contract or in any provision of the Constitution or By-Laws of the Association shall be construed to constitute the Player a member of the Association or to confer upon him any of the rights or privileges of a member thereof.

23. This contract contains the entire agreement between the parties and there are no oral or written inducements, promises or agreements except as contained herein.

NFL PLAYER CONTRACT

THIS CONTRACT is between _____, hereinafter "Player," and _____, a _____ corporation (limited partnership) (partnership), hereinafter "Club," operating under the name of the _____ as a member of the National Football League, hereinafter "League."
In consideration of the promises made by each to the other, Player and Club agree as follows:

1. TERM. This contract covers one football season, and will begin on the date of execution or February 1, 19__, whichever is later, and end on February 1, 19__, unless extended, terminated, or renewed as specified elsewhere in this contract.

2. EMPLOYMENT AND SERVICES. Club employs Player as a skilled football player. Player accepts such employment. He agrees to give his best efforts and loyalty to the Club, and to conduct himself on and off the field with appropriate recognition of the fact that the success of professional football depends largely on public respect for and approval of those associated with the game. Player will report promptly for and participate fully in Club's official pre-season training camp, all Club meetings and practice sessions, and all pre-season, regular-season and post-season football games scheduled for or by Club. If invited, Player will practice for and play in any all-star football game sponsored by the League. Player will not participate in any football game not sponsored by the League unless the game is first approved by the League.

3. OTHER ACTIVITIES. Without prior written consent of Club, Player will not play football or engage in activities related to football otherwise than for Club or engage in any activity other than football which may involve a significant risk of personal injury. Player represents that he has special, exceptional and unique knowledge, skill, ability, and experience as a football player, the loss of which cannot be estimated with any certainty and cannot be fairly or adequately compensated by damages. Player therefore agrees that Club will have the right, in addition to any other right which Club may possess, to enjoin Player by appropriate proceedings from playing football or engaging in football-related activities other than for Club or from engaging in any activity other than football which may involve a significant risk of personal injury.

4. PUBLICITY. Player grants to Club and League, separately and together, the authority to use his name and picture for publicity and promotional purposes in newspapers, magazines, motion pictures, game programs and roster manuals, broadcasts and telecasts, and all other publicity and advertising media, provided such publicity and promotion does not in itself constitute an endorsement by Player of a commercial product. Player will cooperate with the news media, and will participate upon request in reasonable promotional activities of Club and the League.

5. COMPENSATION. For performance of Player's services and all other promises of Player, Club will pay Player a yearly salary of $_____, payable as provided in Paragraph 6; such earned performance bonuses as may be called for in Paragraph 24 of or any attachment to this contract; Player's necessary traveling expenses from his residence to training camp; Player's reasonable board and lodging expenses during pre-season training and in connection with playing pre-season, regular-season, and post-season football games outside Club's home city; Player's necessary traveling expenses to and from pre-season, regular-season, and post-season football games outside Club's home city; Player's necessary traveling expenses to his residence if this contract is terminated by Club; and such additional compensation, benefits and reimbursement of expenses as may be called for in any collective bargaining agreement in existence during the term of this contract. (For purposes of this contract, a collective bargaining agreement will be deemed to be "in existence" during its stated term or during any period for which the parties to that agreement agree to extend it.)

6. PAYMENT. Unless this contract or any collective bargaining agreement in existence during the term of this contract specifically provides otherwise, Player will be paid as follows: If Player has not previously reported to any NFL club's official pre-season training camp in any year, he will be paid 100% of his yearly salary under this contract in equal weekly or bi-weekly installments over the course of the regular season period, commencing with the first regular season game played by club. If Player has previously reported to any NFL club's official pre-season training camp in any year, he will be paid 10% of his yearly salary under this contract in equal weekly installments over the course of the pre-season period, commencing with the end of the first week of Club's official pre-season training camp as designated for Player and ending one week prior to the first regular season game played by Club, and 90% of his yearly salary in equal weekly or bi-weekly installments over the course of the regular season period, commencing with the first regular season game played by Club. If this contract is executed or Player is activated after the start of Club's official pre-season training camp, the yearly salary payable to Player will be reduced proportionately and Player will be paid the weekly or bi-weekly portions of his yearly salary becoming due and payable after he is activated. If this contract is terminated after the start of Club's official pre-season training camp, the yearly salary payable to Player will be reduced proportionately and Player will be paid the weekly or bi-weekly portions of his yearly salary having become due and payable up to the time of termination (prorated daily if termination occurs before one week prior to the first regular season game played by Club).

Appendix

7. DEDUCTIONS. Any advance made to Player will be repaid to Club, and any properly levied Club fine or Commissioner fine against Player will be paid, in cash on demand or by means of deductions from payments coming due to the Player under this contract, the amount of such deductions to be determined by Club unless this contract specifically provides otherwise.

8. PHYSICAL CONDITION. Player represents to Club that he is and will maintain himself in excellent physical condition. Player will undergo a complete physical examination by the Club physician upon Club request, during which physical examination Player agrees to make full and complete disclosure of any physical or mental condition known to him which might impair his performance under this contract and to respond fully and in good faith when questioned by the Club physician about such condition. If Player fails to establish or maintain his excellent physical condition to the satisfaction of the Club physician, or make the required full and complete disclosure and good faith responses to the Club physician, then Club may terminate this contract.

9. INJURY. If Player is injured in the performance of his services under this contract and promptly reports such injury to the Club physician or trainer, then Player will receive such medical and hospital care during the term of this contract as the Club physician may deem necessary, and, in accordance with Club's practice, will continue to receive his yearly salary for so long, during the season of injury only and for no subsequent period, as Player is physically unable to perform the services required of him by this contract because of such injury. If Player's injury in the performance of his services under this contract results in his death, the unpaid balance of his yearly salary for the season of injury will be paid to his stated beneficiary or, in the absence of a stated beneficiary, to his estate.

10. WORKMEN'S COMPENSATION. Any compensation paid to Player under this contract or under any collective bargaining agreement in existence during the term of this contract for a period during which he is entitled to workmen's compensation benefits by reason of temporary total, permanent total, temporary partial, or permanent partial disability will be deemed an advance payment of workmen's compensation benefits due Player, and Club will be entitled to be reimbursed the amount of such payment out of any award of workmen's compensation.

11. SKILL, PERFORMANCE AND CONDUCT. Player understands that he is competing with other players for a position on Club's roster within the applicable player limits. If at any time, in the sole judgment of Club, Player's skill or performance has been unsatisfactory as compared with that of other players competing for positions on Club's roster, or if Player has engaged in personal conduct reasonably judged by Club to adversely affect or reflect on Club, then Club may terminate this contract.

12. TERMINATION. The rights of termination set forth in this contract will be in addition to any other rights of termination allowed either party by law. Termination will be effective upon the giving of written notice, except that Player's death, other than as a result of injury incurred in the performance of his services under this contract, will automatically terminate this contract. If this contract is terminated by Club and either Player or Club so requests, Player will promptly undergo a complete physical examination by the Club physician.

13. INJURY GRIEVANCE. Unless a collective bargaining agreement in existence at the time of termination of this contract by Club provides otherwise, the following injury grievance procedure will apply: If Player believes that at the time of termination of this contract by Club he was physically unable to perform the services required of him by this contract because of an injury incurred in the performance of his services under this contract, Player may, within a reasonably brief time after examination by the Club physician, submit at his own expense to examination by a physician of his choice. If the opinion of Player's physician with respect to his physical ability to perform the services required of him by this contract is contrary to that of the Club's physician, the dispute will be submitted within a reasonable time to final and binding arbitration by an arbitrator selected by Club and Player or, if they are unable to agree, one selected by the League Commissioner on application by either party.

14. RULES. Player will comply with and be bound by all reasonable Club rules and regulations in effect during the term of this contract which are not inconsistent with the provisions of this contract or of any collective bargaining agreement in existence during the term of this contract. Player's attention is also called to the fact that the League functions with certain rules and procedures expressive of its operation as a joint venture among its member clubs and that these rules and practices may affect Player's relationship to the League and its member clubs independently of the provisions of this contract.

15. INTEGRITY OF GAME. Player recognizes the detriment to the League and professional football that would result from impairment of public confidence in the honest and orderly conduct of NFL games or the integrity and good character of NFL players. Player therefore acknowledges his awareness that if he accepts a bribe or agrees to throw or fix an NFL game; fails to promptly report a bribe offer or an attempt to throw or fix an NFL game; bets on an NFL game; knowingly associates with gamblers or gambling activity; uses or provides other players with stimulants or other drugs for the purpose of attempting to enhance on-field performance; or is guilty of any other form of conduct reasonably judged by the League Commissioner to be detrimental to the League or professional football, the Commissioner will have the right, but only after giving Player the opportunity for a hearing at which he may be represented by counsel of his choice, to fine Player in a reasonable amount; to suspend Player for a period certain or indefinitely; and/or to terminate this contract.

16. EXTENSION. If Player becomes a member of the Armed Forces of the United States or any other country, or retires from professional football as an active player, or otherwise fails or refuses to perform his services under this contract, then this contract will be tolled between the date of Player's induction into the Armed Forces, or his retirement, or his failure or refusal to perform, and the later date of his return to professional football. During the period this contract is tolled, Player will not be entitled to any compensation or benefits. On Player's return to professional football, the term of this contract will be extended for a period of time equal to the number of seasons (to the nearest multiple of one) remaining at the time the contract was tolled. The right of renewal, if any, contained in this contract will remain in effect until the end of any such extended term.

17. RENEWAL. Unless this contract specifically provides otherwise, Club may, by sending written notice to Player on or before the February 1 expiration date referred to in Paragraph 1, renew this contract for a period of one year. The terms and conditions for the renewal year will be the same as those provided in this contract for the last preceding year, except that there will be no further right of renewal in Club and, unless this contract specifically provides otherwise, the rate of compensation for the renewal year will be 110% of the rate of compensation provided in this contract for the last preceding year. The phrase "rate of compensation" as used above means yearly salary, including deferred compensation, and any performance bonus, but, excluding any signing or reporting bonus. In order for Player to receive 100% of any performance bonus under this contract he must meet the previously established conditions of that bonus during the renewal year.

18. ASSIGNMENT. Unless this contract specifically provides otherwise, Club may assign this contract and Player's services under this contract to any successor to Club's franchise or to any other Club in the League. Player will report to the assignee club promptly upon being informed of the assignment of his contract and will faithfully perform his services under this contract. The assignee club will pay Player's necessary traveling expenses in reporting to it and will faithfully perform this contract with Player.

19. FILING. This contract will be valid and binding upon Player and Club immediately upon execution. A copy of this contract, including any attachment to it, will be filed by Club with the League Commissioner within 10 days after execution. The Commissioner will have the right to disapprove this contract on reasonable grounds, including but not limited to an attempt by the parties to abridge or impair the rights of any other club, uncertainty or incompleteness in expression of the parties' respective rights and obligations, or conflict between the terms of this contract and any collective bargaining agreement then in existence. Approval will be automatic unless, within 10 days after receipt of this contract in his office, the Commissioner notifies the parties either of disapproval or of extension of this 10-day period for purposes of investigation or clarification pending his decision. On the receipt of notice of disapproval and termination, both parties will be relieved of their respective rights and obligations under this contract.

20. DISPUTES. Any dispute between Player and Club involving the interpretation or application of any provision of this contract will be submitted to final and binding arbitration in accordance with the procedure called for in any collective bargaining agreement in existence at the time the event giving rise to any such dispute occurs. If no collective bargaining agreement is in existence at such time, the dispute will be submitted within a reasonable time to the League Commissioner for final and binding arbitration by him, except as provided otherwise in Paragraph 13 of this contract.

21. NOTICE. Any notice, request, approval or consent under this contract will be sufficiently given if in writing and delivered in person or mailed (certified or first class) by one party to the other at the address set forth in this contract or to such other address as the recipient may subsequently have furnished in writing to the sender.

22. OTHER AGREEMENTS. This contract, including any attachment to it, sets forth the entire agreement between Player and Club and cannot be modified or supplemented orally. Player and Club represent that no other agreement, oral or written, except as attached to or specifically incorporated in this contract, exists between them. The provisions of this contract will govern the relationship between Player and Club unless there are conflicting provisions in any collective bargaining agreement in existence during the term of this contract, in which case the provisions of the collective bargaining agreement will take precedence over conflicting provisions of this contract relating to the rights or obligations of either party.

23. LAW. This contract is made under and shall be governed by the laws of the State of _____.

24. SPECIAL PROVISIONS.

THIS CONTRACT is executed in five (5) copies. Player acknowledges that before signing this contract he was given the opportunity to seek advice from or be represented by persons of his own selection.

Index to Cases

Abendroth v. PGA, 5.1
Alan v. County of Wayne, 7.2
Alexander v. NFL, Ch. 3n.51
Allen Bradley Co. v. Local 3, IBEW, 3.8
Amateur Softball Assn. v. U.S., 1.2
American Football League v. National Football League, 3.2, 4.3
Appalachian Coals, Inc. v. U.S., 1.3
Arizona v. Maricopa County Medical Society, 1.3
Arlosoroff v. NCAA, 6.2
Aspen Skiing Co. v. Aspen Highlands Skiing Corp., 1.3
Associated General Contractors of California, Inc. v. California State Council of Carpenters, 4.1
Austin v. Garrett, 3.7

Bain v. Gillespie, 8.3
Barry v. Barchi, 3.7
Bazell v. City of Cincinnati, 7.2
Berkey Photo, Inc. v. Eastman Kodak Co., 1.3
Bigelow v. Virginia, 8.1
Blalock v. Ladies' Professional Golf Assn., 3.6, 5.1, 5.2

Blanton v. Mobil Oil Corp., 1.3
Blue Shield of Virginia v. McCready, 4.1
Boris v. USFL, Ch. 3n.61
Boston Professional Hockey Assn. v. Cheevers, 3.4, 5.2
Bowman v. NFL, 5.1
Brandes v. Deerfield Beach, 7.2
Breard v. Alexandria, 8.1
Brenner v. World Boxing Council, 5.2
Brick v. Board of Education, 8.2
Broadcast Music, Inc. v. Columbia Broadcasting System, Inc., 1.3, 4.1
Brunswick Corp. v. Pueblo Bowl-O-Mat, Inc., 4.1
Burstyn, Inc. v. Wilson, 8.1

California v. LaRue, Ch. 8n.18
California Retail Liquor Dealers' Assn. v. Midcal Aluminum Co., 4.1
J. I., Case, Co. v. NLRB, Ch. 3n.148
Central New York Basketball, Inc. v. Barnett, 3.3
Central Telecommunications, Inc. v. TCI Cablevision, Inc., 8.3
Charles O. Finley & Co. v. Kuhn, 3.1, 4.3

Chicago Board of Trade v. U.S., Ch. 3n.106, 5.1
Church v. Board of Education, 8.2
Chuy v. Philadelphia Eagles Football Club, 7.1
City of Oakland v. Oakland Raiders, 4.2
Cohen v. California, 8.3
Columbia Broadcasting System, Inc. v. Democratic National Committee, 8.3
Conference of Studio Unions v. Loew's, Inc., 4.1
Coniglio v. Highwood Services, Inc., 4.4
Connell Construction Co. v. Plumbers & Steamfitters Local Union, 3.8
Conrad v. City of Pittsburgh, 7.2
Consolidated Express, Inc. v. New York Shipping Assn., 3.8
Copperweld Corp. v. Independence Tube Corp., 2.2, 4.3
Cordova v. Bache & Co., Ch. 3n.144
Corley v. Daunhauer, 8.2
Crandall v. State of Nevada, 4.3

Dallas Cowboys Football Club, Inc. v. Harris, 3.2
Davis v. Jones, 7.1
Deesen v. Professional Golfers Assn. of America, 3.6, 5.1
DeFrantz v. U.S. Olympic Committee, 6.2
Denver Rockets v. All-Pro Management, Inc., Ch. 1n.34
Detroit Lions, Inc. v. Argovitz, 2.1
Doran v. Salem Inn, Inc., Ch. 8n.18
Dowling v. United States, 3.4
Driskill v. Dallas Cowboys Football Club, Inc., 4.4
Drolet v. New York State Racing and Wagering Board, Ch. 3n.120
Dryer v. Los Angeles Rams Football Co., 8.3
Drysdale v. Florida Team Tennis, Inc., 3.6

East Hartford Educational Assn. v. Board of Education, 8.2
Eastern v. Newcastle United Football Club, Ltd., 3.7

Eastern Railroad Presidents Conference v. Noerr Motor Freight, Inc., 8.3
Eastern States Retail Lumber Dealers' Assn. v. U.S., 1.3
Ellis v. Rocky Mountains Empire Sports, Inc., 7.1
Erving v. Virginia Squires Basketball Club, 3.3

Fashion Originators' Guild of America v. FTC, 1.3
Federal Baseball Club of Baltimore v. National League of Professional Baseball Clubs, 3.1, 4.1, 4.3
Fischer v. United States, 7.1
Flood v. Kuhn, 1.1, 1.3, 3.1, 4.4, 6.1

Giboney v. Empire Storage & Ice Co., 8.2
Ginsberg v. City of Denver, 7.2
Goldfarb v. Virginia State Bar Assn., 4.1
Greenleaf v. Brunswick-Balke-Collender Co., 5.1
Gunter Harz Sports, Inc. v. U.S. Tennis Association, 1.3, 3.6

H. A. Artists & Associates v. Actors Equity Assn., 2.1, 3.8
Hackbart v. Cincinnati Bengals, Inc., 7.1
Hague v. C.I.O., 8.3
Hall v. University of Minnesota, Ch. 1n.72
Haywood v. NBA, 3.3
Hecht v. Pro-Football, Inc., 3.2, 4.2, 4.3
Heldman v. Uniroyal, Inc., 7.1
Heldman v. U.S. Lawn Tennis Assn., 5.1
Henderson Broadcasting Corp. v. Houston Sports Assn., 4.5
HMC Management Corp. v. New Orleans Basketball Club, 6.1, 6.3

International Boxing Club, Inc. v. United States, 3.5, 4.2
International Container Transportation Co. v. New York Shipping Assn., Ch. 3n.144

Index to Cases

Jackson v. Statler Foundation, 6.2

Kansas City Royals Baseball Corp. v. Major League Baseball Players' Assn., 3.1, 4.4
Kapp v. National Football League, 2.1, 3.2, 4.4, 5.1
Kelley v. Johnson, 8.2
Klor's, Inc. v. Broadway–Hale Stores, Inc., Ch. 1n.34, 5.4

Laing v. Minnesota Vikings Football Club, Inc., 4.4
Levin v. NBA, 4.3
Los Angeles Memorial Coliseum Commission v. National Football League, 2.2, 3.2, 4.3
Ludtke v. Kuhn, 5.3, 6.2

McCourt v. California Sports, Inc., 2.1, 3.4, 3.8, 4.4
MacDonald v. Newsome, 8.1
Mackey v. National Football League, 1.3, 3.2, 3.8
Maclean v. First Northwestern Industries of America, Inc., 5.3
Manning v. Zuckerman, Ch. 6n.24
Manok v. Southeastern District Bowling Assn., 3.7, 5.2
Martin v. City of Philadelphia, 7.2
Matuszak v. Houston Oilers, Inc., 6.1
MCI Communications Corp. v. AT&T Co., 4.1
Meat Cutters v. Jewel Tea Co., Inc., Ch. 3n.144
Mid-South Grizzlies v. NFL, 3.2, 4.3
Molinas v. National Basketball Assn., 1.3, 2.2, 3.3, 4.3, 5.2
Molinas v. Podoloff, 3.3
Morio v. North American Soccer League, 4.4
Murdock v. City of Jacksonville, 8.2

Nassau Sports, Inc. v. Hampton, 3.4
National Assn. of Broadcast Employees & Technicians v. International Alliance of Theatrical State Employees, Ch. 3n.144

National Collegiate Athletic Association (NCAA) v. Board of Regents, 1.3
National Constructors Assn. v. National Electric Contractors Assn., 3.8
NFL v. NLRB, 4.4
National Football League (NFL) v. North American Soccer League, 1.3
National Society of Professional Engineers v. United States, 4.1
Neeld v. NHL, 5.1
North American Soccer League v. NFL, 1.3, 2.2, 3.6, 3.7, 4.3, 4.6
Northern Pacific Railway Co. v. United States, 1.3, 2.2, 4.1
Northwest Wholesale Stationers, Inc. v. Pacific Stationery & Printing Co., 1.3

Parker v. Brown, 4.1
Partee v. San Diego Chargers Football Co., 6.1
Pasquel v. New York Yankees, 3.1
Peller v. International Boxing Club, Inc., Ch. 3n.96
People v. Rubin, 8.2
Peto v. Madison Square Garden Corp., 3.4
Pfeiffer v. New England Patriots Football Club, Inc., 4.4
Philadelphia World Hockey Club v. Philadelphia Hockey Club, Ch. 2n.2, 3.4, 3.8
Post Newsweek Station-Conn, Inc. v. Travelers Insurance Co., 8.2
Principe v. McDonald's Corp., 1.3

Radovich v. National Football League, 3.2
Ren-Guey v. Lake Placid 1980 Olympic Games, Inc., 8.3
Reynolds v. National Football League, 3.2
Richards v. U.S. Tennis Assn., 5.3
Robertson v. National Basketball Assn., 2.1, 3.3, 3.8, 4.3
Roth v. United States, 8.2
Rowe v. Baltimore Colts, 7.1

Savin v. Butz, 8.1
Saunders v. National Basketball Assn., 2.1
Scooper Dooper, Inc. v. Kraftco Corp., Ch. 3n.144
Selfridge v. Carey, 8.3
Shapiro v. Queens County Jockey Club, 8.3
Shapiro v. Thompson, 4.3
Shayne v. NHL, 3.4
Siegel v. Chicken Delight, Inc., 1.3
Silver v. New York Stock Exchange, Ch. 4n.5, 5.2
Smith v. Pro-Football, Inc., 2.1, 3.2
Southern Motor Carriers Rate Conference v. United States, 4.1
Standard Oil Co. of New Jersey v. United States, 4.1
State of Arizona v. Maricopa County Medical Society, 1.3
State of California v. La Rue, Ch. 8n.18
State of New Jersey v. Lawn King, Inc., 6.1
State of Wisconsin v. Milwaukee Braves, Inc., 3.1, 4.3, 6.1
Steele v. Louisville & Nashville Railroad Co., 4.4
Stemkowski v. Commissioner, 7.3
STP Corp. v. United States Auto Club, Inc., 3.7, 5.1
Swift & Co. v. U.S., 1.3

Thornhill v. Alabama, 8.2
Times-Picayune Publishing Co. v. United States, 1.3
Timken Roller Bearing Co. v. U.S., 4.1
Tinker v. Des Moines Independent Community School District, 8.2
Tober Foreign Motors, Inc. v. Reiter Oldsmobile, Inc., 6.1
Toolson v. New York Yankees, 3.1, 4.3
Toone v. Adams, 7.1
Tope v. Waterford Hills Road Racing Corp., 7.1
Topps Chewing Gum, Inc. v. Major League Baseball Players' Assn., 7.3

Town of Hallie v. Eau Claire, 4.1
Twin Falls Farm & Dairy Distributing, Inc. v. D & B Supply Co., 6.1

Union Labor Life Insurance Co. v. Pireno, 4.1
United Mine Workers of America v. Pennington, 3.8, 8.3
United States v. Colgate Co., 1.3
United States v. Empire Gas Corp., 1.3
United States v. General Motors Corp., 1.3
United States v. Griffith, Ch. 3n.107
United States v. Grinnell Corp., 1.3
United States v. International Boxing Club, Inc., Ch. 3n.96, 4.2
United States v. National Football League, 3.2
United States v. O'Brien, 8.3
United States v. Quinn, 8.2
United States v. Swift & Co., Ch. 3n.107
United States v. U.S. Trotting Assn., 3.7, 5.1
United States v. Yellow Cab Co., 1.3
United States Trotting Assn. v. Chicago Down Assn., 1.3

Valentine v. Christensen, 8.1
Virginia Pharmacy Board v. Virginia Consumer Council, 8.1

Washington Professional Basketball Corp. v. (National Basketball Assn.) NBA, 3.3
Washington State Bowling Proprietors' Assn. v. Pacific Lanes, Inc., 3.7, 5.1
Weser v. PGA, Ch. 3n.107
Wilson v. Vancouver Hockey Club, 7.1
Winston Realty Co. v. G.H.G., Inc., 6.1
Wood v. National Basketball Assn., 3.8
Wooley v. Maynard, 8.2
WTWV, Inc. v. NFL, 4.5

Zinn v. Parrish, 2.1

Subject Index

Advertising, commercial, 8.1
Agents and managers, 2.1
Agricultural cooperatives, 4.1
Air Force Academy, U.S., 7.1
Airline industry, 4.1
Amateur athletes, Ch. 1n.21, 1.3
Amateur Sports Act (1978), Ch. 1n.21
American Basketball Assn., 3.3
American Bowling Congress, 3.7, 5.2
American League (baseball), 3.1
American Professional Football Assn., 3.2
Arbitration procedures, 3.1, 8.3
Arenas. *See* Stadiums and arenas
Assault upon player, 7.1
Atlanta Braves, 4.3
Attempt to monopolize. *See* Monopolize
Attorney, refusal of union to hire, 4.4
Auto racing, 3.7, 7.1

Baltimore Colts, 7.1
Baseball: antitrust actions involving, 3.1, 4.3, 4.4, 6.1, 7.3; immunity from antitrust, 1.3, 2.2, 3.1
Baseball cards, 7.3
Basketball, 1.2, 1.3, 2.1, 3.3, 3.8, 4.3, 5.2, 6.3, 7.1

Billiard Association of America, 5.1
Blacklisting of an athlete, 3.1
Blackout of games, 4.5
Black Sox Scandal, Ch. 3n.2
Blalock, Barbara Jane, 3.6
Bonds, revenue, 7.2
Boston Braves, 4.3
Bowling, 3.7, 4.1, 5.2
Boxing, 3.5, 4.2, 5.2
Boycotts, group, 1.3, 2.1, 4.1, 5.2, 7.3
Boycotts, horizontal, 3.7
Broadcasting controls, 4.5
Brooklyn Dodgers, 4.4
Buffalo Bills, 4.4

Cable television, 8.3
California antitrust laws, 6.1
California Athletic Agencies Act, 2.1
California Business and Professional Code, 6.1
California Civil Procedure Code, 4.2
California Constitution, 4.2
California Labor Code, 2.1
Canadian Football League, 3.2
Capper–Volstead Act, 4.1
Cartwright Act (California), 6.1
Chicago "Black Sox," Ch. 3n.2

Chinese Taipei Olympic Committee, 8.3
Cincinnati Bengals, 2.1, 7.1
Civil Aeronautics Board, 4.1
Civil Rights Act, 4.4
Clark, Charles "Booby," 7.1
Class actions, 3.2, 7.2
Clayton Act, 3.2, 3.8, 4.1
Collective bargaining agreements, 3.1, 3.2, 3.3, 3.4, 3.8, 4.4
College draft, 3.2
Columbia Broadcasting System (CBS), 3.2
Commerce Clause, 4.3
Compensation rule, 2.1, 3.3, 4.3
Concerted activity, 1.3, 2.2, 4.6
Conspiracy, intra-enterprise, 2.2
Conspiracy in restraint of trade, 4.3, 5.1, 5.2
Conspiracy to monopolize. *See* Monopolize: conspiracy to
Contract liability generally, 7.1, 7.2, 7.3
Cooperatives, farm, 4.1
Cricket, origins of, 1.1
Cross-ownership, 1.3, 4.6

Dallas Cowboys, 4.4
Damages, treble, 3.2
Denver Broncos, 7.1
Denver Rockets, 3.3
Depreciation. *See* Contracts
Detroit Lions, 3.2
Detroit Red Wings, 3.4
Discrimination based on skin color or sex, 4.4, 5.3
Draft system, 2.1
Drysdale, Cliff, Ch. 3n.103

Eligibility rule, 2.1, 5.1
Eminent domain powers, 4.2
English soccer, 3.7
Exclusive dealing, 6.3
Exemption of labor, 1.3, 3.4, 3.8, 4.1, 4.4
Exemptions from antitrust laws, 3.1, 4.1
Export companies, 4.1
Export Trading Company Act (1982), 4.1
"Expression" under First Amendment, 8.1, 8.2, 8.3

Facilities. *See* Playing facilities, control of, plays
Fair representation, duty of, 4.4
Federal Communications Commission, 4.1
Federal Rules of Civil Procedure, Rule 23(b) (1), 3.2
Federal Tort Claims Act, 7.1
Federal Trade Commission, 4.1
Federal Trade Commission acts, state, 6.1
Fifth Amendment, 4.2
Finley, Charles O., 3.1
First Amendment, professional sports as expression of, 8.2, 8.3
First refusal, right of, 2.1, 3.2, 3.3
Fisheries Cooperative Marketing Act (1976), 4.1
Flood, Curt, 2.1
Football, 1.2, 1.3, 2.1, 2.2, 3.2, 4.2, 4.4, 4.5, 5.1, 6.1, 7.1, 7.2, 8.3
Franchise, relocation of, 1.3, 3.6, 3.8, 4.3
Franchise control, 1.3, 3.6, 3.8, 4.3, 6.3, 8.3
Franchise market, 1.3, 3.6, 3.8, 4.3, 6.3, 8.3
"Free agency," 1.3, 2.1, 3.4
Freedom of speech. *See* Speech, freedom of

Gambling, 3.1, 5.2
Gardella, Danny, 1.3
Gate receipts, 4.3
Georgia, University of, 1.3
Golf, 3.6, 5.1, 5.2
Greek athletes, 1.1

Hackbart, Dale, 7.1
Hair regulations, 8.2
Harness racing, 3.7
Harris, David, 7.3
Haywood, Spencer, 3.3
Hockey, 1.2, 1.3, 2.1, 3.4, 3.8, 4.4, 5.1, 7.3
Holmes, Oliver Wendell, 3.1
Horses: trotters, 1.3, 3.7, 5.1; urine samples of, 3.7

Subject Index

Horse trainer, suspension of, 3.7
Houston Oilers, 3.2, 6.1

Idaho antitrust laws, 6.1
Immunity of professional baseball, 1.3, 3.1, 4.1
Impermissible exclusionary practices, 1.3
Income-averaging, 4.3
Income-splitting, 4.3
Indemnity rule, 3.3
Indianapolis 500 race, 5.1
Insurance exemption, 4.1
Internal Revenue Code, 4.3
International Boxing Club, 3.5, 4.2
Investment Advisory Act, 2.1
Iowa antitrust laws, 6.1

Johnson, Jack, 3.4
Joint-selling agency, 1.3
Joint venture, 2.2
Journalists, women, 5.3, 6.2
"Jumping" contract, 3.1, 3.2

Kansas City Royals, 3.1
Kapp, Joe, 3.2
Kennedy, Robert F., Stadium, 4.2
Kerr, Dickie, 3.1

Labor exemption, 1.3, 3.4, 3.8, 4.1, 4.4
Labor unions, 3.8, 4.1
Ladies' promotions, 5.3
Landis, Judge Kenesaw Mountain, 3.1
League, professional sports, 1.3, 2.2, 4.3, 4.4
Lease of stadium, 4.2, 6.1, 6.3
Liability, tort and contract, generally, 7.1, 7.2, 7.3
Little FTC Acts, 6.1
Little League baseball, 7.1
Los Angeles Dons, 3.2
Los Angeles Kings, 3.4
Los Angeles Raiders, 4.2, 4.3
Los Angeles Rams, 4.3, 8.3
Louis, Joe, 3.5, 4.2
Louisiana antitrust laws, 6.3

McCarran-Ferguson Act, 4.1
McNally, Dave, 2.1, 3.1

Madison Square Garden, 3.5
Managers. *See* Agents and managers
Market division, 4.1
Massachusetts antitrust laws, 6.1
Meadowlands Complex, 4.3
Media coverages, control of, 4.5
Messersmith, Andy, 2.1, 3.1
Mexican League, 3.1
Milwaukee Braves, 4.3, 6.1
Minnesota Vikings, 3.2, 4.4
Molinas, Jack, 5.2
Molinas, Jack, 5.2
Monopolies, 1.3, 2.2, 3.1, 3.2, 4.1
Monopolize: attempt to, 1.3, 2.2; conspiracy to, 1.3, 2.2
Monopsony, 1.3
Municipality: identification of, 1.2; regulation by, 4.1, 7.2

National Basketball Association (NBA), 1.2, 1.3, 2.1, 3.3, 3.8, 4.3, 5.2, 6.1
National Collegiate Athletic Assn. (NCAA), 6.2; television plan of, 1.3
National Football League (NFL), 1.2, 1.3, 3.2, 4.2, 4.6, 5.1, 7.1, 8.3; Player Contract, 7.1
National Football League Players' Assn., 1.2, 2.1, 3.2, 4.4
National Forest Service, 8.1
National Hockey League (NHL), 1.2, 1.3, 2.1, 3.4, 3.8, 4.4, 5.1, 5.2
National Hockey League Players' Assn., 2.1, 3.4, 4.4
National Labor Relations Act, 3.8, 4.4
National League (baseball), 3.1
National Professional Soccer League, 3.7
National Wrestling Alliance, 3.5
New England Patriots, 3.2, 4.4
New Jersey antitrust laws, 6.1
New Orleans Jazz, 6.3
Newspapers, tying arrangements with, 1.3
New York City business community, 4.3
New York Giants, 4.5
New York Human Rights Law, 5.3
New York Jets, 4.3
New York Knickerbockers, 4.3

New York Nets, 4.3
New York Yankees, 3.1, 4.5, 6.2
Nimmer, Professor, 8.3
Norris-LaGuardia Act, 3.8
North American Soccer League, 3.7, 4.6
North Carolina antitrust laws, 6.1

Oakland Athletics, 4.3
Oakland Raiders, 2.2, 4.2, 4.3
Oklahoma, University of, 1.3
Olympic Committee, U.S., 6.2, 8.3
Olympic Games, 1.1, 1.2, 6.2, 8.3
Option clause, 2.1, 3.2
Organized Baseball, 1.3, 3.1. *See also* Baseball

Performative speech, 8.2
Philadelphia Eagles, 3.2, 4.4, 7.1
Philadelphia Phillies, 3.1
Pittsburgh Steelers, 7.2
Playing facilities, control of, 4.1
Price-fixing, 1.3, 3.8, 4.1, 6.3
Professional athlete, 1.1, 1.2
Professional Baseball Rules, 2.1
Professional Golfers Association (PGA), 3.5, 5.1
professional management contract, 2.1
Professions defined, 4.1
Psychiatrists and psychologists, 4.1
Public Law 15, 4.1
Public Law 87-331, 3.2, 4.5
Public Law 93-107, 3.1, 4.5

Radio. *See* television and radio rights.
Refusal, first. *See* First refusal, right of
Regulation, state, 6.1, 6.2, 6.3
Rehnquist, Mr. Justice William, 1.3
"Reserve system," 2.1, 5.2
Rhode Island antitrust laws, 6.1
Richards, Renee, 5.3
Robertson, Oscar, 3.3
Robinson, Jackie, 4.4
Rozelle Rule, 1.3, 3.2, 5.1
Rugby, 1.1, 8.3
Rule of Reason, 1.3, 3.2, 3.5, 4.1, 7.3

St. Louis Cardinals, 3.1
Salary cap, 1.3
San Diego Chargers, 6.1
San Francisco Clippers, 3.2
Seattle Supersonics, 3.3
Seitz, Peter, 2.1
Self-regulation, 1.2
Sex-chromatin test, 5.3
Sex discrimination, 4.4, 5.3
Shea Stadium, 4.3
Sherman Act, 1.3, 2., 2.2, 4.1, 4.2, 4.3, 4.4, 4.6, 5.2, 6.1, 7.3
Sims, Billy, 2.1
Skating exhibition, 8.2
Skiing, 1.3, 8.1
Skin color discrimination, 4.4
Soccer, 1.3, 3.7, 4.3, 4.4
Speech, freedom of, 8.1, 8.2, 8.3
Sports Broadcast Act (1961), 3.2, 4.5
Sports business defined, 1.1
"Sports law" defined, 1.1
Sports Violence Act (1980), 7.1
Stadiums and arenas, 4.2, 6.3, 7.2, 8.2
Standard Player's Contract, 2.1, 5.2
Standing to sue, 4.1, 6.3
State action, 4.1, 6.1, 6.2, 8.3
State antitrust regulation, 4.3, 6.1, 6.2, 6.3
statutes of limitations, 7.1
Subchapter S corporations, 4.3
Sullivan, John L., 3.5
Surfing, professional, 8.1
Symbolic speech, 8.2

Taiwanese athletes, 8.3
Tampering with players, 4.4
Taxes, federal, 4.3, 7.3
Taxpayers' suits, 7.3
Tax-saving devices, 4.3, 7.3
Team transfers, 4.3
Telecast revenues, 4.3
Television and radio rights, 3.2, 8.2, 8.3
Television pool arrangements, 4.5
Tennis, 1.3, 3.6, 5.1
Tennis rackets, 1.3, 3.6
Texas antitrust laws, 6.1

Subject Index

Tickets, season, 4.4
Ticket-selling joint venture, 1.3
Ticket tying arrangements. SEE Tying arrangements
Tomjanovich, Rudy, 7.1
Tose, Leonard, 3.2
Tracks, racing, 5.1
Transfers. *See* Team transfers
Trotting. See Horses, trotters
Tying arrangements, 1.3, 4.4

Umpires. *See* Referees and umpires
United States Department of Justice, 4.1
United States Football League, 3.2

United States Lawn Tennis Association, 5.1
United States Tennis Association, 5.3

Washington, Kermit, 7.1
Washington Redskins, 3.2, 4.2
Webb–Pomerene Act, 4.1
Whitehall Evening Post, 4.5
Wimbledon, 3.6
Wingfield, Walter C., 3.5
Wisconsin antitrust laws, 6.1
WJZ radio station, 4.5
World Boxing Council, 5.2
World Hockey Association, 2.1, 3.4
Wrestling, 3.5, 7.1, 8.2

About the Author

WARREN FREEDMAN, member of the New York, Federal, and U.S. Supreme Court Bars, served as corporate counsel to Bristol-Myers Company for 20 years in addition to his private law practice. He is the author of *The Right of Privacy in the Computer Age* (Quorum Books, 1987), *Frivolous Lawsuits and Frivolous Defenses* (Quorum Books, 1987), *Federal Statutes on Environmental Protection* (Quorum Books, 1987), *International Products Liability* (3 vols.), *Products Liability for Corporate Counsels, Controllers, and Product Safety Executives, Allergy and Products Liability,* and *Richards on Insurance,* as well as two travel books and three sociology textbooks. Over the years he has contributed extensively to various law journals and reviews. He has taught on the graduate level at Rutgers University School of Law and the New School for Social Research.